Peer Mentor Companion

Peer Mentor Companion

Marni Sanft
Eldon McMurray
Michael Jensen
Utah Valley State College

Houghton Mifflin Company
Boston   New York

Executive Publisher: Patricia A. Coryell
Executive Editor: Mary Finch
Sponsoring Editor: Shani B. Fisher
Marketing Manager: Edwin Hill
Development Editor: Amy Gembala
Senior Project Editor: Margaret Park Bridges
Art and Design Manager: Jill Haber
Cover Design Director: Tony Saizon
Senior Photo Editor: Jennifer Meyer Dare
Senior Composition Buyer: Chuck Dutton
New Title Product Manager: Susan Brooks-Peltier
Editorial Assistant: Amanda Nietzel
Marketing Assistant: Erin Timm

Cover image: © Royalty-free Corbis

Acknowledgment is made to the following sources for permission to reprint selections from copyrighted material: P. 5: Definition of *mentor*, copyright © 2006 by Houghton Mifflin Company. Adapted and reproduced by permission from *The American Heritage Dictionary of the English Language*, Fourth Edition. P. 21: Excerpt on Schlossberg's transition theory from Evans, Forney and Guido-DiBritto, "Schlossberg's Transition Theory," *Student Development in College*, Jossey-Bass, 1998. Reprinted with permission of John Wiley & Sons, Inc. P. 28: List and discussion of first-year student needs from M. Lee Upcraft, John N. Gardner, Betsy O. Barefoot and Associates (eds.), *Challenging and Supporting the First-Year Student*, Jossey-Bass, 2005, pp. 8–9. Reprinted with permission of John Wiley & Sons, Inc; p. 28: *The First-Year Experience* is a service mark of the University of South Carolina. A license may be granted upon written request to use the
(Acknowledgments continued on page 233)

Printed in the U.S.A.

Library of Congress Control Number: 2006937984

Instructor's examination copy
  ISBN-10: 0-618-83400-1
  ISBN-13: 978-0-618-83400-6

For orders, use student text ISBNs
  ISBN-10: 0-618-76641-3
  ISBN-13: 978-0-618-76641-3

23456789-DOC-11 10 09 08 07

Contents

Part II Increasing Awareness of Self and Others

Part III Learning Effective Peer Mentoring Skills

Preface

Working with the peer mentors in our program at Utah Valley State College has been the highlight of our careers. These students are highly motivated, both to succeed in their own academic endeavors and to help others succeed. They are excited about learning and want others to feel the same excitement. They are connected to their campus community and actively work to get others involved. In short, they represent the college experience at its best! Our hope is that through this book we will be able to inspire new mentors and empower them to have the most successful and rewarding experience possible.

Shaping a Text for Successful Peer Mentors

In 1999, the College Success Studies department at Utah Valley State College, in partnership with the Student Life and Student Services departments, began a pilot of an extended orientation first-year experience course called College Student Success 1000. Each section of the course had a peer mentor assigned to work with the instructor. Each mentor was specifically trained to present topics that are more meaningful to students when presented by another student. The mentors brought an added level of energy to the classroom, and the students' feedback was overwhelmingly positive. We had fewer than twenty mentors that first year. Since then, the program has grown to include forty selected mentors with another forty in training each year.

We work with the mentors for several semesters and want to see all of them succeed. Over the years, we have become more and more aware of what factors drive their success. While we have always emphasized the importance of communication and facilitating learning, we have come to realize that we must also help the mentors understand the purpose of first-year experience programs and provide opportunities for them to reflect on their experience and increase their self-awareness. In 2003, we helped revise our mentor-training curriculum to reflect what we had learned about mentors' needs. Students now take a course called Leadership Mentoring I before they apply to the program. Students who are accepted then take Leadership Mentoring II during their first semester in the program, a course that requires them to meet regularly with other first-time mentors to discuss concerns and review important concepts. After that semester, all of the mentors enroll in the Leadership Mentoring Practicum, which gives them college credit for their service as a mentor and provides a vehicle for ongoing reflection and accountability.

As we developed the curriculum for these courses, we realized that there were very few resources available that focus on students mentoring other students. We wrote *Peer Mentor Companion* so that students would have a text that specifically addresses the purpose of peer mentoring in college, the role of self-awareness in successful mentoring, and essential mentoring skills and techniques. Along the way, we made sure that every chapter was presented to and evaluated by current peer mentors and mentors in training.

This book is therefore the product of a synergistic effort between the mentors and us, combined with feedback from our colleagues and the results of our own ongoing research. It presents the most up-to-date strategies for mentoring other students combined with insights from students themselves. We believe that all students who use it will develop greater confidence in their mentoring abilities and become familiar with techniques that have been proven to work.

Features of the Text

Each chapter of *Peer Mentor Companion* has a number of features that have been carefully designed to help mentors in training. These features help bridge the theoretical background mentors need with the strategic application of knowledge and skills to their mentoring.

A **Case Study** introduces each chapter and creates a context for applying the skills addressed in the chapter. All of the case studies are based on the experiences of actual students who were enrolled in our Student Success course. Each case study is revisited in a series of **Case Study Discussion** questions at the end of the chapter that prompt students to reflect on how the skills presented in the chapter can be used to help resolve the particular situation.

Each chapter is bookended by features that invite students to pause and evaluate where they are on their path to becoming a successful mentor. **Where Are You Going?** follows the case study and presents the key terms and concepts that students will learn from reading the chapter. **Where Are You Now?** at the end of each chapter asks students to answer review questions about the chapter concepts. **Where Do You Want To Be?** poses a series of questions to prompt further reflection on how to apply those concepts to the practice of mentoring. As students write about their mentoring insights, they are building skills that we hope they will continue to use in the future: We encourage mentors to keep a reflective journal throughout their mentoring experience.

Throughout, we use relevant quotes from our program's peer mentors and from experts to bring an authentic "voice of experience" to the chapters. **Mentor's Voice** quotes come from the students who read and reviewed this book during its development. We felt their insights reinforced the importance of certain concepts. **Expert's Opinion** statements are drawn from a wide variety of experience areas, from education and leadership to literature and history. They help illustrate the broad application of the concepts in this book.

The **Activities** in the chapters were created to provide readers with opportunities to apply learning in three possible ways—individually, one-on-one, or as a group. Each activity is marked with one or more icons indicating the intended number of participants:

 for one individual,

for two, or

for groups of three of more.

These activities provide extensive opportunities for self-evaluation by completing a variety of assessments; for personal reflection through writing about significant experiences and insights; and for practical application by putting mentoring concepts into practice. We hope this text will provide mentors with a hands-on training experience in which they will complete the activities in the book and take frequent opportunities to meet with other mentors to discuss their experiences and insights. Bulleted lists of **Strategies** appear periodically throughout the book to help highlight crucial information.

Additional Resources

The **Online Study Center (college.hmco.com/pic/sanft)** provides students with more resources to help them succeed, including a Student Success Toolbox.

Visit the **Online Teaching Center (college.hmco.com/pic/sanft)** for a Facilitator's Guide containing suggestions for facilitating the case studies and additional activities to supplement those in the book; detailed guidance on how to develop a mentoring program from the ground up; and peer-mentoring success stories from the mentors at Utah Valley State College.

The **Myers-Briggs Type Indicator® (MBTI®) Instrument**[1] is the most widely used personality inventory in history—and it is available for packaging with *Peer Mentor Companion*. The standard Form M self-scorable instrument contains ninety-three items that determine preferences on four scales: Extraversion-Introversion, Sensing-Intuition, Thinking-Feeling, and Judging-Perceiving. Talk to your sales representative about completing our qualifications form for administering the MBTI on your campus. Please contact your Houghton Mifflin Sales Representative for more details. MBTI and Myers-Briggs Type Indicator are registered trademarks of Consulting Psychologists Press, Inc.

For more than a decade, **Houghton Mifflin's College Survival Consultants** have led the way in providing Student Success course expertise through on-campus consulting, training, and national workshops.

• Our consultants have extensive experience in teaching and administering the first-year course and in facilitating trainings at national educational conferences throughout the year.

---

[1] MBTI and Myers-Briggs Type Indicator are registered trademarks of Consulting Psychologists Press, Inc.

- Our workshops and conferences provide educators with strategies and tools that improve student retention.

- Our year-round on-site teacher training and curriculum consultation provide Houghton Mifflin client schools with effective pedagogical strategies that can be applied to all disciplines and that have been proven effective in a variety of Student Success course curricula.

College Survival is part of Houghton Mifflin's TeamUP initiative. For more information on these services, as well as information on TeamUP's faculty programs, consulting, and media integration, visit **teamup.college.hmco.com.**

Acknowledgments

There have been countless contributors to the success of the peer-mentoring program at UVSC. The hundreds of peer mentors who have participated in our program have contributed in truly remarkable ways semester after semester. The success of our program would not have been possible without them. We would especially like to thank the following mentors for their direct contributions to the final contents of this book:

Robbie Adams	Megan Hull	Shirley Rosser
Logan Alkema	Juliann Jensen	Chelsea Seegmiller
Jen Barney	Camile Johnson	Whitney Shaw
Billy Beeston	Megan Larkin	Natalie Smith
Lex Bourgeous	Melissa Long	Neil Smith
Bryan Boyd	Mona Manning	Samantha Jo Spor
Megan Brinkerhoff	Seth Mathers	Gaynor Tafuna
Lori Bridges	Ashton McMullin	John Talbot
Sam Cardenas	Annie Miller	Kirk Teuscher
Brian Chin	Nathan Miller	Darren Tintle
David Clay	John Moyes	Ella Tomlin
Marcie Dabell	Jake Nelson	Mele Vaitohi
Heather Dehart	Audrey Oldham	Amy Valentine
Vince Dilley	Aaron Olsen	Alissa Walcott
Jessica Dollar	Spencer Olsen	Carina Walker
Ben Duffy	Marc Palmer	Melissa Walker
Jeffrey Engh	Ben Perkins	Cheryl Walter
Ken Foster	Reed Perkins	Jessica Williams
Jessica Fraga	Lacey Peterson	Ben Woodruff
Cody Gray	LaShana Price	Deanna Yocum
Bill Hennen	Scott Robinson	Sandy York

In addition to the peer mentors, the members of the UVSC Partnership for Student Success and our College Success Studies Department also deserve to be mentioned for their numerous contributions to the program over the years. Thank you to Julie Bagley, Elaine Byrd, Elaine Carter, Phil Clegg, Denise Hodgkin, Michelle Lundell, Bob Rasmussen, Diana Stafford and Stacy Waddoups.

We are grateful to the following reviewers for their valuable contributions to this book:

Stephanie M. Adams, *William Woods University*, MI
Anita N. Blowers, *University of North Carolina at Charlotte*

David Campaigne, *University of South Florida*
Mary Carstens, *Wayne State College,* NE
Melissa Crawford, *University of Central Arkansas*
Gail Dillard, *Abraham Baldwin Agricultural College,* GA
Dawn Dillon, *Peace College,* NC
Tracy Florence, *Marymount University,* VA
Allen Goedeke, *High Point University,* NC
Beverly Low, *Colgate University,* NY
Katie Lynch, *Mississippi State University*
Brenda Marina, *University of Akron*
Beth Marsh, *Appalachian State University,* NC
Judith Miller, *Clark University,* MA
Rusmir Music, *Brandeis University,* MA
Jeanne M. Pettit, *Northern Kentucky University*
DeLaine Priest, *University of Central Florida*
Tiffany Sanchez, *American University, Washington* DC
Diane Savoca, *St. Louis Community College,* MO
Shannon Schans, *Trinity Christian College,* IL
Vicki Steietha, *Northern Kentucky University*
Jeffrey D. Swanberg, *Rockford Business College,* IL
R. Steven Turley, *Brigham Young University,* UT
Beverly Walker, *North Central State College,* OH
Lisa Wasson, *Niagra University,* NY
Paige King Wilmeth, *University of Hawaii at Manoa*
Paula Wimbish, *Hinds Community College,* MS
Marta Wyrodek, *Boston University,* MA

We would also like to thank the staff at Houghton Mifflin who assisted us. Mary Finch and Shani Fisher recognized the potential in this project and encouraged us to submit the initial proposal and first manuscript. Amy Gembala helped us develop the final manuscript and understand all the details related to publishing. We literally could not have completed this project without their constant help along the way.

Finally, and most important, we wish to thank our families, in particular our spouses—Doran, Rebecca, and Diane—for their continued support, especially for assuming the extra responsibilities this project added to our family lives.

Marni B. Sanft
Michael Jensen
Eldon McMurray

Introducing Peer Mentoring

Part I introduces concepts you need to understand to effectively help other students. Chapter 1 focuses on "Becoming a Peer Mentor." Chapter 2 identifies the reasons many colleges and universities include peer mentoring in first-year programs that are "Helping Students Make the Transition to College." Chapter 3 illustrates both the peer mentor's and student's responsibilities by "Defining Roles," and Chapter 4 discusses the stages involved in "Establishing and Maintaining Relationships."

Becoming a Peer Mentor

Case Study: "To Be or Not to Be?"

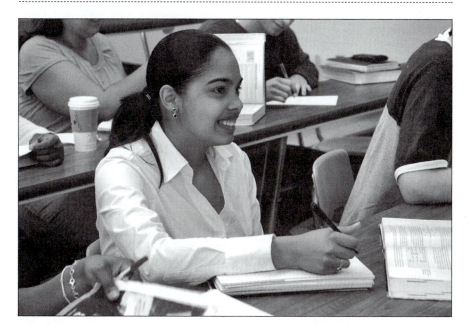

As a student, Laura has always been involved in her studies and in extracurricular activities as well. She was a student officer throughout her high school career. In her student success course, Laura had a peer mentor who helped her adjust to the rigor of college life. Now she is thinking that she would like to become a peer mentor.

Laura has maintained a fairly high GPA. She has a scholarship from the Biology Department that covers the cost of her tuition. She works part-time at a popular local clothing store, participates in an interfaith group on weekends, and has a pretty full social calendar. Everyone views her as a "together" person who never seems to let anything bother her. She is always upbeat and willing to take on another challenge.

3

Online Study Center college.hmco.com/PIC/sanft1e

To qualify as a peer mentor, Laura will need to complete extensive training and commit to spending several hours each week mentoring students. She has also been recruited by her college's student government to lead a committee. Her parents are worried that she may be taking on too much and that her grades might suffer.

After listening to everyone, Laura realizes that she can't do everything she wants to do—or everything others want her to do. She must make some difficult choices.

As you discuss the following questions with other mentors in your program, remember that this case study has been written about a real student facing real challenges. We encourage you to imagine the complexity of the situation and not to oversimplify the issues. You may not feel experienced enough to completely answer the questions, but you will have an opportunity to revisit this case study after learning the concepts in this chapter.

How could Laura prioritize her options in an effective way?

Have you found yourself in a similar situation? How did you decide what to do?

If Laura came to you seeking input, what advice would you give?

Where are you going?

After reading this chapter, you should be familiar with the following concepts related to mentoring.

- Definition of *peer mentoring*
- Formal and informal peer mentoring
- Comparison of peer mentoring and tutoring

- Benefits of peer mentoring
- Motivation and peer mentoring
- Balancing needs and responsibilities as a peer mentor

Key Terms

In this chapter, you will encounter the following terms, which appear in bold. You can highlight the definitions as you read or look for the terms in the glossary at the end of the book.

Formal mentoring   **Peer mentor**
Informal mentoring   **Self-focused**
Mentor   **Transferable skills**
Other-focused   **Tutor**
Peer

What Is a Mentor?

In Greek mythology, as Odysseus prepared to leave to fight the Trojans, he chose Mentor, his wise and trusted friend, to guard and teach his son, Telemachus. *The American Heritage Dictionary* refers to this Greek character in the definition it gives for **mentor**:

> Odysseus's trusted counselor, [who] became the guardian and teacher of Telemachus.

Common synonyms for *mentor* include *guide, adviser, counselor, and teacher.* The word has come to mean a more-experienced friend who assists someone with making an important transition, learning a new skill, or facing an unknown challenge. A **peer** is someone who is of equal standing with you—a friend, a colleague, a fellow student. A **peer mentor** is not just any student, but is rather a student who has learned from experience and has developed skills to successfully guide other students through college.

A peer mentor must blend in and connect with the rest of the class. The peer mentor is not another teacher or authority figure, but is instead usually most effective when leading by example. When several college students were asked to describe common characteristics of a mentor, the trait they valued most was optimism about life. A peer mentor's positive attitude is the basis for the encouragement and support that helps students discover their own abilities to succeed.

MENTOR'S VOICE

The most prominent aspect of the peer mentoring program to me is the reality that you have college students willing to take the time to mentor, teach, and facilitate the success of other college students. Think about it, college students concerned for the success and welfare of other students, a rare and precious find indeed.

Lex Bourgeous, peer mentor

Can you think of people who have been mentors to you? You can most likely think of people who have been positive, guiding influences at home, in school, at work, or in other settings—a teacher who always complimented you, a sibling who cheered you on, a friend who expressed belief in your ability to accomplish a task, or a roommate who exhibited good study habits. Sometimes these people were formally identified as mentors, but much of the time they mentored you in informal ways. The following activity is designed to help you identify who these people were and what you admired most about them.

What Is the Difference between Formal and Informal Mentoring?

The mentors you identified in Activity 1.1 may not have been assigned to be mentors. They might have become natural mentors because of your relationship with them. **Informal mentoring** describes the situation in which someone takes on the mentor role without being assigned. This type of mentoring often occurs in a family or friendship setting.

ACTIVITY 1.1   Identifying Your Mentors

Answer the following questions to articulate your concept of mentors.

1. Identify at least three different people who have mentored you in some way. Write their names, and explain how you knew them and what they did to influence you.

_____

_____

_____

2. Describe specific traits that you admired in each of them. Do you think these traits are important for a mentor to have? Explain.

_____

_____

_____

3. Discuss at least one trait that you would like to develop as you become a peer mentor. What can you do to develop this skill?

_____

_____

_____

Formal mentoring usually takes place in a work or educational setting. Someone is either assigned or sought out to help another "learn the ropes." If you are in a training course to become a peer mentor, you will be assigned to work with a specific student or group of students, which means that you will probably find yourself in a formal mentoring situation. You should be aware of things you will need to do to be more effective in the formal peer mentor situation.

Help students understand your role. Chapter 3 provides an in-depth look at your roles as a peer mentor. Students may not understand why you have been assigned to be their peer mentor and what you can do to help them. It is your responsibility to communicate your expectations and understand theirs.

Focus on building a relationship. In a formal mentoring relationship, you must consciously work to build trust and develop a relationship. Your genuine interest in the students who are assigned to you will help you close the gap that initially exists between you and them. We examine relationship building in Chapter 4.

Give students space. Don't be overbearing. Sometimes peer mentors are overly enthusiastic about helping new students. Give students an opportunity to decide what kind of help they need, and don't be discouraged or offended if they don't want your help.

Make the most of the time you have. You have a limited amount of time to work with these students. If you plan to meet often, you will be more successful at building solid relationships and accomplishing your learning objectives. Chapters 9 and 10 cover facilitating learning and planning with students.

Share ideas with other mentors. When you are part of a mentoring program, you have the advantage of a network of mentors. You can support each other and help each other meet the responsibilities of your assignments.

Ask for help. If you are having difficulty mentoring a student, you can turn to others for assistance. Talk to your fellow peer mentors, your peer mentoring program administrator, or a faculty member to get ideas about how to make the relationship more successful.

How Is Mentoring Different from Tutoring?

While a peer mentor can also be a tutor and vice versa, it is important to recognize that the two involve fundamentally different approaches. A **tutor** may develop a relationship with the student being tutored, but the role in most tutoring situations is to teach or clarify content specific to a course. The tutoring relationship is typically limited to a specific time and place. Mentoring, on the other hand, does not have those limitations. A peer mentor may also tutor, but a mentor is more focused on promoting success for the whole student, not just developing proficiency in a particular subject. A peer mentor attempts to establish a more personal relationship that will allow insight into the student's wants and needs in many aspects of the college experience.

A tutor	A peer mentor
• focuses on an assignment	• focuses on building a relationship
• teaches a specific subject	• teaches critical thinking and study skills
• demonstrates skills	• demonstrates effective behavior
• must be knowledgeable	• must be trustworthy
• provides information	• provides support
• is seen as an expert	• is seen as a peer
• affects performance in a course	• affects overall success

Being a peer mentor is more than doing a job. It requires a commitment of time and energy to one or several students who want to improve. Your interaction with each student will be unique because of the nature of your relationship, and you must be prepared to deal with a variety of different issues and circumstances.

How Confident Are You in Your Mentoring Knowledge and Skills?

If you are reading this book, you are probably involved in some type of peer mentor training to help you prepare for being a mentor. The purpose of this book is to help you understand why college students need mentors and how you can help them deal with the challenges of college. The following activity will help you assess your own strengths and weaknesses as they relate to your mentoring knowledge and skills. While you may be tempted to give yourself a high score in each area so that you appear confident, it is more important to honestly assess your understanding and abilities so that you can identify which chapters in this book will be most beneficial to you.

👤 ACTIVITY 1.2   Mentoring Confidence Inventory

Use the following scale to rate your confidence in each of the following areas.

0 Not Confident
1 Slightly Confident
2 Somewhat Confident
3 Fairly Confident
4 Quite Confident
5 Completely Confident

Becoming a Peer Mentor

0 1 2 3 4 5   1. I know what it means to be a mentor.

0 1 2 3 4 5   2. I know the difference between mentoring and tutoring.

0 1 2 3 4 5   3. I know why I want to become a peer mentor.

0 1 2 3 4 5   4. I understand how my motivation affects my performance.

0 1 2 3 4 5   5. I am prepared to balance peer mentoring responsibilities with my other life responsibilities.

Total __ /25

Helping Students Make the Transition to College

0 1 2 3 4 5   1. I can explain why college students need peer mentors.

0 1 2 3 4 5   2. I understand the differences between high school and college.

0 1 2 3 4 5   3. I am aware of how peer mentors can help students make the transition to college.

0 1 2 3 4 5   4. I am aware of the objectives of the first-year-experience program on my campus.

0 1 2 3 4 5   5. I understand how involvement can affect my development as a student.

Total __ /25

Defining Roles

0 1 2 3 4 5   1. I understand my role within the mentor program.

0 1 2 3 4 5   2. I know the different roles I have with the students I mentor.

0 1 2 3 4 5   3. I understand the student's role in the mentoring relationship.

0 1 2 3 4 5   4. I am capable of fulfilling the different roles of a peer mentor.

0 1 2 3 4 5   5. I know how to develop my mentoring skills in each of the different roles I have as a mentor.

Total __ /25

Establishing and Maintaining Relationships

0 1 2 3 4 5   1. I can explain what makes a mentoring relationship different from other relationships.

0 1 2 3 4 5   2. I know what students are looking for in a mentoring relationship.

0 1 2 3 4 5   3. I know how to establish an effective mentoring relationship.

0 1 2 3 4 5   4. I know what to do to maintain a good mentoring relationship.

0 1 2 3 4 5   5. I know how to end a mentoring relationship in a positive way.

Total __ /25

Understanding Self-Awareness

0 1 2 3 4 5   1. I understand why self-awareness is necessary to a mentor.

0 1 2 3 4 5   2. I know the differences between self-concept, self-esteem, and self-efficacy.

0 1 2 3 4 5   3. I understand how self-efficacy affects agency.

0 1 2 3 4 5   4. I am aware of my thoughts, feelings, and actions.

0 1 2 3 4 5   5. I know the different types of awareness essential for college students.

Total __ /25

Becoming a Role Model

0 1 2 3 4 5   1. I understand the differences between being a peer mentor and being a role model.

0 1 2 3 4 5   2. I am comfortable being honest about my strengths and weaknesses.

0 1 2 3 4 5   3. I can identify my own personal values.

0 1 2 3 4 5   4. I am aware of how my choices and actions reflect my values.

0 1 2 3 4 5   5. I am confident in my ability to help others recognize their own values.

Total __ /25

Developing Cultural Sensitivity

0 1 2 3 4 5   1. I understand the benefits of diversity on a college campus.

0 1 2 3 4 5   2. I respect and value the diversity of the students I mentor.

0 1 2 3 4 5   3. I recognize how cultural influences affect my perspective.

0 1 2 3 4 5   4. I am aware of my own attitude toward cultural differences.

0 1 2 3 4 5   5. I employ effective strategies for cross-cultural interaction.

Total __ /25

Communicating Effectively

0 1 2 3 4 5   1. I understand how communicating as a mentor is different than communicating in other relationships.

0 1 2 3 4 5   2. I have effective listening skills.

0 1 2 3 4 5   3. I am aware of my verbal and nonverbal messages.

0 1 2 3 4 5   4. I am confident in my presentation and group discussion skills.

0 1 2 3 4 5   5. I understand how to effectively give and receive feedback.

Total __ /25

Facilitating Learning

0 1 2 3 4 5   1. I know what it means to facilitate learning.

0 1 2 3 4 5   2. I know the differences between adolescent learners and adult learners.

0 1 2 3 4 5   3. I understand that I must use different facilitation techniques for different types of learners.

0 1 2 3 4 5   4. I can incorporate active learning techniques in my teaching.

0 1 2 3 4 5   5. I can explain the value of peer-to-peer teaching.

Total __ /25

Planning and Problem Solving

0 1 2 3 4 5   1. I know how to plan to be an effective mentor.

0 1 2 3 4 5   2. I could help other students plan for the semester.

0 1 2 3 4 5   3. I can demonstrate effective goal setting for other students.

0 1 2 3 4 5   4. I understand different decision-making styles.

0 1 2 3 4 5   5. I know what skills are required to conduct effective problem solving.

Total __ /25

Utilizing Campus Resources

0 1 2 3 4 5   1. I can explain to students why it is important to be aware of campus resources.

0 1 2 3 4 5   2. I am familiar with academic resources available on campus.

0 1 2 3 4 5   3. I am familiar with student support services available on campus.

0 1 2 3 4 5   4. I have a network of people to whom I can refer students who need help.

0 1 2 3 4 5   5. I can recognize the signs of stress and help students identify the resources that can help them manage their stress.

Total __ /25

Evaluating Your Mentoring

0 1 2 3 4 5   1. I understand the importance of critical reflection.

0 1 2 3 4 5   2. I know how to evaluate my skills and performance.

0 1 2 3 4 5   3. I am comfortable asking others for feedback.

0 1 2 3 4 5   4. I understand the benefits of reflective journaling.

0 1 2 3 4 5   5. I am aware of how my motivation can change.

Total __ /25

Consider your total score in each area to assess your confidence in your mentoring knowledge and skills.

0–5   Not Confident
6–10   Slightly Confident
11–15   Somewhat Confident
16–20   Fairly Confident
21–24   Quite Confident
25   Completely Confident

1. In which areas are you most confident about your mentoring knowledge and skills?

   _____

   _____

2. In which areas are you least confident about your mentoring knowledge and skills?

   _____

   _____

3. Which chapters will be most beneficial to you as you prepare to be a peer mentor?

   _____

   _____

What Are the Benefits of Becoming a Peer Mentor?

Though peer mentoring programs differ from campus to campus, the benefits of participating in those programs are similar. You could take advantage of many of the following benefits or even come up with others.

- Connect and contribute to your campus community
- Develop leadership and mentoring skills
- Empower others to succeed
- Enjoy camaraderie with other peer mentors
- Enrich your college experience
- Experience the satisfaction that comes from serving others

- Gain experience that looks good on a résumé
- Improve communication and people skills
- Increase academic confidence
- Learn to navigate the college system
- Make new friends
- Master key learning strategies
- Network with faculty and students
- Participate in service-learning opportunities
- Receive a scholarship or other form of compensation
- Take responsibility for your own success
- Have fun!

Many of the benefits listed above are **transferable skills**—skills that will be useful in a future career or workplace. They will help you in any job, no matter what your major or chosen career. In a world that changes as rapidly as ours, they will be invaluable as you pursue both academic and career opportunities in the future.

After considering the list of benefits, do you see that you could gain as much or more from peer mentoring than can the students you help? You may look to the future and recognize the benefit peer mentoring might have on your resume. You might be altruistic and want to help struggling students, or you may recognize that someone helped you succeed and want to return the favor by helping others. You could also participate in programs that provide scholarships or paychecks. Whatever your reasons for taking on this important responsibility, thinking, writing, or talking about them will help you clarify your motives and make a personal commitment to become an effective mentor.

How Does Your Motivation Affect Your Mentoring?

After completing Activity 1.3, can you determine whether your motivation is **self-focused**, **other-focused**, or both? The source of your motivation will affect the amount of satisfaction you gain from mentoring others. You need to find a balance between what you can do for others and what you need to do for yourself. Consider the difference between Kevin and Emily.

Kevin is self-focused. He is so motivated by his own personal gain that he sees the time and energy required by his assignment as an imposition. He is inflexible and becomes irritated with his students. He puts in his time without making a difference, and eventually he leaves the peer mentor program to find more satisfying ways to achieve his desired ends.

ACTIVITY 1.3   Identifying Your Motivation

As you answer the following questions, refer to the benefits of peer mentoring listed in the previous section. Highlight the benefits that are most appealing to you. Be honest. There are no right or wrong answers. People choose different benefits based on their personal situations.

1. List the top three benefits for you of becoming a peer mentor.

_____

_____

2. Explain how these benefits motivate you to be a peer mentor.

_____

_____

_____

_____

3. In what ways will your motivations to be a peer mentor affect your future performance in this role?

_____

_____

_____

Emily is other-focused. She is willing to devote endless hours to her students. She is becoming burned out and has created dependency in her students. She wants her students to like her so much that she will do just about anything, including helping them with all their homework and checking resources for them. She also eventually leaves the program because it has consumed her life.

Neither of these people was effective. Kevin was too self-focused, and Emily was too other-focused. Your goal as a peer mentor should be to help students become independent and confident about their abilities. You will not do this by enabling them with constant help or overprotecting them from the reality that success takes real effort on their part. You also will not accomplish it if you do not provide them with enough encouragement or time.

Successful peer mentors learn to strike a balance between their students' and their own needs. You are there to help the students, but some hurdles are low to the ground and easily cleared without your help. Other hurdles require students to put in extra effort or to seek your mentoring support before they can get over them. When particularly high hurdles seem insurmountable, you can help students learn from each attempt until the right combination of moves yields success. But if you do not pay attention to your own needs and challenges, you will not be able to clear your own hurdles, and you will be left without the personal strength you need to help others.

How Do You Balance Your Needs and Your Responsibilities as a Mentor?

The fact that you are in peer mentor training is a good indicator of your ability to achieve. Remember that the academic success of your students cannot be achieved at the sacrifice of your own. Try to keep the following guidelines in mind as you plot your course on the path to success.

Be aware. Learn as much as you can about yourself and about how you deal with both challenges and opportunities. Chapter 5 focuses on awareness.

Know what you want. Decide what you want as a peer mentor and from your college experience. What do you hope to accomplish after you graduate?

Set goals. Continuously focus on both your long-term and short-term goals. Decide how much effort it will take for you to succeed and how much you are willing to put forth. Refer to Chapter 10 for ideas on goal setting.

Plan consistently. Determine your plan of attack each day, each week, and each semester to gain the most from every opportunity. You can also refer to Chapter 10 for suggestions about planning.

Be optimistic. Assess your attitude. Do you truly feel that you can succeed? Do you view challenges as possibilities?

Study smarter. Take stock of your study strategies. Can you use more help in any areas, such as time management, critical reading, taking notes, or writing? If so, seek assistance from other peer mentors, program administrators, faculty members, tutors, study groups, or other support services.

Reflect often. Finally, learn the value of reflection and of real conversation with people. Objectively reflect on accomplishments and setbacks, and evaluate both the process and the result. Seek constructive feedback from people you respect. Chapter 12 provides more evaluation ideas.

Only you know your reasons for becoming a peer mentor. Whatever they may be, give your best effort to create a peer mentoring relationship that will benefit all involved. This chapter has briefly introduced some important aspects of peer mentoring. Subsequent chapters provide more specifics on how to put it all together.

Online Study Center college.hmco.com/PIC/sanft1e

⊕ Where are you now?

These questions are designed to help you review the important concepts covered in the chapter. Answering these questions can help you assess your own understanding or prepare for a test.

1. In your own words, define *peer mentor*. What characteristics do effective mentors have in common?

2. Describe how you have either mentored or been mentored in both formal and informal peer mentoring situations. How did the formal and informal situations differ for you?

3. Explain the fundamental difference of approach between tutoring and mentoring.

4. What specific benefits of being a peer mentor might appeal to different people?

5. How can a peer mentor's motivation affect the way he or she mentors and his or her overall satisfaction with the mentoring relationship?

6. What can you do to ensure that you maintain a good balance between peer mentoring and your own education?

Case Study Discussion

Review the case study at the beginning of this chapter, and answer the following questions as they relate to the concepts you learned in the chapter. Discuss your answers with other mentors in your program so that you can explore different perspectives and gain greater insight into how to help this person.

Why is Laura's experience relevant in this chapter?

What would you need to know to help a student like Laura?

If you had to help Laura, how would you approach the situation?

If your initial idea didn't work, what else could you do to help Laura?

⊕ Where do you want to be?

Reflect on what you have learned about mentoring in this chapter, and consider how you will apply these ideas to your specific responsibilities as a mentor.

1. What do you consider the most valuable concept in this chapter?

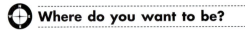

2. Why was it significant to you?

_____

_____

_____

_____

3. How will you apply this concept as a mentor?

_____

_____

_____

_____

Helping Students Make the Transition to College

Before starting college, Danielle spent her life working on the family farm. She was recruited and awarded an athletic scholarship because she was an outstanding softball player in high school. Even though it is not softball season, she works out and attends softball practice for several hours a day.

This is Danielle's first experience away from her family and living on her own in a larger city. She appears to be distracted by the different places and activities to explore. In class, Danielle flirts with the boys sitting around her and sends text messages on her cell phone, so she misses a lot of information and rarely takes notes.

Danielle attends class, but apparently she doesn't study effectively. She has not completed many assignments and currently has a D+ average. If she does not earn at least a C average this semester, she will

18

not only be ineligible to play, but she will also be in jeopardy of losing her scholarship.

When you asked Danielle if you could help her, she blew you off. She acted like she wasn't bothered by her poor grades. When she was a high school athlete, someone was always checking on her and making sure she got passing grades. Other things were always "taken care of" by Mom and Dad. Perhaps she figures the same will happen with her professors in college.

As you discuss the following questions with other mentors in your program, remember that this case study has been written about a real student facing real challenges. We encourage you to imagine the complexity of the situation and not to oversimplify the issues that the student faces. You may not feel experienced enough to completely answer the questions at this point, but you will have an opportunity to revisit this case study after learning the concepts in this chapter.

What problems may Danielle be facing in her transition to college life?

What challenges does this situation present for the mentor?

What would you do as a mentor to help Danielle resolve some of her problems?

 Where are you going?

After reading this chapter, you should be familiar with the following concepts related to mentoring.

- Factors affecting a student's transition to college
- Differences between high school and college
- Steps to make successful transitions

- Purpose of first-year programs
- Effect of peer mentors on student development

Key Terms

In this chapter, you will encounter the following terms, which appear in bold. You can highlight the definitions as you read or look for the terms in the glossary at the end of the book.

First-year Experience® (FYE)
Interdependence
Learning community
Retention

Schlossberg's transition theory
Student involvement
Transition

What Factors Affect a Student's Transition to College?

Psychologists have defined a **transition** as "any event that results in changed relationships, routines, assumptions, and roles."[1] Danielle was clearly experiencing a transition in which her role as a student had changed; some of the assumptions she made in high school were not applicable in college. Many students like Danielle have trouble making the transition to college because they are overwhelmed by their new situation and don't understand how to manage their time, study effectively, meet new people, or ask for help. Some students overcome these challenges with only a little assistance, but others are so unprepared that they don't know why they are even in school, let alone what they hope to accomplish.

A Tale of Two Students

Student A started his college experience with apprehension. He would be the first in his family to seek higher education. How would college be different from high school? In high school he had been on the honor roll, active in clubs, and part of a large social circle. He enrolled in the large local university and immediately recognized some of his inadequacies. How could he compete with so many students who were more mature than he and who seemed to understand what was going on? He felt isolated. Each day after class, he worked at a part-time job, and he returned home around 11:00 P.M. each night. He struggled in his classes. After two semesters, he had failed one course, received Ds in two others, and earned a few Cs and Bs. He had a 1.9 GPA and ended his first full year of college on academic warning.

Student B also began college with apprehension. He was the first in his family to try to obtain higher education. He enrolled in a local community college and wondered how he would fare competing with so many students. He also worked at a part-time job and got home around 11:00 P.M. each night. But his communications professor took him under her wing and began to informally mentor him. She taught him study strategies that improved his ability to perform well in class. Over the course of two years, he took three classes from the professor, and she helped him apply for and receive a scholarship at the community college. Later she encouraged him to continue his education at a university. He believes that her influence led to his selection as an outstanding student at the end of his second year.

What made the difference in the transition experiences of these two students? Would it surprise you to know that they are really one person?

Mitchell's first year of college is described in the story of Student A. He left the university and attended the community college as Student B. Why did he succeed in the second transition, but not in the first? Mitchell would tell you that he failed because he felt isolated and suffered through his first year on his own. When he transferred to the second college, someone took an interest in him and mentored him to become a successful, effective student. To this day, he credits the communications professor with keeping him in school and setting him on a path to graduate magna cum laude, complete a master's degree program, and enjoy a successful career in higher education.

Schlossberg's Transition Theory: The Four Ss

A mentor was able to help Mitchell make a more successful transition at the local community college. As a mentor, you can be instrumental in helping students adapt to the college environment, but it is important to understand that many complex issues affect an individual's ability to make a successful transition. In *Counseling Adults in Transition*, Schlossberg, Waters, and Goodman identified four main factors that affect how well a person deals with change.[2] These factors are known as **Schlossberg's transition theory**.

1. **Situation**. In most cases, students choose to enter college, and they view the available opportunities as positive. But they may find themselves in new situations that are out of their control and difficult to manage because they lack previous experience. Many students also deal with other concurrent stresses such as relationships, health, and finances.

2. **Self**. The factors that influence a student's sense of self include gender, age, ethnicity, and socioeconomic status, as well as the student's outlook, commitment, and values. As discussed in Chapter 5, students' perceptions of themselves affect the decisions they make and the outcomes they achieve.

3. **Support**. A student's sources of social support include close relationships, family, groups of friends, and a sense of belonging to the campus community. In Mitchell's case, support from someone on campus was the most significant factor in his making a successful transition to college. A recent national survey found that "The primary factor directly impacting whether or not a student stays in college and graduates is the quality of the interaction he or she has with a concerned person in the campus community."[3] As you can see, many students need the type of support that a mentor can offer.

4. **Strategies**. These include strategies for adapting to new situations and managing different types of stress as students move through the transition to college. A transition involves changes in a student's relationships, roles, and routines, and students need to adopt new strategies to deal with the various changes in their lives.

As a mentor, you can try to understand each student's individual attributes and unique situation, and you offer support and share your own strategies for being successful in college. In

> ## ◤MENTOR'S VOICE
>
> *It was very difficult for me to make the needed transition, even though I wanted very much to be in school. I know that there are students out there that are like I was and I hope that I can apply the skills I learned to help them.*
>
> **Sam Cardenas**, peer mentor

ACTIVITY 2.1   Analyzing the Transition to College

Answer the following questions to better understand your own transition to college. Discuss these questions with another student. This will give you practice in discussing key transition issues with other students as well as help you develop a broader perspective about how students deal with the transition to college.

1. **Situation**
   - Was beginning college a major or minor event in your life? Explain.

   _____

   _____

   - What stresses affected you as you made the transition to college?

   _____

   _____

2. **Self**
   - Did you feel that your personal attributes (such as gender, age, ethnicity, and socioeconomic status) were an advantage or disadvantage? Explain.

   _____

   _____

   - How would you describe your attitude toward your new experience in college?

   _____

   _____

3. **Support**
   - What types of support did you have as you were making the transition?

   _____

   _____

   - How significant was this support in helping you move through the transition?

   _____

   _____

4. Strategies

- What strategies helped you adapt to new situations and deal with stress?

_____

_____

- What strategies do you know of now that would have been helpful as you were making the transition to college?

_____

_____

Mitchell's case, support made a significant difference in his ability to succeed. In his first attempt, he was frightened and alone, and he nearly failed. In the second, a mentor guided him to strategies he needed to build his confidence. Like the communications professor, you can be a friend and teach key strategies to help students deal with problems they will encounter as they cross from high school to college. But you must also remember that you are a single factor among many complex factors. It may be difficult to recognize a student's challenges and needs at a particular moment, and in some cases it will be beyond your ability to deal with those challenges and needs.

How Is College Different from High School?

As a peer mentor, you have many things in common with other students at your educational institution. You entered higher education within the last couple of years, so you understand many of the changes involved in the transition. You have successfully joined a new culture with its own set of rules, both spoken and unspoken. You can help new students recognize and adjust to some critical differences between high school and college. The sooner students understand these differences and the obstacles they may cause, the sooner they can deal with them on their own.

New academic standards. Often professors assign more reading and give fewer tests in college than in high school. They expect you to spend more time studying, but they give less guidance about what or how to study.

Differences in teaching styles. Instructors in higher education are often immersed in their subject matter. They might struggle to make the subject as interesting to you as it is to them, and they may not try to connect with the students in their classes.

An abundance of choices. A high school student typically takes classes in only a few buildings and knows many of the students and teachers for several years. Decisions about what classes to take are often governed by state guidelines, which limit the options. A college student can be easily overwhelmed by the number of courses, departments, buildings, and instructors. They can add up to a confusing array of choices for new students.

Pressure to select a major. Students often feel pressure to select a major when they register. Some students have clear ideas about what they want to do in their future careers, while other students do not even know what the advisor means when talking about majors.

Larger, more diverse classes. Colleges may enroll hundreds or thousands more students than even the largest high schools. The different class sizes, educational experiences, cultures, and values of instructors and other students are adventures into the unknown for most students.

Attendance. In many classes, attendance is not required or even checked. Most professors view attendance as the student's responsibility, and students who do not attend classes pay the consequences. Research has shown that there is a strong correlation between attendance in class and student success.

Time management. In reality, students do not need to manage time; they need to learn to manage themselves. Students spend less time in class in college than they did in high school, but they are expected to spend more time studying. They need to plan to spend quality time studying.

Meeting new people. Though this may seem like an insignificant problem to many students, almost half the students who were surveyed at one college listed difficulty making friends as one of the reasons they dropped out.[4] Some students have been in the same peer group for most of their lives, and they lack the social skills to make new friends. They are overwhelmed by the number of unknown faces they see in the college environment.

Roommates. Moving away from the familiar confines of home can be extremely stressful. For some students, living in an unfamiliar place with people who have very different habits and values can be overwhelming.

Social activities. While social activities are not necessarily unique to college, students often experiment with, and indulge in, their newfound freedom. Lack of self-control at parties or poor judgment on a date can create additional challenges and stresses for some students.

Change in sleeping and eating habits. Many first-year students adopt poor health habits. Some eat mostly junk food, while others party all night. They compromise their health and their ability to learn because they don't get adequate rest and proper nutrition.

Questions about identity and values. The identities of many teenagers revolve around family or peer group values. Many new students have never considered what their values are or how new ideas might affect their behavior inside and outside the classroom. The process of developing their own identities and values can be stressful for many students.

ACTIVITY 2.2   Understanding Different Perspectives

Interview three students about their transition from high school to college. Record their responses and reactions below. Look for people in different situations who can help you identify a variety of issues that students deal with when they are making the transition.

1. In your experience, what was the most significant difference between high school and college?

_____

_____

_____

2. How did you adapt to this change?

_____

_____

_____

Financial difficulties. Many students come to college with no prior experience managing a budget. The study cited earlier showed that eight out of ten students listed financial reasons for dropping out of school.[5]

Unfamiliar campus. Most college campuses are significantly larger than even the largest high schools, and many students do not want to be seen using campus maps. Finding classes and moving between classes and buildings can be disorienting during the first few weeks of the semester.

Despite the challenges new students face, if they can cope with their initial discomforts they will one day enjoy the opportunities that come with all these changes. Higher education presents students with new freedom to express themselves along with new choices—what classes to take, how to structure their time, what to study, and with whom to associate. Peer mentors can help students as they learn to make significant choices about their futures.

How Can Mentors Help Students Make Successful Transitions?

Experienced students can help new students make decisions about classes and majors, take on academic challenges, and face personal problems because they have struggled with many of the same things. A mentor's experience is

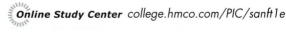
Online Study Center college.hmco.com/PIC/sanft1e

recent and relevant to other students. You can become a trusted friend who can help students overcome minor frustrations or significant challenges. The students you interact with are likely to look to you and use your guidance and advice as they figure out what they can do to become successful college students.

The ABCs of Mentoring Students in Transition

Students may not be aware that many of the issues they are struggling with are related to their transition. The following steps will help you address transition issues that your students may have and help them identify strategies for dealing with these issues.

Acknowledge the student's reality. You cannot help a student if you do not understand his or her perspective. When you hear concern or frustration, do not assume that you understand the student's circumstances. Transition is a complex process involving many factors. Ask the student to explain his or her concern, and listen to the answer. Also ask the student to consider his or her assumptions, and help the student see the effect of these assumptions.

Be strategic *and* student-focused. After you have all the information the student is willing to share, ask what the student thinks she or he should do. Listen carefully to the response. What the student thinks she or he should do is often the best way for the student to solve the problem. She or he may not have thought it through, and rephrasing the response may make the student realize the solution.

Many times, mentors want to solve students' problems for them, but it's important to focus on a student's goals, not your goals for the student. You can help the student determine whether the outcome is reasonable and, if so, how to go about realizing it. If the student cannot see beyond the immediate situation, perhaps you can offer an alternative point of view.

Commit student to do it! The student will not commit to a plan of action unless he or she has been involved in developing the plan. Help the student clarify his or her intentions, and promise to follow up. Most students are more likely to keep a commitment if they know that they will have to be accountable to someone.

Your encouragement and guidance could help other students deal with the frustrations and challenges they face in college. Preparing answers to common concerns of first-year students will help you acknowledge their reality, be strategic, and help them commit to success in this phase of their lives.

If you were a mentor to each of these students, how would you respond?

Class is so boring. I could just read the book. Why do I have to go?

I'm homesick. I don't have any friends here.

I didn't want to come to college. My parents made me come

I freak out whenever I have to take a test—especially math tests.

Homework takes up all my time. I don't have time for anything I want to do.

Between my job and my roommates, I don't have any time to study.

I am so busy with school, work, and friends that I'm not eating well or getting enough sleep. When I get home, my whole body just shuts down.

ACTIVITY 2.3   Helping Students Make Successful Transitions

Choose one of the statements above, and role-play a conversation with another student. Acknowledge the student's concern, and find out more about his or her situation. Help the student identify a specific goal and strategy to address the concern. Commit the student to follow through. Together, answer the following questions. Then switch places and act out the scene again, with the person who played the student acting as the mentor.

1. Summarize the student's concerns and the peer mentor's advice.

_____

_____

_____

2. How effective do you think the peer mentor's strategy was?

_____

_____

3. What, if anything, would you do differently if you encountered the same situation with one of the students you are mentoring?

_____

_____

Why Do Campuses Have First-year Experience Programs?

In 1989 *The Freshman Year Experience* was published by M. Lee Upcraft and John N. Gardner. Your position as a mentor is more than likely a result of the national movement in higher education that this book began. The research shows that students' experiences during the first year significantly affect their success in college. Campuses across the United States have implemented programs and initiatives that address the critical needs of first-year students, including

- Developing intellectual and academic competence
- Establishing and maintaining interpersonal relationships
- Exploring identity development
- Deciding on a career
- Maintaining health and wellness
- Considering faith and spiritual dimensions of life
- Developing multicultural awareness
- Developing civic responsibility[6]

Peer Mentor Companion will help you increase your awareness of these needs and understand how you can assist students who are struggling with these issues.

First-year Experience® **(FYE)** programs involve campus-wide efforts to help students make successful transitions to college. Specifically, the programs aim to improve student success during the first year of college and to increase

retention by keeping students enrolled from the first year through graduation. First-year programs have received more attention and support from campus administrators and faculty in the last twenty-five years. Campus administrators, student service personnel, and academic faculty members have come together to adopt initiatives to help students succeed in the first year and achieve their educational goals. Your peer mentoring program is evidence of first-year initiatives on your campus.

Retention of students through graduation is one of the main objectives of first-year programs. Students leave school for many reasons. Some choose to transfer to different schools that have better programs in their fields. Others choose to take breaks because of financial or health concerns. The term *stopping out* is used to describe these students. Students who drop out entirely cause the greatest concern to administrators tracking retention because such students will not enjoy the benefits and opportunities available to those who have completed their education. An extensive amount of research has been done to determine how the campus community can better meet the needs of students so that they can stay in school. Table 2.1 illustrates common reasons why students do not continue their education.

As a peer mentor, you should be aware of the retention concerns on your campus. As you can see in Table 2.1, financial concerns are common among

Table 2.1: Common Reasons Students Do Not Continue Their Education

REASON	FOR TRANSFERRING	FOR STOPPING OUT	FOR DROPPING OUT
Academic Program Not Offered at Current College	X		X
Acceptance at Higher-Ranked College	X		
Family/Child-Care			X
Financial Aid Difficulties	X		
Financial Concerns	**X**	**X**	**X**
Health Concerns		X	
Lack of Academic Success	**X**	**X**	**X**
Marriage		X	X
Relationship Problems	X		
Relocation	X		
Travel/Taking a Break		X	
Working Full Time/Job Conflict		X	X

Source: J. Hoyt and M. Lundell, "Why Students Drop Out: A Retention Study at Utah Valley State College," *National Association for Developmental Education (NADE)* (Fall 1999).

all three groups of students who leave college. If you are aware of students who are struggling with financial concerns, you can connect them with professionals on your campus who can help. Many students know that financial aid is available, but they are intimidated by the process to qualify for it. If you are mentoring a student with financial concerns and you know someone in the financial aid office on your campus, you might suggest setting up a time for the two of them to meet. You may be able to help a student stay in college because you were able to intervene at a critical time.

The other most common concern is lack of academic success. According to a report by the National Center for Education Statistics, "Fewer than half of seventeen-year-olds 'can [read and] understand complicated literary and informational passages,' fewer than one in ten can perform algebra, and about six in ten can perform 'moderately complex' math."[7] A grim reality is that without help these students are likely to fail.

Your campus may offer a freshman seminar designed to help students learn more effectively. During the 1990s, researchers estimated that somewhere between 80 percent and 90 percent of all institutions of higher learning in the United States provided some type of first-year course designed to help under-prepared students.[8] Each year the number of college students enrolling in these personal development courses increases. In fact, almost 42 percent of all freshmen enrolled in public two-year colleges in 1999 were enrolled in freshman seminar courses.[9] As a peer mentor, you may be involved in this type of course. Students are often more willing to accept guidance from a peer, and you can help by recognizing their needs and helping them apply the strategies they learn in their FYE courses.

Many campuses have moved beyond a single FYE course to implement broader-based **learning communities**. In their most basic form, learning communities are a kind of coregistration or block scheduling that enables students to take courses together. The same students register for two or more courses, forming a sort of study team. Researcher Vincent Tinto discovered that being part of these shared learning experiences with adult and peer mentors led students to develop their own supportive peer groups during the first year.[10] The groups often extended beyond the classroom in ways that many students saw as an important part of their being able to persist in college. As one older student put it, "my learning group was like a raft carrying me over the rapids of my life."

For many students, the friendships formed in the learning community continued beyond the academic year, and they formed networks of friends that influenced the rest of their college experience. For some, the friendships were short-lived, simply a part of the FYE program. But even those students spoke highly of the experience and of the value of the friendships and the support. As a peer mentor, you may be involved in a learning community. You can help facilitate these relationships by providing opportunities for students to interact with one another.

Peer mentors can be a key part of any FYE program. Chapter 3 discusses your role and the mission of your program in more detail. The most important thing to remember is that you can make a difference in students' experience during their first year that will influence the rest of their college experience.

What Is the Effect of Peer Mentors on Student Development?

Students experience significant intellectual and personal growth during their years in college, and both you and the students you mentor may have a greater influence on each other than you realize. Peer groups not only provide emotional support and social interaction, but they can also help students adjust to their newfound independence, develop a sense of identity, and establish personal academic and career goals. While Astin acknowledges that you and your classmates have a "potent" effect on each others' development, he emphasizes that **student involvement** has a very strong influence on your personal development as well. Astin defines involvement as "the amount of physical and psychological energy"[11] that you invest in your college experience.

> ### EXPERT'S OPINION
>
> "The student's peer group is the single most potent source of influence on growth and development during the undergraduate years."
> **Alexander Astin**, *What Matters in College: Four Critical Years Revisited*

As a mentor, you devote an incredible amount of energy to helping others improve their academic experience, and you have the opportunity to interact with a variety of different people. Ironically, your efforts are focused on others, but the most noticeable effect may be on your own development. As you help others define and pursue their goals, you may find your own path to success becoming clearer and your confidence increasing. You may experience any of the following benefits.

- Clarifying personal values
- Developing your own sense of identity
- Gaining self-confidence
- Improving interpersonal skills
- Increasing self-awareness
- Recognizing the value of **interdependence**

Because you understand the benefits of getting involved, you positively affect another student's experience by encouraging that student to get more involved. Studies have shown that mentors dramatically increase student participation and positively affect the grade point averages of the students they mentor.[12] Vincent Tinto has done extensive research on the factors that affect student success in the first year of college. He claims that students need academic, social, and personal support, and they need to get involved and make frequent contact with faculty and students in the institution.[13] A mentor can provide

 Online Study Center *college.hmco.com/PIC/sanft1e*

the individual support and the incentive to get involved with a larger peer group. As students respond to your encouragement and take the initiative to create their own academic experience, they will receive the same benefits that you have received.

 Where are you now?

These questions are designed to help you review the important concepts covered in the chapter. Answering these questions can help you assess your own understanding or prepare for a test.

1. Identify the four Ss of Schlossberg's transition theory, and describe how they relate to making the transition to college.

2. Based on the reading and your discussions with other students, identify the five most-significant differences between high school and college for students on your campus.

3. List the ABCs of mentoring students in transition.

4. Explain the purpose of first-year programs.

5. Describe the effect of peer mentors on student development.

Case Study Discussion

Review the case study at the beginning of this chapter, and answer the following questions as they relate to the concepts you learned in the chapter. Discuss your answers with other mentors in your program so that you can explore different perspectives and gain greater insight into how to help this person.

Why is Danielle's experience relevant in this chapter?

What would you need to know to help a student like Danielle?

If you had to help Danielle, how would you approach the situation?

If your initial idea didn't work, what else could you do to help Danielle?

 Where do you want to be?

Reflect on what you have learned about mentoring in this chapter, and consider how you will apply these ideas to your specific responsibilities as a mentor.

1. What do you consider the most valuable concept in this chapter?

_____

_____

2. Why was it significant to you?

_____

_____

_____

_____

3. How will you apply this concept as a mentor?

_____

_____

_____

_____

3 Defining Roles

Case Study: "Keeping It All Inside"

Josh is a nineteen-year-old fresh-man majoring in international business. He was pleased with his first semester of college and his 3.6 GPA. He has exciting plans to do a study abroad program in Tokyo later this summer.

One month into the current semester, Josh's father took him out to dinner to tell Josh that he was planning to divorce Josh's mother. Josh's father told him not to talk to his mother about it until he was given permission. Two months later, Josh's father still has not confronted the mother, so only he and Josh know of his intentions. Josh is an only child, and his parents have begun to complain about each other to him. Josh has distanced himself from his father because he is angry that his father put him in this position.

When Josh comes to class, he sits alone against a wall and doesn't seem to pay attention. The instructor you work with informs you that Josh, who was an A student, is not turning in assignments and is in jeopardy of receiving a poor grade.

As you discuss the following questions with other mentors in your program, remember that this case study has been written about a real student facing real challenges. We encourage you to imagine the complexity of the situation and not to oversimplify the issues that the student faces. You may not feel experienced enough to completely answer the questions at this point, but you will have an opportunity to revisit this case study after learning the concepts in this chapter.

In your opinion, what are the greatest problems Josh is facing?

What challenges does this situation present for the mentor?

What would you do as a mentor to help Josh resolve some of his problems?

Where are you going?

After reading this chapter, you should be familiar with the following concepts related to mentoring.

- Peer mentor's roles with students
- Peer mentor development within each role
- Student's role with the mentor
- Peer mentor's role with the program

Key Terms

In this chapter, you will encounter the following terms, which appear in bold. You can highlight the definitions as you read or look for them in the glossary at the end of the book.

Connecting link
Facilitator
Learning coach

Peer leader
Student advocate
Trusted friend

What Are the Mentor's Roles in the Mentoring Relationship?

You are already aware that there are as many reasons that college students need mentors as there are college students, and it may appear that you will have to assume a different role for every need that each student has. As you think about Josh's story, you can probably identify different roles that you could take on.

Mentoring may seem like an overwhelming and impossible task if you believe that you must be everything to everybody. Chapter 2 mentioned Alexander Astin's finding that peers have the greatest influence on other college students. He also wrote that "One person in the right place and the right time can make a life-changing difference."[1]

As a peer mentor, you may be the right person, or you may help a student find the right person to help him or her succeed. You do not need to be everything to everybody, but if you understand a mentor's key roles and know which role is the right role at the right time, you will be able to influence your peers and help them identify their own needs.

The most significant roles a peer mentor has are trusted friend, connecting link, learning coach, student advocate, and peer leader.

> **Trusted friend.** As a peer mentor, you have a unique relationship with the students you serve because you consciously work to build trust and develop a friendship with each. Students are more likely to view you as a peer leader, a connecting link, a learning coach, or a student advocate if they first see you as a trusted friend. Your relationship with the student will give you more leverage than will all the knowledge you share.

FIGURE 3.1: The Five Roles of the Peer Mentor

Connecting link. A college campus provides countless opportunities to meet new people and discover new interests. As an experienced student, you have become acclimated to the campus environment. You can help students become part of the larger campus community. As a connecting link, you help students find their individual niches and feel like they belong on your campus.

Learning coach. Like a coach who helps team members reach their athletic potential, you will be expected to teach fundamental skills and strategies to help your students achieve academic success. Students who are entering college from high school or students who are returning to college after years in the work force often struggle to adapt to the rigor and pace of their studies. You can coach them through the process of acquiring successful study habits.

Student advocate. As an advocate, you protect the best interests of your students. You can advocate for them in many ways if you are aware of their rights and responsibilities. You can also help them become familiar with services that provide advising support, that help with policy solutions, that offer accessibility options, and more. You must be able to see and hear when they need support and help them network with people who can do more for them than they can do for themselves.

Peer leader. A leader is simply someone who works collaboratively

MENTOR'S VOICE

Being a peer mentor gives me an extra push or incentive to be better than an average student. It helps bring out the best in us because we are examples of doing exactly what is being taught.

Lori Bridges, peer mentor

with others and inspires them with his or her own vision. As a mentor, you are no longer solely focused on your individual success. You have become a leader within a community of students who are all striving for success. As you demonstrate success for your students, they will be inspired to follow your example.

How Do You Develop Your Abilities to Be an Effective Mentor in Each Role?

Trusted Friend

A mentor's role is more complex than that of a tutor or teaching assistant because a mentor is committed to developing a relationship with students that extends beyond the classroom setting. In Chapters 4 and 8, you will learn more about building relationships and communicating with the students you mentor. Because the relationship is critical to mentoring, being a trusted friend is the first and most important role you will fill. If you are a friend, you will know enough about your students to help guide their transition to the college experience.

Your ability to make friends begins with the impressions you give of yourself. One of the most important traits to develop as a mentor is approachability. You need to make people whom you haven't met before feel comfortable in your presence.

The following checklist provides valuable concepts to keep in mind as you attempt to create friendships with the students you mentor. Look carefully at each to determine your levels of proficiency. Are there areas to work on to improve the way you develop friendships with and influence people? If so, set goals and follow through.

- ✔ **First impressions.** Smile! You have seven seconds to begin creating lasting impressions. It is very difficult to change negative ones.
- ✔ **Acknowledgement.** Listen carefully. Nod and question. Demonstrate that you care by paying attention.
- ✔ **Charisma.** Be a positive influence on others by making a personal connection with them.
- ✔ **Courtesy.** Just say "please," "thank you," and "excuse me."
- ✔ **Gratitude.** Don't just say it. Show it. Send a note.
- ✔ **Image.** It's not just looks; image is a powerful force. It's the way you carry yourself physically, emotionally, and intellectually.
- ✔ **Reputation.** It's not just what you say. What message does your behavior send?
- ✔ **Presence.** Be consistent; maintain confidence in yourself and enthusiasm about the potential of others.

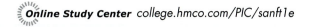
Online Study Center college.hmco.com/PIC/sanft1e

After the first impressions are made, developing trust takes time and patience. Begin by clarifying students' expectations of you and of how your mentoring roles relate to their needs. Some of their expectations will be realistic, and some will be unrealistic, but you need to address all of them. Come to a formal or informal agreement about what you are able and qualified to do for them. As students understand your roles and you begin to satisfy their needs, they will see you as a competent mentor. If they know that you are genuinely concerned about them, they will begin to respect you for your character. You need to demonstrate both character and competence to begin to develop trust. Once trust is established, do all you can to maintain it.

EXPERT'S OPINION

"To be truly effective in any area, a person must have a balance of high character and high competence. As people balance these two elements, they build personal trustworthiness and their trust with others."

Stephen R. Covey,
The 7 Habits of Highly Effective People

Your relationships with students will grow as you interact with them. Keep in regular contact with them, and listen when they need to talk about the stresses in their lives. Keep confidences and promises. It is important to note, however, that you should not become a therapist or a surrogate parent. Part of being trustworthy is defining and maintaining proper boundaries.

STRATEGIES FOR becoming a trusted friend:

- Be available.
- Make regular contact.
- Clarify expectations.
- Establish and maintain boundaries.
- Keep confidences.
- Show empathy

Connecting Link

Developing students' connections to campus is critical to their success and the college's retention of students. Your role as a connecting link is vital in helping students find ways, both inside and outside of the classroom, to get involved with their education.

Students are drawn to higher education for various reasons. Some want to attend class and then leave. Others want to fit in. Still others want to enjoy the social aspect. You can provide students with a connecting link to

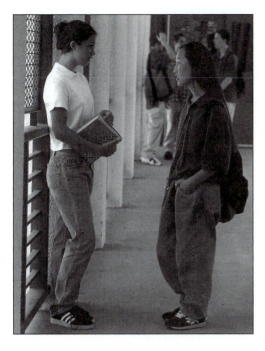

campus if you believe that your campus has something to offer everyone. Your attitude will help shape the attitudes of your students as they connect with available opportunities.

The thing that determines success on campus will not be heredity, intellect, opportunity, or even educational experience. These factors may heavily influence it, but the determining factor is attitude. Psychologist and philosopher William James said, "The greatest discovery of my generation is that a human being can alter his life by altering his attitudes."[2] Students may be ambitious or lazy, interesting or dull, responsible or undependable, successful or unsuccessful, all based on their attitudes. The willingness to seek out connecting activities will help your students make the most of their higher education experience.

Campuses have a myriad of extracurricular resources available to students. Chapter 11 tells how to utilize them. A peer mentor who knows what is available can often link students with activities related to their interests faster than the students can link to them on their own. The connections

ACTIVITY 3.1 Students' Attitudes toward Campus

After you have answered the following questions on your own, talk with several other students to get their answers to the questions. Their responses can provide insights that may be useful as you mentor students whose perspectives are different than your own.

1. How do you feel about your campus?

_____

_____

_____

_____

2. Why did you choose to attend this school?

_____

_____

_____

_____

3. What opportunities have you enjoyed at this school that you might share with the students you mentor?

_____

_____

_____

_____

4. Do you believe most students can benefit from becoming involved in your campus community? Why?

_____

_____

_____

_____

can be with faculty and staff members, student activities, clubs, departments, and so on.

Make the effort to attend some activities with your students. When you demonstrate how you take advantage of the educational and recreational learning experiences offered on your campus, you truly become a connecting link. Table 3.1 lists resource areas that are found on many campuses. You can revise this list to reflect what is available at your own institution.

STRATEGIES FOR becoming a connecting link:

- Help students identify activities that are meaningful to them.
- Know what opportunities are available.
- Participate in campus activities.
- Understand the social dynamics on your campus.

Table 3.1: Campus Resources for Students in Transition

ACADEMIC TUTORING

Academic Workshops and Seminars	Multicultural Center
Advising Center	Music and Theater Productions
Art Gallery	Outdoor Recreation and Education
Athletic Events	Planetarium Presentations
Career Services	Service-Learning Center
Clubs and Organizations	Student Activities (dances, concerts,
Faculty Members	etc.)
Guest Speakers	Student Government
Health and Wellness Centers	Student Media and Publications
Intramural Activities	Study Groups
Library Tutorials	Workout Facilities
Math Lab	Writing Lab

Learning Coach

Peer mentors work to help students identify learning strengths and achieve their potential. Students are often unaware of their own learning styles. A mentor can help identify certain learning preferences and guide students through a process of discovering how to approach learning based on those preferences.

Some learners are primarily interested in personal meaning. These students tend to seek a purpose, yet they may struggle to understand why they want what they want. To successfully create a positive experience for students with this learning style, the mentor's coaching role is to be a motivator. Peer mentors may have similar views about the value of a college education and can be more effective than professors in helping these students find their own motivation for becoming successful.

Other students are primarily interested in facts. They want explicit instructions, and they focus on the details of an assignment. A mentor can help students with this learning style by introducing them to experts. The mentor may not fill the role of expert, but he or she can direct the student to a qualified tutor or teaching assistant.

Many students are more interested in hands-on learning experiences than in theoretical discussions. These students want to stop talking and start doing something. They look to mentors to coach them through learning processes and experiments. They are most interested in the mentor's practical application of course information. For example, if you are mentoring in a study skills course, you could teach the strategies you use for taking effective notes in different types of classes.

Finally, some students want to pursue alternate applications. They want to do things differently than they have been done before. They want to come up with something that is creative and new. A mentor will get the best response from students with this learning style by encouraging creativity and offering suggestions for improvement.

One of the best ways to effectively coach your students through the learning process is to be an example of good study and learning habits. Chapters 9 and 10 explore some of these ideas in more depth. You will need to pay close attention to the wants and needs of your students if you desire to do your best with this role.

STRATEGIES FOR becoming a learning coach:

- Be aware of learning styles.
- Demonstrate effective study strategies.
- Facilitate study groups.
- Make time for one-on-one mentoring.
- Prepare appropriate presentations.
- Remember that a question can be better than an answer.
- Set learning goals.

Student Advocate

An advocate is a person who defends or maintains a cause for someone else. Peer mentors serve as advocates for the needs, interests, and rights of first-year students who are making the transition to college. This role includes making students feel at ease by advocating for them when their inexperience or lack of knowledge causes hardship. A lot of students simply need a temporary advocate— someone who can step in with crucial information at the right moment.

A popular, if cynical, belief is that it isn't *what* you know but *whom* you know that counts. As a peer mentor, you know things and you know people who can do things for students. If you have vital information about campus services, you can be one of the greatest resources they have. You can be a part of the solution if you know the resources and your students know that you know. Chapter 11 will help you identify available resources.

The advocate role requires you to be a trusted friend to your students. You need to be aware of warning signs that students may be in trouble or experiencing difficulties. You will want to pay attention to things like whether your students are attending class, paying attention, and completing assignments on time. These clues can often lead you to larger problems your students may be having. They may not be doing homework, and the reason could be that they are having trouble with landlords, bosses, family, roommates, finances, and so on.

Some warning signs to watch for are

Change in attitude about school

Sleeping in class

Not attending class

Missing or being late with assignments

Ambivalence about their performance

Negative changes in appearance

Negative comments about themselves

Negative comments about others

Being quickly angered or bothered

Remember that you are a peer mentor, not a magician. You cannot wave a wand and make everything better. You also do not need to take on responsibility for your students' needs. You are a resource that can lead them to the help they need. Do not allow them to abuse your relationship by making you an equal partner in their problems. If you notice that a student is being clingy or wants you to enable him or her in inappropriate behavior, seek guidance from your program administrators and instructors immediately.

Advocates should observe ethical standards as they strike a balance between needs and wants. You will want to make sure to stay focused on your student's needs, not just on their wants. Your students will usually learn more from experiencing the consequences of poor decisions than from finding loopholes in the system.

Does your program have an identified code of ethics for mentors? If not, you may want to refer to these basic ethical guidelines.

Commitment. Fulfill your obligations to your program.

Competence. Know what you are talking about.

Integrity. Be honest with your students, yourself, and the program.

Respect. Value and support the differences of others.

Responsibility to self. Adhere to program policies of professional conduct.

Responsibility to students. Maintain appropriate confidentiality.

MENTOR'S VOICE

A student advocate knows people and services on campus. They practice ethical behavior and they know the students' rights and responsibilities. A student came to me with her story of how a professor humiliated her in front of her class by insulting her race and gender. I encouraged her to talk to the professor and state her expectations and needs as his student. When she approached him she received more excuses and insults and the situation was still unresolved. I helped her know her rights as a student and what resources (Judicial Affairs) were available for her needs. If I hadn't learned my advocate role I wouldn't have had an idea of how to help her.

Deanna Yocum, peer mentor

 Online Study Center *college.hmco.com/PIC/sanft1e*

STRATEGIES FOR becoming a student advocate:

- Know people and services on campus.
- Know rights and responsibilities.
- Practice ethical behavior.

Peer Leader

It is likely that you are already familiar with several of the most commonly held leadership traits, including self-confidence, adaptability, empathy, influence, and collaboration. There are several other important traits you will want to develop to effectively lead those who see you as a peer: authenticity, initiative, goal identification, planning, delegation, support, and attitude. Perhaps the best way to demonstrate these traits is by example.

Authenticity. As a peer mentor you want to be authentic with your students. You don't want to pretend to be something you are not. People usually can recognize when you are being phony. Another word for being authentic is transparency. Be who you are. It is okay for students to see your strengths and weaknesses. Knowing that you also have struggles will help students view you as one of them, and you will be more believable.

Initiative. A peer leader takes initiative to get things done. You can't just sit around waiting for your students to come to you with questions or concerns. Unless you have already demonstrated your interest in them, they probably won't come to you. If you are paying attention, you will often be aware when something needs to be addressed, and you may be the person who gets the ball rolling. Peer mentors who wait for students to come to them often miss opportunities to help until it is too late.

Goal identification. One of the most useful things you can do is assist students in the identification of individual or group goals. Some students will be proficient at setting goals, but many will not have experience with it. You can facilitate setting students' personal educational goals, and you can also help students determine goals on class projects and study groups.

Planning. You can be a leader to your students if you show how to plan for success. You will want to utilize your students' skills and input as you develop plans together. Good planning takes organizational skills. Once goals have been identified, take the necessary time to organize a plan of action that makes sense and has clear objectives.

Delegation. Effective leaders know they can't do everything by themselves. It is important to delegate responsibilities to students. This provides them with opportunities to develop and strengthen their own skills. Peer mentors can often learn as much from their students as their students learn from them. It never hurts to allow for different perspectives.

Support. Providing the right amount of support in a given situation is key to leadership. At times you may need to provide direction, but resist the urge to take over, even if you feel you could do things better and/or faster by yourself. You are part of an institution of learning, and personal experience is often the best teacher.

Attitude. Leadership is a battle often won or lost with the attitude of the leader. Your attitude affects the whole group. Students often mirror their mentors. If the peer mentor indicates that an assignment is pointless, students will be inclined to agree. Be optimistic. Let students know that you believe in them and in the things you ask them to do.

Example. As a peer mentor, perhaps the best thing you can do is to be an example to your peers. When you lead by example, you show students how you have become a successful student. Students don't always want to be told what they should do. Most will watch to see what you do. You will not be able to lead them if you don't "walk the talk." You demonstrate your example through the habits you employ.

How Will Your Habits Affect Your Mentoring?

Widely recognized as one of the greatest powers is habit or ritual—you obey your habits. A habit is often stronger than discipline or willpower. Habit is to success what the rails and ties are to a train; as the rails support and guide the engine, each of the cars willingly follows. Nearly unseen as the train goes by are the dozens of ties under the rails to help distribute the load of the speeding train. In this same way, habit supports and guides your personal success as well as the success of your students. The rails and ties represent your knowledge of and experience with the terrain. Do your rails and ties make a solid track? Will your students succeed if they emulate your habits? Activity 3.2 on page 47 will help you evaluate this.

The following habits are essential if you want to be a successful student: study habits, work habits, thinking habits, and planning habits. You cannot fake these habits. How well do you perform in each of these areas?

Study habits. Inability to manage time is the most frequently identified cause of college failure. Many students achieve academic success by setting aside time to study and knowing exactly what needs to be accomplished during that time. Study time by itself is not enough; the study *habit* is all-important. You should plan not only when you will study, but also where you will study and how you will prepare yourself to make the most of your study time.

Work habits. There is no excellence without labor, and there are very few things that you can do well before your muscles have committed them to memory. You can listen forever to instructions on how to play basketball, but if the skill is not established in your muscle memory as a habit, you will not be a good basketball player. Anyone desiring success will utilize the power of good work habits and practice, practice, practice until he or she achieves the desired results.

Thinking habits. Scientists, scholars, and philosophers at the time of Galileo embraced flawed ideas; no amount of energy or effort would make the world flat. Many student problems develop because of poor thinking habits. Before you can get someone else to think, you must become a critical thinker. Your demonstration of critical thinking skills— asking questions, analyzing data, being open to different possibilities, utilizing a systematic approach to study—will be a good example for students to follow.

Planning habits. It has often been said that "if you fail to plan, you plan to fail." Effective planning includes identifying what you want, gathering information, assessing your alternatives, listing pros and cons, creating a plan of action, and continually evaluating your choices. If you would like to instill particular habits in your students, you need to be certain that you first include those habits in your own life.

TRATEGIES FOR becoming a peer leader:

- Be authentic.
- Take the initiative.
- Identify individual or group goals.
- Plan for success with organization.
- Delegate responsibilities.
- Resist the urge to take over.
- Remember that your attitude affects the whole group.
- Be an example.

What Is the Student's Role in the Mentoring Relationship?

As students become engaged in the mentoring relationship, they will begin to take responsibility and learn from their own experiences. Table 3.2 will help you clarify the distinction between your responsibility and the student's responsibility in that relationship.

Table 3.2: Roles and Responsibilities

STUDENT'S RESPONSIBILITY	MENTOR'S RESPONSIBILITY
• Make personal discoveries.	• Encourage thoughtfulness.
• Determine intentions.	• Identify tasks.
• Make and evaluate decisions.	• Clarify issues.
• Generate a plan.	• Suggest possible strategies.
• Take action.	• Follow up.

Students will gain the most from mentoring when they realize that they must play an active part and accept responsibility for their own success. You are a **facilitator**; you can assist with planning, processing information, and clarifying issues, but your goal is to help each student become independent and self-directed.

Students also have responsibilities in each of the five roles previously outlined for the peer mentor. Some students will naturally understand what

---

ACTIVITY 3.2 **Assessing Your Habits as a Student**

Identify your personal strengths and weaknesses for each of the habits listed below. Then consider the following questions: What have you done to develop good habits? What can you do to change poor habits? Identify a specific action plan to help you improve in one area.

1. Study habits

_____

_____

2. Work habits

_____

_____

3. Thinking habits

_____

_____

4. Planning habits

_____

_____

they can do within the roles, while others will rely on you to show them what their options are.

The first role addressed was the trusted friend. Students need to partner with you in building the relationship. As they show that they trust you by coming to you with questions or concerns, let them know that you find them trustworthy also. Friendship is a reciprocal relationship that requires both giving and taking. You will quickly learn that some of the people you are assigned to mentor will not be interested in developing a relationship with you. That is OK. Watch for the signs they give you, and try to keep the relationship within their comfort levels.

For you to be a connecting link to your students, they will need to make you aware of their areas of interest. They need to tell you about extracurricular activities that appeal to them. You may need to get the conversation started. But you cannot do it all. Students become part of a connecting network by making others aware of, or getting them to attend, activities of interest. When students share their interests with the rest of the class, the network expands naturally and quickly.

After relying on your example for a while, your students need to become their own learning coaches. Learning becomes more engaging when students take control of it and share the experience with others. Through study groups and casual discussions about course topics or life experiences, students can take learning out of the classroom and gain tremendous amounts of knowledge. You want to support them as needed, but let them take responsibility for facilitating their own learning. Students will not have you to lean on throughout their entire educational experience, so the sooner they take responsibility for their own learning, the better.

As students learn more about the resources available to help them, they develop more personal responsibility in the student advocate role. Each institution has identified rights and responsibilities to protect its students. Your students need to be aware of what their rights and responsibilities are. Talk to them about their needs, but let them do as much on their own as they can to advocate for themselves. Encourage them to share what they know with their peers as well.

Many of the students you mentor have the ability to lead others. Provide them with opportunities to be peer leaders to other students. Let them take the lead in study groups or share examples of how they do things with students in their classes. They can assist you with a presentation or with organizing an activity or service project. Often students will thrive when given opportunities for personal growth and development.

As a peer mentor, you can encourage your students to accept responsibility for their own learning by showing how you do it yourself. By your example, you teach them how they can teach themselves and get involved in their education. They cannot assume they will be completely entertained and engrossed by their courses and professors. As they make personal discoveries, decisions, and plans, they become more aware of what they can do to make the most of their learning. They learn to employ strategies on their own instead of relying on others to do it for them.

What Is the Mentor's Role within the Program?

Peer mentoring programs vary from campus to campus. In general, they focus on helping students make important transitions, but some mentors serve as orientation leaders, while others assist instructors in freshman seminar courses. Whatever your position in the program, it is important to understand how that position relates to the vision that the institution has for the program. If you understand the strategic directions of your program and the professional dynamics within it, you will be better prepared to contribute and to find satisfaction in what you do for the students.

You need knowledge of the program, the people, the procedures, and your personality.

Knowledge of the program. It is imperative to understand why you are in a peer mentoring position and what the expectations for that position are. You should understand the possibilities and the limitations. You should receive guidelines from your program that outline your rights and responsibilities as well as the goals and vision of the program.

Knowledge of the people. You may already know a lot about the demographics of the students you will serve because you are one of those students. You probably understand many of their needs and wants and ambitions. But do you know whom to turn to when you have a question about a student? Do you know the administrators who will support you in your role as a peer mentor? It is helpful to develop relationships with these people and to allow them to mentor you through the program.

Knowledge of the procedures. Your program has procedures for selecting peer mentors, making mentoring assignments, demonstrating accountability, and assessing your effectiveness. You should ask about these procedures and their purposes. Experienced mentors can help you understand the program's requirements and give you suggestions for working within the program. They will be able to share best-practice ideas they have developed through experience.

Knowledge of your personality. You must increase your own self-awareness. It is essential to have a clear understanding of yourself, of what is important to you, and of how you operate (what makes you tick). You need to know why you do things and how to develop self-mastery. You must create your own motivation, regulate your own learning, and follow through on your intentions. You are the only one who can account for the quality of the effort you make.

Knowing how to gather information and whom to approach with questions are vital and relate to the most important mentoring skill for you to acquire—the ability to communicate. As you increase your personal knowledge, you will also increase your confidence in your ability to utilize these important resources. Activity 3.3 is designed to help you build relationships within your program.

ACTIVITY 3.3 Understanding Your Program

Consult other peer mentors and/or program administrators to find answers to the following questions. Keep some of this information where it will be easily accessible, especially the requirements of your program, so you can access it when needed.

1. Does your program have a mission or vision statement? If so, what is it? If not, describe the mission of the program as you understand it.

_____

_____

_____

2. Briefly outline the basic requirements and procedures of your program.

_____

_____

_____

3. List the names of and contact information for the people who will mentor you within the program.

_____

_____

_____

4. Explain whether you think this program is a good fit for you and your personality.

_____

_____

_____

Where are you now?

These questions are designed to help you review the important concepts covered in the chapter. Answering these questions can help you assess your own understanding or prepare for a test.

1. Describe what peer mentors can do to become trusted friends to their students.

2. What are some of the most important connections you should know to link your students to?

3. What are the most important skills a peer mentor should employ while serving in the learning coach role?

4. As a student advocate, how can a peer mentor determine appropriate levels of involvement in solving a student's personal problems?

5. What do you believe are your greatest strengths and weaknesses as a leader, and what do you plan to do to improve?

6. In your own words, explain the difference between your role and the student's role.

Case Study Discussion

Review the case study at the beginning of this chapter, and answer the following questions as they relate to the concepts you learned in the chapter. Discuss your answers with other mentors in your program so that you can explore different perspectives and gain greater insight into how to help this person.

Why is Josh's experience relevant in this chapter?

What would you need to know to help a student like Josh?

Which peer mentoring roles would be most appropriate for you to use to help Josh?

If your initial idea didn't work, what else could you do to help Josh?

 ## Where do you want to be?

Reflect on what you have learned about mentoring in this chapter, and consider how you will apply these ideas to your specific responsibilities as a mentor.

1. What do you consider to be the most valuable concept in this chapter?

_____

_____

_____

2. Why was it significant to you?

_____

_____

_____

_____

Online Study Center college.hmco.com/PIC/sanft1e

3. How will you apply this concept as a mentor?

    _____

    _____

    _____

    _____

Establishing and Maintaining Relationships

Case Study: "Nowhere to Go"

Reneé is a freshman who has an hour commute from her parent's home to school. She takes care to look her best and is always dressed nicely. She is popular and always seems happy to be in the freshman-year-experience class you are assigned to mentor. She consistently contributes effectively when assigned individual and group work and has an A average in the class.

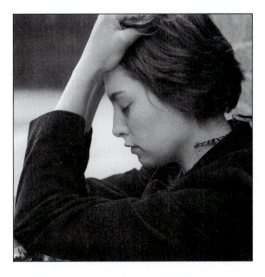

About midway through the semester, Reneé misses every class for a week and never indicates why she is not there. The next week you see a girl in the hallway who looks like Reneé but is dressed in dirty, wrinkled clothes and looks as though she has not bathed for a week. As you get closer, you realize that it is Reneé. She seems embarrassed and pretends she does not see you. You are genuinely concerned about her, so you approach her.

You discover that Reneé had a terrible argument with her parents, and they kicked her out of their home. She has been living out of her car for the past week. She has no friends living in the city where the college is located. She appears somewhat dazed and confused about what to do.

As you discuss the following questions with other mentors in your program, remember that this case study has been written about a real student facing real challenges. We encourage you to imagine the complexity of the situation and not to oversimplify the issues that the student faces. You may not feel

53

experienced enough to completely answer the questions at this point, but you will have an opportunity to revisit this case study after learning the concepts in this chapter.

In your opinion, what are the greatest problems Reneé is facing?

As a mentor, how would you establish a trusting relationship with Reneé so that she will be willing to open up to you?

What can you envision Reneé doing to resolve some of her problems?

What do you believe your role is in assisting her with her problems?

 Where are you going?

After reading this chapter, you should be familiar with the following concepts related to mentoring.

- Unique aspects of a mentoring relationship
- Positive attributes in a mentoring relationship
- Stages of a mentoring relationship

Key Terms

In this chapter, you will encounter the following terms, which appear in bold. You can highlight the definitions as you read or look for them in the glossary at the end of the book.

Boundaries
Confidentiality

Credibility
Mentoring relationship

What Makes the Mentoring Relationship Unique?

According to Rey Carr, a professional mentoring consultant, "Mentoring is primarily about creating an enduring and meaningful relationship with another person."[1] Both mentor and student must find meaning in order to actually achieve success. This idea can be overwhelming for some potential mentors because relationships require commitment, commitment spawns involvement, and involvement can place the mentor in a position of vulnerability. You cannot avoid this possibility. As the author Madeleine L'Engle said, "To be alive is to be vulnerable."[2] Accepting the challenge and learning to develop mature interpersonal relationships will be a significant part of your own development.

Chapter 3 identified your roles as a mentor and emphasized the importance of being a trusted friend. Your friendship with your students will be the foundation for everything else you do as a mentor, but it is important to understand that simply being a friend is not enough. Sometimes a friend may give in to peer pressure and fail to do things that need to be done. A friend may not respect certain **boundaries** or conditions that guide your behavior and limit the extent of your interaction in a mentoring relationship. As a mentor, you can definitely be a friend, but you also need to motivate your students to be effective.

The mentoring relationship needs to be a partnership rather than a subordinate relationship. The peer mentor and the student need to give equal effort. When the two parties collaborate as a team, things can work beautifully and at times can lead to unbelievable results. Peer mentors have described this type of interaction as exhilarating. However, if the person you are trying to mentor is not also committed to the mentoring relationship, it is frustrating to continue with your best efforts. Many peer mentors find it extremely difficult to work with a student who resists assistance. Sometimes a student may ask for help but refuses to make an effort to improve the situation.

The demands of a mentoring relationship multiply with every student you are assigned to mentor. You will more than likely be responsible for mentoring several different students, and each will present you with unique challenges as you work together to establish a relationship. Can you see that you are quite possibly in for a roller coaster ride as you serve in your mentoring role? To be as successful as possible, you need to understand how to generate and maintain good relationships with others. As you model your relationship skills, your students develop similar skills.

What Attributes Improve the Mentoring Relationship?

Students have identified certain attributes of their mentors that help them establish and maintain good relationships. The attributes include care for others, confidence, dependability, optimism, respect, and trustworthiness. They are essential in developing a relationship and becoming a trusted friend.

Other important attributes are not as obvious to students. The following list identifies attributes that your students will come to value as they learn more about your role as a mentor. In each of your roles, you will develop traits necessary to make your relationship with your students more effective.

Connecting link:

• Be aware of your student's interests.

• Get involved on campus.

• Include your students in activities.

• Show enthusiasm.

Learning coach:

• Apply effective learning strategies.

• Facilitate study groups.

• Focus on learning goals.

• Share personal experiences.

Student advocate:

• Be sensitive to your student's needs.

• Know your campus resources.

• Resolve conflicts within your group.

• Show empathy.

Peer leader:

• Be authentic.

• Be a positive influence.

• Encourage collaboration between students.

• Show initiative.

The last skill on the list may be the most important. In a mentoring relationship, it is your responsibility to show initiative and to put forth the effort necessary to get to know your students. You will not be an effective mentor if you wait for students to introduce themselves to you.

If you are committed to becoming the best possible mentor, keep these attributes in mind. They will make a difference in your relationship with students. Some of the attributes may come naturally to you, but others can be learned.

What Are the Stages of a Mentoring Relationship?

As in building any type of relationship, you will go through several identifiable stages in a **mentoring relationship**. The following questions will help you identify each stage.

Who are you?

Why are we here?

Where are we going?

How are you doing?

ACTIVITY 4.1   Attribute Awareness and Reflection

Speak to at least five other people. Ask them what attributes they want a peer mentor to have.

1. What responses were of most interest to you? Explain.

_____

_____

_____

_____

Reflect on what you've learned so far in this chapter and from this activity. Answer the following questions about yourself.

2. What attributes do you want in a peer mentor?

_____

_____

_____

3. Do you see these traits in yourself? If you do, in what ways do you demonstrate them? If you do not, which would you like to develop, and how might you do so?

_____

_____

_____

What is working? What is not working?

Are we there yet?

Each step in Figure 4.1 represents a stage in building a relationship with your students. The stages identified as "How are you doing?" and "What is working? What is not working?" continue throughout the relationship.

As shown in Figure 4.1, the model also incorporates the factor of time. You are involved in a formal mentoring relationship that is limited by time, and you must consider how you will move through each stage within the time frame. Trust must build through the entire process. Ask yourself at each stage what you can do to develop and maintain trust with those you mentor.

Online Study Center college.hmco.com/PIC/sanft1e

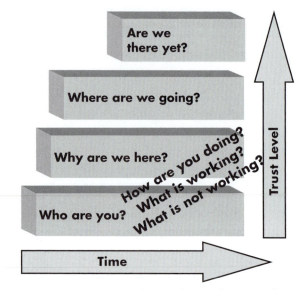

FIGURE 4.1: Mentoring Relationship Timeline

Who Are You?

This stage is the foundation for your relationship with your students. The question "Who are you?" will help you remember to begin by getting to know your students and letting them get to know you. Peer mentors who have taken time to contemplate their initial approach usually have the best experiences with this initial stage of the mentoring process.

You have probably heard the expression "You only get one chance to make a first impression." How will you approach your students for the first time so that they will be comfortable with you and will believe in your ability to help them? You can express confidence without appearing to be a know-it-all. You can also be personable and remain within the bounds of students' comfort levels. It is most important to keep the interaction real. Don't try to be someone you are not. You don't need to be perfect in everything you do. The fact that you have struggles now and then will increase your **credibility**; your challenges as a student make you more believable as a mentor. Students will recognize that you are just like them in some ways, but that you have "been there and done that," so they can learn from you.

The greatest caveat in this initial stage is to avoid doing something that will glaringly remove your credibility. This may sound obvious, but now and then a new peer mentor is so nervous about meeting students for the first time that she or he unwittingly says something offensive or so self-deprecating that it takes several meetings to get back to square one. The initial loss of potential effectiveness can be difficult to overcome.

 ACTIVITY 4.2 Making First Impressions

Think back to an occasion when you met a teacher, an advisor, or another campus employee for the first time.

1. Briefly describe a positive experience you had when meeting someone for the first time.

_____

_____

2. Briefly describe a negative experience.

_____

_____

3. What made the positive experience different than the negative experience?

_____

_____

4. What can you learn from this experience that will help you make meeting your students a positive experience?

_____

_____

STRATEGIES FOR helping you get to know your students:

- Create a getting-to-know-you survey.
- Break the ice with a name game.
- Get students' phone numbers and e-mail addresses.
- Take pictures with a digital camera to help you connect names and faces.
- Talk with students about their interests.
- Add other ideas:

_____

_____

 Online Study Center college.hmco.com/PIC/sanft1e

One of the best things to do early on is to make a concerted effort to know the names of the students you mentor. Do a getting-to-know-you activity that will help those involved discover things they have in common. Knowing things like where people are from and what their educational goals are can help break down some of the barriers that form when people begin new relationships. Make sure you are truly interested in the information you obtain. If it has no meaning to you, it will have no meaning to the students.

Why Are We Here?

The next stage involves clarifying your role as a mentor. Students may not respond well to your efforts to get to know them if they do not understand your motives. The question "Why are we here?" will remind you to be upfront about your responsibilities as a mentor and genuine about your interest in the other student.

The people you mentor need to know that you have a real concern for their well-being and success as students. This attitude will go a long way in getting the relationship started. It is also important for them to understand what you will not and cannot do for them. As discussed in Chapter 3, both the mentor and the student have roles in making the relationship successful. Review Table 3.2, which outlines the student's and the mentor's responsibilities. If you step out of these roles, you could be headed for trouble. If you have mutual understanding about the nature of the relationship, it will be strong and successful.

Typical ground rules for the mentoring relationship include honesty, commitment, boundaries, confidentiality, and expectations.

Honesty. If you expect your students to be honest with you, you must be honest with them. Don't overinflate your abilities or education.

Remember that you are a peer and that the students you mentor are on equal footing with you. It will not hurt your credibility if you say "I am not sure about that, so give me a chance to find out, and I will let you know." Students must also be honest with you. Hold them accountable for what they say or do. Let them know how it affects you as well as them.

Commitment. If you promise to do something, follow through on it. If a student promises to do something, he or she should follow through. A mentor who sets up a study group and fails to show up permanently damages his or her credibility. Similarly, a student who agrees to come to a study session and doesn't is also showing a lack of commitment. As the mentor, you must first model the behavior you expect. You can expect the same behavior from your students, and if they fail to follow through, you can let them know that you expect accountability.

Boundaries. One important thing to establish early in the relationship is a clear idea of boundaries. You are a student, but you are also in a position of authority and represent the educational institution. Just as there are boundaries to protect both faculty members and students, there need to be boundaries between you and the students you mentor. It is important for students to trust you and open up about their problems, but you need to avoid becoming too involved in personal issues. Always meet in a public place, and limit the amount of time you spend with students. If a student engages in inappropriate behavior or crosses the line, contact your program administrator immediately. For example, a student may call you repeatedly at all times of the day and night. Do not tolerate this situation. Your program administrator can help you confront the student and establish clearer boundaries.

Confidentiality. It is extremely important to understand the policies and procedures of **confidentiality** at your institution. Recognize when something is said in confidence, and protect the person by not sharing that information with unauthorized people. There are some things you can have access to and other things that you should not know. It is also important to keep confidences when students ask you to do so. If a situation is desperate, ask the professional staff in your program for guidance, but never break a confidence unless there is danger to the student or to other people.

Expectations. You don't want the students you mentor to become clones of you. Each is unique and has her or his own strengths and weaknesses. Know your students. Know what they want to achieve. Know what their abilities are. Encourage them without becoming overbearing. Help students achieve their best without feeling like they have to live up to someone else's expectations.

STRATEGIES FOR helping to clarify your role:

- Be available to students.
- Express willingness to help.
- Give students your contact information.
- Help connect students with campus activities.
- Refer students to resources they need.
- Add other ideas:

_____

_____

Where Are We Going?

The next stage involves establishing a clear direction in your relationship. As a mentor, you are expected to do more than simply hang out with your students. The question "Where are we going?" will remind you to work with the students to identify a clear objective and to set measurable goals.

You may wonder how to identify the needs of the students you mentor. Early in the relationship you will not automatically know what they need, but as the relationship builds you will become more adept at identifying their needs—perhaps even more adept than the students are. In the case study at the beginning of this chapter, for example, Reneé was unable to indicate what kind of help she needed.

Chapter 2 introduced the ABCs of mentoring and emphasized the need to be student-focused. The same principle applies in this stage of the mentoring relationship. Each student is different and has a unique set of needs. Do not assume that students need the same things you need. If you are struggling to identify a student's needs, talk to the student; he or she can give you more insight. An instructor or program administrator might also help you identify students who need you the most.

One way to get information is to ask questions. Asking questions will likely help you know what to do to help your students. Many students will be open to discussions and will freely provide answers. As you interact with your students, you might ask these questions.

What are your expectations of a mentoring relationship?

What are some things you want to accomplish with your education?

Tell me some of the greatest challenges you are facing at school right now.

What is the most difficult thing you have experienced in your transition to college?

If you weren't afraid of failing, what would you attempt to do?

What is something I can do that would be helpful to you?

What are your greatest strengths and weaknesses related to study habits?

If you are working with students in a classroom setting, pay attention to what is going on with them in class. Arrive early and listen to or participate in their conversations. In such an informal situation, you can often get the scoop on what is really going on. Walk with your students after class, and the same thing will often happen. Spending time with students outside of regular class time puts you on a level playing field.

Whatever you do, make sure your interactions with students come from sincere interest. They will see right through you if you appear to only want information from them. You also need to share information about yourself and your opinions and feelings. A successful relationship requires openness on both sides.

ⓈTRATEGIES FOR giving your relationship direction:

- Decide on specific goals. Let students set the goals; don't set the goals for them!
- Keep copies of students' goals.
- Monitor students' progress by following up.
- Respect students' personal limitations and boundaries.
- Add other ideas:

  _____

  _____

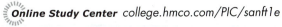

Ⓜ️ENTOR'S VOICE

My favorite thing about being a mentor this semester was becoming friends with my students and building relationships with them. Just being able to talk to them one on one about life, school, work, and other things. I know for myself I must be friends with someone and feel comfortable around them before I will ever go to them for help or advice.

Ashton McMullin, peer mentor

How Are You Doing?

This stage begins with your initial contact and may continue long after your formal mentoring relationship has ended. The question "How are you doing?" is a simple reminder to keep in touch with your students. Your efforts in this area may help you develop trust. You may also notice that as you interact more and more with the students both in and out of the classroom, your mentoring assignment becomes less of a chore and more enjoyable.

Friendship is part of the mentoring relationship. Do you consider a person who only nags you about what you should do to truly be a friend? Is someone who allows you to drop the ball on important things you want to accomplish truly a friend? As a mentor you need to be prepared and willing to talk to your students about all kinds of things that are going on in their lives—school, work, family, social life, and more. You need to walk a careful line as you interact with so many different types of people with different needs. For some students, a weekly e-mail reminder about homework assignments or a text message about meeting for a campus activity will be enough to maintain the relationship. Other students need personal contact for the relationship to succeed. As you demonstrate your concern for and interest in your students, they will begin to believe that you are trustworthy and will be more open to you.

All contact does not need to be done on an individual basis. Contacting an entire class by e-mail or text messaging can be an effective way to keep everyone informed. Some students who feel comfortable and are prepared to go it alone can benefit from your messages without feeling like you are pressuring them to interact with you. Group contact is also a great way to help students start to interact more with each other. Whatever you choose to do, make sure you have

Ⓢ️TRATEGIES FOR keeping in touch with your students:

- Attend a campus activity together.
- Plan weekly study groups.
- Send a text message or an e-mail message, or call if you haven't seen students.
- Set up a time to meet with students individually.
- Add other ideas:

_____

_____

the permission of all involved before you give out personal information such as e-mail addresses or phone numbers.

What Is Working? What Is Not Working?

This stage also continues throughout the relationship. The questions remind you to evaluate how the mentoring relationship is working. Periodically assess what is happening between you and your students, and make any needed changes along the way. Use both formal and informal methods to solicit feedback from a variety of different people. The more points of view you consider, the more accurate your assessment will be.

It is imperative to be open to the feedback you receive and completely honest with yourself and others. Look for feedback in the comments students make and in their attitude toward you. Lead a casual discussion about what is and is not working. If you want to conduct a more formal evaluation, prepare a survey with questions that look at all aspects of the relationship, including goals, communication, mentor responsibility, and student responsibility.

You may want to ask yourself the following questions to prompt guided reflection on how the relationship is going. You can also ask your students the questions that apply to them.

Are the goals of the mentoring relationship established and clear?

- If so, what about them is working?
- If not, what needs to be done to make them so?

Do I demonstrate effective listening skills that

- clarify and confirm?
- show concern, interest, and empathy?

Am I remembering to

- recognize that different students learn at different speeds?
- try diverse methods to meet students' needs?
- suspend judgment, respect and accept differences, and be patient?
- challenge students to try the strategies?
- provide students with my own personal examples?
- always be honest?

Am I monitoring myself to remain

- nonjudgmental, respectful, and open to students who differ from me?
- appropriate and a positive example for students?
- responsible by meeting expectations of the mentoring program and my students?

Do I demonstrate to students that I understand the material we discuss in class and that I am trying to be a successful student as well?

If things are going well, be grateful and pat yourself on the back. If something is amiss in the relationship, recommit yourself and do all you can to get it back on track. You may need to recommit your students as well. Remember that honesty is one of the ground rules.

ⓈTRATEGIES FOR soliciting feedback:

- Ask for constructive criticism.
- Be aware of informal feedback in casual conversation.
- Conduct an anonymous survey asking about strengths and weaknesses.
- Discuss your observations, and ask for suggestions.
- Add other ideas:

_____

_____

Are We There Yet?

Every mentoring relationship needs to come to a close. The "Are we there yet?" stage gives you and your students an opportunity to reflect on what you have accomplished together. Reaching this stage does not mean the end of interacting with your students; it does mean that your relationship will take on a different form. As a mentor, one of your goals is for your students to become successful on their own.

Just as each student is unique, so is the length of time you will spend in the mentoring relationship with each. Some students don't want or need your help; others are ready to take off on their own within a few weeks; and others will seek you out for an entire semester. Remember that you are not in this relationship to carry people along for the duration of their educational careers; you are there to provide good examples, encouragement, and knowledge of the college experience. Over time, your students will have their own experiences to build on. They may even become mentors to others. It is not uncommon to see mentoring relationships develop among students in your class as one student reaches out to help another. When formal mentoring is not so much needed, the parties involved often turn their focus to friendships or to their own individual interests.

As discussed in Chapter 12, reflection and evaluation are necessary if you want to improve your skills as a mentor. Reflection can reinforce experience and offer insights that you previously overlooked. When you take time to reflect with your students, you may find that you all gained more from the relationship than you had previously assumed. Reflecting and carefully considering what you have learned that will help you in future assignments will help you improve your performance each semester as you become the best possible mentor.

STRATEGIES FOR wrapping things up:

- Ask students to reflect on what they have learned.
- Discuss goals and progress toward achieving those goals.
- Write a letter expressing your confidence in students' ability to continue successfully.
- Add other ideas:

_____

ACTIVITY 4.3   Mentoring Timeline

Create a mentoring timeline that indicates when your formal mentoring relationship will begin and end. Indicate when and how you will incorporate each of the six stages of the mentoring relationship.

First day of contact   **Last day of contact**

——▶

1. **Who are you?** What will you do to get to know your students? When do you plan to do this?

_____

_____

2. **How are you doing?** How will you maintain regular contact with students? When do you plan to do this?

_____

_____

3. **Why are we here?** What will you do to clarify your role? When do you plan to do this?

_____

_____

4. **Where are we going?** How will you learn about your students' needs and help them set appropriate goals? When do you plan to do this?

_____

Online Study Center college.hmco.com/PIC/sanft1e

_____

_____

5. **What is working? What is not working?** What will you do to solicit feedback about the effectiveness of the relationship? When do you plan to do this?

_____

_____

_____

6. **Are we there yet?** What will you do to encourage your students to reflect on the value of the relationship? When do you plan to do this?

_____

_____

_____

 Where are you now?

These questions are designed to help you review the important concepts covered in the chapter. Answering these questions can help you assess your own understanding or prepare for a test.

1. Explain the unique aspects that make a mentoring relationship more than just a friendship.

2. Describe one positive attribute related to each role in a mentoring relationship. How comfortable are you with each of these attributes?

3. Describe each stage of a mentoring relationship, and explain when it is appropriate to initiate each stage.

Case Study Discussion

Review the case study at the beginning of this chapter, and answer the following questions as they relate to the concepts you learned in the chapter. Discuss your answers with other mentors in your program so that you can explore different perspectives and gain greater insight into how to help this person.

Why is Reneé's experience relevant in this chapter?

What would you need to know to help a student like Reneé?

If you had to help Reneé, how would you approach the situation?

If your initial idea didn't work, what else could you do to help Reneé?

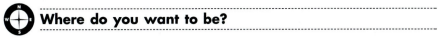

Where do you want to be?

Reflect on what you have learned about mentoring in this chapter, and consider how you will apply these ideas to your specific responsibilities as a mentor.

1. What do you consider to be the most valuable concept in this chapter?

_____

_____

2. Why was it significant to you?

_____

_____

_____

_____

3. How will you apply this concept as a mentor?

_____

_____

_____

_____

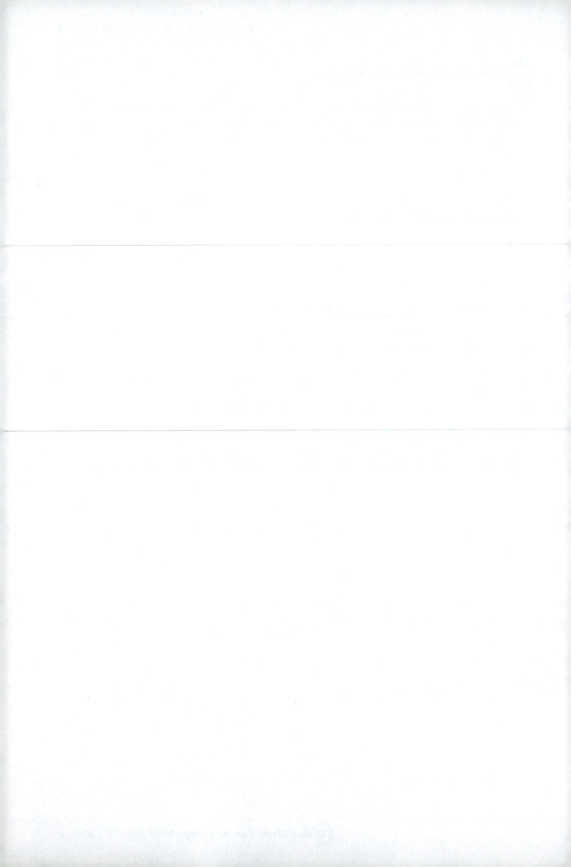

Increasing Awareness
of Self and Others

Part II builds on the foundation for successful peer mentoring established in Part I. Chapter 5 explains the importance of "Understanding Self-awareness" to provide you with a deeper understanding of yourself. Chapter 6 focuses on "Becoming a Role Model" in order to positively influence other students. Chapter 7 helps you to recognize and appreciate cultural influences in your life and the lives of the students you serve by "Developing Cultural Sensitivity."

Understanding Self-Awareness

Case Study: "Where Do I Begin?"

Juan moved to the United States from Honduras nearly five years ago. He was seventeen years old at the time. He is now in his first semester of college. A few weeks after the semester has begun, he confides that he does not know how to perform better in class. He is the first person in his family to attend college, and he says that no one at home can help him.

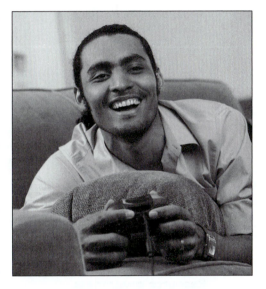

Juan is taking developmental English and math courses as well as a student success course. He attends all of his classes but currently has Ds in both English and math and a C in the success course. He struggles to understand what is required, so he has several incomplete assignments.

Juan goes home immediately after class and usually takes a nap, helps his father around the house, or plays video games with his brother. In the evening, he goes to his part-time job and then spends a few hours with his girlfriend. He claims he has a desire to change, but does not know where to begin.

As you discuss the following questions with other mentors in your program, remember that this case study has been written about a real student facing real challenges. We encourage you to imagine the complexity of the situation and not to oversimplify the issues that the student faces. You may not feel experienced enough to completely answer the questions at this point, but you will have an opportunity to revisit this case study after learning the concepts in this chapter.

73

In your opinion, what are the greatest problems Juan is facing?

How might self-awareness help Juan deal with his problems?

What direction would you give Juan to help him improve his situation?

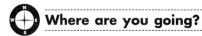 **Where are you going?**

After reading this chapter, you should be familiar with the following concepts related to mentoring.

- Relationship between self-awareness and mentoring
- Self-awareness and the self-system
- Definition of *agency*
- Developing awareness of thoughts, feelings, and actions
- Awareness and change
- Types of awareness essential for college students

Key Terms

In this chapter, you will encounter the following terms, which appear in bold. You can highlight the definitions as you read or look for them in the glossary at the end of the book.

Agency
Emotional awareness
Empowerment
Habits of mind
Intellectual awareness
Physical awareness
Resource awareness

Self-awareness
Self-concept
Self-efficacy
Self-esteem
Self-system
Social awareness
Spiritual awareness

Why Is Self-Awareness Necessary to Be an Effective Peer Mentor?

Self-awareness is vitally important to your success as a student. In fact, it is necessary to even understand what success means to you. Chapter 2 identified the most critical issues that students face during the first year of college. Exploring identity development is one of them. The first year of college often brings students a new level of independence. To successfully deal with the challenges and opportunities, they must consider who they want to be and how they will become that person.

The fact that you are training to become a peer mentor suggests that the choices you are making will help you and others succeed. Students who struggle with self-awareness do not recognize how their choices affect their lives. They often feel that they have no options, and they do not realize how their decisions have contributed to the situations they are in.

> ### MENTOR'S VOICE
>
> *For people to grow at all, they need to be aware of themselves so they know what they can improve.*
>
> **Logan Alkema**, peer mentor

If you understand how increasing your self-awareness affects your success as a student, you can help other students understand the same thing. Your goal as a mentor is to help students understand themselves well enough to recognize what they need to change and to take appropriate steps to improve their situations and their chances of success. You can help students feel a sense of **empowerment** as they realize that they have the ability to improve their own circumstances and that self-awareness allows them to take control of their lives.

In Chapter 1, a peer mentor is described as a student who has learned from experience and has developed skills in guiding other students through college. If you want to effectively guide other people, you need to become increasingly aware of how you view others and of how others view you. You must also be aware of your own experiences and of all that you have learned from them. But you must recognize the limitations of your experience when you are helping others. Your experience does not make you an authority on another person's life. Discuss the importance of self-awareness with your students, and allow them the freedom to discover themselves.

> ### EXPERT'S OPINION
>
> "The fundamental task of the mentor is a liberatory task. It is not to encourage the mentor's goals and aspirations and dreams to be reproduced in the mentees, the students, but to give rise to the possibility that the students become the owners of their own history....to assume the ethical posture of a mentor who truly believes in the autonomy, freedom, and development of those he or she mentors."
>
> **Paulo Freire**, *Mentoring the Mentor*

What Is Self-Awareness?

Simply stated, **self-awareness** means understanding your own thoughts, feelings, and actions. Johann Diaz, cofounder of ExecutiveAwareness.com, describes self-awareness as "the art of waking up, of realizing who you really are and why you do the things you do, in the way you do them."[1] Though it sounds simple, becoming self-aware is an involved process that requires time and intentional, conscious effort. Cognitive psychologists suggest that self-awareness

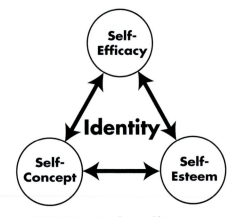

FIGURE 5.1: The Self-System

can be best understood in the larger context of the **self-system**, an approach to explaining human identity. When you understand the components of the self-system, you will better understand your own thoughts, feelings, and actions, and your self-awareness will increase.

The three major dimensions of the self-system are self-concept, self-esteem, and self-efficacy. These three aspects are closely related and affect each other in various ways, as Figure 5.1 shows.

Self-concept is your perception of yourself in comparison to other people. In other words, you see yourself as similar to or different from others in your life, especially significant others, and the way you describe yourself reflects the language used by defining influences in your life. The combined influence of the media and your family, culture, religion, and education creates a context that you use to articulate who you are. This context can be negative or positive depending on how you internalize the feedback you receive from the various sources.

Part of developing self-awareness is understanding how you see yourself and evaluating the accuracy of your own perception. While some of your beliefs about yourself may persist for years, others change from moment to moment. It takes time and effort to discover that some of your beliefs and assumptions about yourself may be based on misconceptions that you have accepted as valid. As you increase your knowledge and interact with a variety of different people, you develop a larger context that you can use to understand yourself.

Self-esteem is the value you see in yourself based on how your "real" self compares to an "ideal" self you have mentally constructed throughout your life. Your real self is based on your perception of yourself, or your self-concept. Your ideal self has also been influenced by your culture, family, religion, and education and the media, but you may not be conscious of how these sources have determined your expectations of yourself. You may be struggling to realize an unrealistic ideal, or you may have adopted someone else's ideal because you don't have a clear concept of who you want to be. You can increase your self-awareness by becoming conscious of the expectations you have of yourself and considering whether your ideal self is a realistic or unrealistic expectation to impose.

Self-efficacy is the confidence you have in your ability to accomplish certain things. *Efficacy* literally means "power or capacity to produce a desired effect."[2] If you have a strong sense of self-efficacy, you believe that you have the power to accomplish what you want to accomplish.

Your level of confidence varies depending on your abilities. Some students are confident about their skills in English but have no confidence about their math skills. Others excel in athletic challenges while they struggle in the classroom. You can probably identify things you know you do well. You have high self-efficacy in these areas. You may also be able to recognize things you avoid because you do not feel confident that you can succeed. Becoming aware of your self-efficacy in various academic endeavors will help you better understand why you do the things you do and will give you more choices about how to deal with challenges.

Understanding the three aspects of the self-system will help you understand yourself and others better because you will appreciate the complexity of each individual's identity. You will be more effective as a mentor if you have a generally positive self-system. People who view themselves and their abilities negatively often look to other people to help them feel better about themselves. They are dependent on the approval of others. However, a mentor cannot guide other people if he or she is constantly seeking validation. The mentoring process must be its own reward. As a mentor, you should not need validation from your students to make your efforts seem worthwhile.

You cannot change another person's negative self-system. You are a mentor, not a professional counselor. You are not qualified to analyze the conscious and subconscious beliefs that define another person's self-system. If a student is seeking more help than you can give, turn to your program administrator for advice. You will be more effective when you establish and maintain appropriate boundaries about personal issues. You can, however, make a concerted effort to better understand yourself and then share your insights with other students as appropriate. Your insights on how to gain greater self-awareness may motivate another student to make an effort to increase his or her self-awareness as well.

> ## MENTOR'S VOICE
>
> *"Every time I have a rough day, I sit down and think about these concepts:*
>
> *"First, self-concept: Who did I compare myself to today? How did it make me feel?*
>
> *"Second, self-esteem: What do I really want to become?*
>
> *"Third, self-efficacy: Do I believe in myself? Why or why not?*
>
> *"After I ask myself all of these questions, I feel better about who I am and who I want to be."*
>
> **Megan Larkin**, peer mentor (in training)

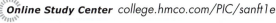

Online Study Center *college.hmco.com/PIC/sanft1e*

ACTIVITY 5.1   Understanding Your Self-System

This activity will help you consider your own self-concept, self-esteem, and self-efficacy. Spend at least thirty minutes on the activity in order to achieve the level of thoughtfulness necessary to understand your own self-system. You can also discuss your answers with another student to help her or him better understand the self-system.

Self-Concept

1. List twenty words that describe you.

_____ _____ _____ _____

_____ _____ _____ _____

_____ _____ _____ _____

_____ _____ _____ _____

_____ _____ _____ _____

2. Circle all the words that have negative connotations for you. Explain below how you would change these negative traits if you could.

_____

_____

_____

Self-Esteem

3. Describe your ideal self in two or three sentences. Explain the influences that have affected this ideal in your mind.

_____

_____

_____

4. Do you think your ideal is realistic? Why?

_____

_____

Self-Efficacy

5. Describe something you know you can do well.

_____

_____

6. Describe something you want to accomplish in the next five years.

_____

_____

7. Describe one aspect of your life in which a lack of confidence might be a barrier to your success.

_____

_____

Self-Awareness

8. Would you describe your self-concept as generally positive?   Yes   No

9. Do you believe your ideal self is attainable?   Yes   No

10. Do you have the power to produce desired results in your own life?   Yes   No

If you answered No to any question above, explain below.

_____

_____

What Is Agency?

Albert Bandura, author of *Self-Efficacy: The Exercise of Control*, claims that self-efficacy is a critical component of the construct of agency. Self-efficacy is confidence in your own abilities, and **agency** is the power to decide how to use your abilities to achieve desired results. Bandura defines *agency* as an intentional action for a given purpose—it is the "core belief that one has the power to produce effects by one's actions."[3] Many researchers claim that this power is a fundamental human desire. Babies demonstrate agency when they notice whether their behavior has an effect and then intentionally repeat the behavior, expecting the same effect. Students study with the expectation of learning more about a subject. Musicians practice with the intention of improving their technique. You choose to do certain things because you believe that the effort will result in a particular outcome. The desire for agency persists throughout life and is so powerful that people become depressed and helpless when they begin to feel there is no relationship between what they do and what happens.

Agency affects both an individual and his or her environment. The consequences of your actions will affect your thoughts and feelings about yourself as well as your confidence. Poor decision making or harmful behavior can contribute to a negative self-concept and low self-esteem, while productive behavior can improve self-confidence and provide motivation to persist in a particular effort. Your actions also affect your environment, including the people, circumstances, and opportunities you encounter. Self-awareness includes the awareness of how your decisions and behaviors affect you and your environment. Agency allows you to choose both your actions and your responses in a given situation.

As a mentor, you can address issues of agency with your students. You can discuss taking responsibility for their actions or choosing responses to events beyond their control. You can help them see that they are more likely to get what they want when agency involves planning, clarifying expectations, and anticipating outcomes. Students will begin to recognize their power to improve their circumstances when you ask appropriate questions about their expectations and desired outcomes. As they begin to plan for success, you can encourage them to monitor their behavior and reflect on the outcome.

How Does Self-Awareness Affect Your Agency?

While understanding the complexity of the self-system is essential, it may be simpler to remember that self-awareness means that you understand your thoughts, feelings, and actions. The model in Figure 5.2 may help you analyze a situation by considering how the three components of self-awareness affect a person's agency.

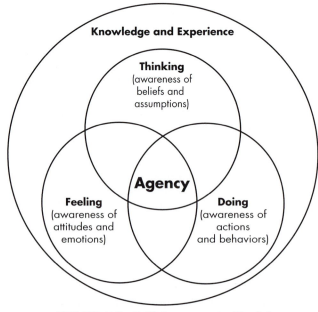

FIGURE 5.2: Self-Awareness Model

Knowledge and experience define the limits of your awareness. Your thoughts, feelings, and actions are limited by your knowledge and experience. For example, a child who encounters a horse for the first time may call it "dog" because he or she does not have another word to describe it. The child needs additional knowledge to differentiate between dogs and horses. You will also encounter new ideas and try new things that will expand your knowledge and experience and increase your self-awareness.

Thinking incorporates your beliefs and assumptions in a situation. Your thoughts can be so powerful that they control your emotions and your actions. If you believe you are in danger, you may be overcome with fear and choose to run. On the other hand, you may perceive danger as a thrill and feel exhilaration when you take on the challenge. The difference is simply what you think about the situation. Developing an awareness of your thoughts can help you better understand what you feel and do.

Feeling includes both emotions and attitudes. Often your emotions manifest themselves spontaneously in a situation. You may cheer wildly when your favorite team scores. While your emotions may be manifest in the moment, your attitudes are learned over time and often influence how you react. You may be cheering wildly because you love this team, and it is the first game of the season. Your roommate, on the other hand, is completely indifferent to this team and thinks you are overreacting. Learning to recognize your attitudes and how they affect your responses to people and situations can help you better understand your emotions.

Doing describes both your actions and your behavior. Action defines what you do in a particular situation, whereas behavior relates to how you conduct yourself on a regular basis. You may attend a study group for the history test, but you regularly avoid completing your reading assignments. Generally speaking, one positive action will not compensate for repeated negative behavior. If you want to achieve your desired results, you have to consider the effects of all that you do.

In this particular model, *agency* is synonymous with *success*. As you already know, agency is the power to act and achieve desired results. When you achieve your desired result, you have a successful outcome. The model illustrates that your thoughts and feelings affect the outcome as much as your actions do.

The following examples will help you to see how all three factors work together to affect a person's circumstances.

John has struggled with math throughout his education and thinks that math is too difficult. He feels frustrated and has the attitude that trying to learn math is a waste of time. His actions reflect his thoughts and feelings, and he quits attending class.

Jaime also thinks that math is difficult, but she believes that she must learn how to do math. She feels a sense of determination to succeed in math class. She works hard and meets regularly with a math tutor. She eventually gets a passing grade in the class.

As a mentor, you need to become aware of how your own thoughts and feelings affect your actions. It is just as easy to model negative behavior as it is to model positive behavior, so be careful what you do. If you are self-aware, you will model more effective behaviors and help motivate your students to do the same.

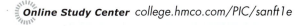
Online Study Center college.hmco.com/PIC/sanft1e

⬥ ACTIVITY 5.2   Recognizing Thoughts, Feelings, and Actions

The following activity asks you to consider how your thoughts and feelings affect your actions in both positive and negative ways. The objective is to increase your self-awareness, so think carefully about your responses.

1. Describe a positive behavior that you see in yourself. Identify the thoughts and feelings that motivate this behavior.

_____

_____

_____

2. Describe a negative behavior that you see in yourself. Identify the thoughts and feelings that may contribute to the behavior. What can you do to change the behavior?

_____

_____

_____

How Does Awareness of Your Thinking Lead to Change?

In 1910, in *How We Think*, John Dewey described how **habits of mind** influence the way people think without conscious awareness.[4] These habits can best be described as a consistent tendency or inclination to think in a certain way. Many scholars today believe that awareness of one's thinking habits is necessary to become a more effective critical thinker.

Awareness of thinking habits is the first step to changing behavior. Some habits of mind, if undetected, can be destructive over time. Some students fail repeatedly and do not know why. Albert Einstein wisely said, "We cannot solve the significant problems we face with the same level of thinking that created them."[5] If you remain at the same level of thinking, you will not be able to solve your problems or empathize with other people's problems.

To recognize your habitual responses, allow others to question and challenge your thinking. A mentor can engage a student in a thoughtful discussion about beliefs or assumptions. When the student begins to recognize the value of an alternative point of view, she or he begins to recognize and evaluate her or his own thinking patterns. When subconscious habits of mind are brought to a conscious level, one's perception of reality begins to change. Experiencing a dramatic change in your awareness can be a powerful moment of truth. It is difficult to describe these realizations in words, but they can leave you a different person.

As a student in a first-year student success class, Maria Martinez tried to find words to describe her own altered awareness:

> It was shortly after I had participated in a discussion about relationships in my Student Success class. As I was driving along the freeway from my home, I was stunned as I had never been before. I had to stop and park on the shoulder of the freeway as the full intensity of what had happened became clear to me. For the first time in my life, I realized that a relationship is fundamentally about an unconditional commitment to someone, something, some idea, etc., and that it did not begin with "what do I get" from the relationship. My first impulse was to dismiss such a realization as at best paradoxical, or at worst nonsense. It was in opposition to everything I had ever learned and experienced about being related to another person. To my initial discomfort, this new knowledge framing my relationships simply would not go away. It was as though I had gone through a door,

👥 ACTIVITY 5.3 *Evaluating Thinking Habits*

The following activity asks you to consider an example of how your thinking on a particular issue has changed. Recognizing your own habits of mind can be difficult. Share your answers with another person, and ask that person to share his or her answers with you. Your discussion may help you think of other experiences in which your perspective changed.

1. Describe an assumption you made that proved to be inaccurate.

_____

_____

2. What happened to change your perspective?

_____

_____

3. Can you identify other assumptions that have become habits?

_____

_____

4. What can you do to determine whether your thinking habits are valid?

_____

_____

Online Study Center college.hmco.com/PIC/sanft1e

which disappeared the moment I walked through it. Every time I attempted to return to my old way of operating, I felt like a fraud or a liar. I finally came to accept my *altered way of being* in relationships with both personal and professional friends. The filter had been removed. As a result, the nature of my relationships has taken on a significantly improved quality and, correspondingly, a quantitative reduction in conflict and stress.

Initially it may be difficult to consider another way of thinking. But once you start noticing certain thinking habits, it will become easier to notice them again and again. You will begin to see how they affect different aspects of your life. The awareness can provide the motivation you need to change, and change can lead to the discovery of other habits of mind.

What Types of Awareness Are Essential for College Students?

So far in this chapter, you have learned about self-awareness from a psychological perspective. This section focuses on the day-to-day reality of college students and identifies the types of awareness necessary to be successful. You will see how awareness is necessary in every aspect of your life.

Intellectual awareness includes knowledge of both your own thinking processes and effective learning strategies. *Metacognition*, a concept covered

in Chapter 9, is another term for this type of awareness. If you are using metacognition, you can recognize when you are learning and when you are not. You regulate your learning by using effective learning strategies that ensure that you are learning and making the most of your study time.

For example, a student who does not understand Einstein's theory of relativity after reading about it in a textbook asks the professor to clarify the concept. This student knows that he is an auditory learner and that the verbal explanation will be easier than the written explanation for him to understand. After talking to the professor, he rereads the textbook to see if his comprehension has improved. This student chose a study strategy based on his learning style or preferred approach to learning. Understanding your learning preferences helps identify learning strategies that are effective for you. Another important aspect of intellectual awareness is your ability to think critically about your assumptions and biases and how they affect your ability to learn.

Resource awareness involves recognizing time and money as resources that must be used responsibly. Successful students manage their money and their time in a way that allows them to accomplish their goals. A student who wants to continue in school meets with a financial aid adviser to learn about available options. She knows the tuition payment deadlines and budgets accordingly. Another student creates a semester calendar so that he knows when his major assignments are due. This calendar helps him plan ahead and balance the requirements of several classes.

You may realize that you are often guilty of wasting your time or money. Sometimes you may follow your impulses instead of your goals. An impulse is often driven by the desire for instant gratification. A goal is defined by a future expectation and delaying gratification, which means waiting to get what you want. If you know what you want and are aware of the limitations of your resources, you can make better decisions about how to use them.

Physical awareness is the consciousness of the positive and negative effects of certain behaviors on your body. College is the first time many students are living on their own and are completely responsible for what they eat, when they sleep, and a myriad of other lifestyle choices. Some students develop problems with sleep, weight, drugs, and alcohol—all of which may have a profound influence on their physical well-being. Their problems may be reactions to stress. For example, a student may be so worried about a difficult class that she takes stimulants to stay awake longer and get more homework done. The effect of the drugs and the lack of sleep negatively affect both her health and her ability to learn.

If you want to improve your health, you have to change the way you think about yourself and your circumstances. You can reduce stress by changing your expectations, managing your resources, or exercising.

Emotional awareness involves understanding how negative feelings, such as fear, anger, and depression, affect your performance and how to cope with those feelings. Left undiscovered, these emotions can distort your perspective. A student who is attending college and is away from his home for the first time might experience depression. He may feel home-sick or alone. These feelings could lead to lack of confidence in his ability to succeed.

Understanding your emotions begins with recognizing how your feelings about yourself affect the way you react to the circumstances in your life. If you are content with who you are, you may be more comfortable with taking risks and dealing with change. If you struggle with some aspect of your self-system, your negative emotions may be related to how you feel about yourself. If you are open to exploring your emotions, you can develop strategies to handle them in an effective and timely manner.

Social awareness includes recognition of social influences and their effects on your interpersonal relationships. You may not realize how pressure from family, friends, society, and the media often dictate your choices. A student may come from a family with a long history of working as teachers, and her parents might assume that she will continue the custom. If she wants to pursue something other than teaching, her personal choice may create unexpected problems with her family. Social expectations and limitations, whether they are expressed or unexpressed, often affect your ability to succeed. You can deal with them if you are aware of the expectations and of your own desires, interests, and potential. As you become more comfortable with who you are, you will become more tolerant of others and enjoy the company of many different people.

Spiritual awareness is the consciousness of one's attitudes and perspectives about life and reality. Experts in student development are focusing more and more on the relevance of a student's spiritual perspective. This perspective defines purpose in your life. You know how to find inner peace and seek balance. Your perspective gives you the strength to face adversity and challenges. Most important, you recognize that your contribution makes a difference in the world, which motivates you to serve others.

A student was particularly talented in graphic arts and multimedia. Though he received significant recognition, he was not satisfied with his work. The student took advantage of different service opportunities available in the community. He felt more satisfied when serving others than when he focused on his art. After personal reflection, he changed his major to sociology and found meaningful work with a nonprofit agency.

Some experts, like Daniel Goleman, author of *Emotional Intelligence*, would argue that self-awareness is more important than academic abilities when it comes to being a successful student and mentor. If you have self-awareness, you will be able to help others recognize the importance of self-awareness and motivate them to be more successful in school and in life. You will also gain greater insight and improve your relationships with the students you mentor and other people in your life.

EXPERT'S OPINION

"If you don't have self-awareness . . . if you can't have empathy and have effective relationships, then no matter how smart you are, you are not going to get very far."

Daniel Goleman, *Emotional Intelligence*

ACTIVITY 5.4 College Student Awareness Assessment

This activity will help you consider your levels of self-awareness in different areas of your life. Complete the assessment, and calculate your score for each section. Reflect on the results to answer the questions that follow. You can also use this activity to help the students you mentor recognize areas where they need to improve their self-awareness.

	NEVER		SOMETIMES		ALWAYS

Intellectual Awareness

	NEVER		SOMETIMES		ALWAYS
1. I make informed decisions about how I study.	0	1	2	3	4
2. I think of creative ways to learn new concepts and difficult subjects.	0	1	2	3	4
3. I relate new information to things I already know.	0	1	2	3	4
4. I understand my own learning process and preferences.	0	1	2	3	4
5. I think critically about my assumptions and biases.	0	1	2	3	4

Total   _____ /20

Resource Awareness

	NEVER		SOMETIMES		ALWAYS
6. I can resist impulses and delay gratification.	0	1	2	3	4
7. I recognize the limitations of my resources.	0	1	2	3	4
8. I set goals and use my resources to achieve those goals.	0	1	2	3	4
9. I take responsibility for my use of time and money.	0	1	2	3	4
10. I view time and money as resources, not as restrictions.	0	1	2	3	4

Total   _____ /20

Physical Awareness

	NEVER		SOMETIMES		ALWAYS
11. I get sufficient sleep to maintain my health.	0	1	2	3	4
12. I make regular exercise a priority.	0	1	2	3	4
13. I recognize how stress affects my mind and body.	0	1	2	3	4
14. I recognize the effects of alcohol, drugs, and tobacco on my body.	0	1	2	3	4
15. My eating habits will ensure my long-term health.	0	1	2	3	4

Total   _____ /20

Online Study Center college.hmco.com/PIC/sanft1e

Emotional Awareness

16. I am comfortable taking risks.	0	1	2	3	4
17. I am content with myself and others.	0	1	2	3	4
18. I adjust well to changing circumstances.	0	1	2	3	4
19. I am objective about what other people think of me.	0	1	2	3	4
20. I avoid feeling sorry for myself.	0	1	2	3	4

Total   _____ /20

Social Awareness

21. I recognize the influences of other people and the media in my life.	0	1	2	3	4
22. I am comfortable with the expectations others have of me.	0	1	2	3	4
23. I value people who are different than I am.	0	1	2	3	4
24. I am comfortable around other people.	0	1	2	3	4
25. People are generally comfortable around me.	0	1	2	3	4

Total   _____ /20

Spiritual Awareness

26. I embrace opportunities to serve others in my community.	0	1	2	3	4
27. I know how to find a sense of inner peace.	0	1	2	3	4
28. I recognize a purpose in my life.	0	1	2	3	4
29. I see challenges as a learning opportunity.	0	1	2	3	4
30. I seek balance in my life.	0	1	2	3	4

Total   _____ /20

1. What type of awareness do you consider to be the most important? Why?

_____

_____

2. In which area did you give yourself the highest score? Would you consider this type of awareness a strength of yours? Why?

_____

_____

_____

3. In which area did you give yourself the lowest score? Would you consider this type of awareness a weakness of yours? How can you improve in this area?

_____

_____

_____

 Where are you now?

These questions are designed to help you review the important concepts covered in the chapter. Answering these questions can help you assess your own understanding or prepare for a test.

1. Why is it important for a mentor to understand self-awareness?
2. Describe the three main parts of the self-system.
3. Define *agency*, and explain how it is related to the self-system.
4. Explain how thinking, feeling, and doing are interrelated.
5. Define *habits of mind*. Explain how awareness of your thoughts can change your feelings and behavior.
6. Describe the six types of awareness essential for college students.

Case Study Discussion

Review the case study at the beginning of this chapter, and answer the following questions as they relate to the concepts you learned in the chapter. Discuss your answers with other mentors in your program so that you can explore different perspectives and gain greater insight into how to help this person.

1. Why is Juan's experience relevant in this chapter?
2. What would you need to know to help a student like Juan?
3. If you had to help Juan, how would you approach the situation?
4. If your initial idea didn't work, what else could you do to help Juan?

 Where do you want to be?

Reflect on what you have learned about mentoring in this chapter, and consider how you will apply these ideas to your specific responsibilities as a mentor.

 Online Study Center *college.hmco.com/PIC/sanft1e*

1. What do you consider the most valuable concept in this chapter?

    _____

    _____

2. Why was it significant to you?

    _____

    _____

    _____

    _____

    _____

3. How will you apply this concept as a mentor?

    _____

    _____

    _____

    _____

    _____

Becoming a Role Model

6

Case Study: "The Freewheeling Junior"

Courtney, a twenty-one-year-old student beginning her junior year, is known as a fun-loving party girl. She always puts play time ahead of schoolwork. Courtney tends to miss morning classes because she stays out late most nights and is too tired to get up in time to attend. In her mind, her college years are more about having a good time and enjoying her freedom than about getting a degree and preparing for a future career. She has never held a job; her wealthy family has taken care of all her financial needs.

Though Courtney seems to have the intellect and ability to do respectable work, her grades don't show it because she doesn't follow through. She was placed on academic warning after her second semester, academic probation after her third semester, and academic suspension after her fourth semester. The only way for her to appeal the suspension is to enroll and succeed in a student success class.

Courtney believed that her parents would always support her lifestyle choices. However, after learning about the suspension letter, they have decided to withhold financial support until Courtney improves her grades and takes more responsibility for her actions. Until now, she has never worried about the effect of her choices.

As you discuss the following questions with other mentors in your program, remember that this case study has been written about a real student facing real challenges. We encourage you to imagine the complexity of the situation and not to oversimplify the issues. You may not feel experienced enough to completely answer the questions at this point, but you will have an opportunity to revisit this case study after learning the concepts in this chapter.

91

What do you think Courtney needs to do to resolve her situation?

As a mentor, how could you approach Courtney to talk about her choices?

What do you believe you can do to assist her?

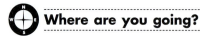 **Where are you going?**

After reading this chapter, you should be familiar with the following concepts related to mentoring.

- Comparison of *role model* and *mentor*
- The role of being authentic
- Common peer mentor values
- Value identification and clarification for others

Key Terms

In this chapter, you will encounter the following terms, which appear in bold. You can highlight the definitions as you read or look for them in the glossary at the end of the book.

Authentic
Role model
Value

How Is a Role Model Different from a Mentor?

A mentor is a trusted advisor, guide, or counselor. As a peer mentor, you might be assigned to guide students through the transition to college or help them network with vital campus resources. In these cases, you influence your fellow students through what you are able to do for them. You interact with them on a very personal level.

A positive **role model** is someone who exemplifies values and behavior that others want to imitate or follow. A role model's influence on another person can be great. The role model inspires others to emulate the attributes or attitudes that make him or her an exceptional person. You do not need to know a role model on a personal level. People you observe or know about who exhibit qualities you admire can be role models. They can even be historical figures whose lives inspire you. Anyone from Abraham Lincoln to Oprah Winfrey may possess qualities people want to adopt. Role models are not necessarily positive. Sometimes we learn how not to behave from negative experiences with people.

> **EXPERT'S OPINION**
>
> "What we are communicates far more eloquently than what we say or do."
>
> **Stephen Covey**, *Principle-Centered Leadership*

ACTIVITY 6.1   Identifying a Role Model

In earlier activities, you identified people who were mentors to you. In this activity, identify people you view as role models. They can be people you know personally or people you only know about. Answer the following questions.

1. Think of several people who have been role models for you, and explain how they influenced you.

_____

_____

_____

2. Did any of these people also serve as mentor to you? If so, in what way?

_____

_____

3. How would you describe the difference between a role model and mentor?

_____

_____

_____

A mentor does not automatically become a positive role model, but a good mentor tries to become one. You will become a role model if you earn students' respect by demonstrating attributes they value. They will respect you and want to be like you if you are honest with yourself and others about your values and your choices. This is an important responsibility. Along with being an example, you especially want to build and maintain relationships with the students you mentor.

Why Is It Important for a Positive Role Model to Be Authentic?

Becoming a positive role model is not only about becoming the person you want to be; it is also about embracing who you are now. It is important to remember that "the goal of a good role model is not perfection but openness to being genuinely human and willing[ness] to understand and develop oneself."[1] In other words, a good role model needs to be honest, not perfect. Honesty allows you to be an **authentic** person who does not pretend to be something he or she is not.

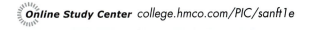
Online Study Center college.hmco.com/PIC/sanft1e

MENTOR'S VOICE

*A declaration of where you currently
stand is imperative to moving forward.
One first has to come to grips with
where he is in life. If an addict does not
admit the problem he will never move
forward. This applies to all aspects of life.*

Albert Mitchell, peer mentor

The first step in becoming an authentic person is to tell yourself the truth about yourself and to accept your limitations. You must ask yourself searching, sometimes uncomfortable or difficult questions about who you are and what you want to be. You must also have the maturity to honestly assess whether your actions reflect the values that are most important to you. Taking these steps will enable you to recognize your own strengths and weaknesses and to develop an authentic sense of self. This honest analysis of your values, strengths, and weaknesses is part of self-awareness, as discussed in Chapter 5. Presenting your authentic self in mentoring relationships means admitting to your students that you have weaknesses, and also letting them know that you are working to improve in those areas.

What Are Common Values Peer Mentors Successfully Model to Others?

The ideals that you cherish or esteem as important are your **values**. Values influence and guide your choices, including the moment-to-moment choices that manifest themselves in your behaviors and attitudes. Your values define you as an individual. As a mentor, you are in a position to become a significant role model to the students you are helping. Identifying your values and aligning your behavior with those values will give you the power to affect their lives. Students will recognize and respect your values in all that you do and say.

EXPERT'S OPINION

"Emotional maturity is a preface for a sense of
values. The immature person exaggerates
what is not important."

Vince Lombardi, *What It Takes To Be #1*

As the old adage goes, "Actions speak louder than words." You can talk to students about important values to have as a college student, but if you don't model those values in your own behavior, your words won't make much difference. All people have strengths. Play to yours while you work on improving your weaker areas. If you choose to model certain values to your students, try implementing them effectively in your own student experience first.

The objective of this section is to help you identify values that will increase your personal effectiveness and improve the quality of your mentoring interactions. Consider the power of each of the following values in your own life and in your mentoring relationships. Try to identify what you do on a consistent basis to model these values to others.

Purpose. The power of purpose is the power to discover what you want. When you value purpose, you seek to understand the reasons for doing what you do. Henry David Thoreau wanted to "live deliberately . . . and not, when [he] came to die, discover that [he] had not lived."[2] Like Thoreau, you can learn from every experience and make the most of every day. When other students recognize that your sense of purpose gives you the strength and motivation to work toward your goals, they will begin to consider their own reasons for doing what they are doing.

Adaptability. The power of adaptability is the power to see ideas as tools. This power allows you to suspend judgment when you are presented with a new idea. Your own preconceived notions do not limit your ability to think. Edward R. Murrow said, "A great many people think they are thinking when they are merely rearranging their prejudices."[3] Murrow was a famous journalist who was not afraid to look at ideas. If you are willing to discuss new ideas, students may be more open to new ideas they encounter in their education. They will be inspired by your openness and willingness to learn.

Creativity. The power of creativity is the joy of discovering new ideas. Albert Einstein claimed that "Imagination is more important than knowledge."[4] He believed that the true value of education lay in a person's ability to "think something that cannot be learned." When you value creativity, you actively seek new and exciting approaches to living, learning, and even problem solving. You value other people because they can feed your creativity with their own perspectives and approaches. You will encourage other students to develop their own powers of creativity when they see the energy you find in new ideas.

Focus. The power of focus is the power to be in the present moment. This may seem like a simple concept, but many of us fail to fully experience the here and now because we are distracted. The ability to focus is the ability to forget worries and concentrate your consciousness on the present situation. You are aware of the task in the moment and can pay attention until it is complete. When other students recognize that you can eliminate distractions and concentrate, they may be more willing to persist with difficult tasks themselves.

Perspective. The power of perspective is the power to see problems as opportunities. The word *problem* comes from the ancient Greek word *proballein*, which means "to throw forward." In other words, problems encourage and sometimes force you to learn new skills or change your circumstances. Perspective is the ability to see the problem in a larger context and value the opportunities that it creates. Ironically, when you see a problem as an opportunity, it is no longer a problem. Wayne Dyer, one of America's most successful businessmen, said, "When you change the way you look at things, the things you look at change."[5] This ability to see beyond obvious barriers is the power to literally "throw" yourself forward and progress beyond your problems. Anyone who has this power will inspire others to reevaluate their own problems.

Open-mindedness. The power of open-mindedness is the power to realize your assumptions. According to psychologist William Glasser, our minds store our experiences like pictures in a photo album.[6] We try to make sense of the world based on the pictures in our mind. We think and act in ways that make the world around us match the pictures. We can develop the power of open-mindedness by becoming aware of our pictures and letting go of those that limit our view of the world. We thus open ourselves to appreciate the diverse points of view of the people around us. Other students will respect this quality in you when they see that you are willing to engage with their new ideas and not dismiss them without consideration.

Responsibility. The power of responsibility is the power to accept the circumstances in your life as if you created them. Abraham Lincoln warned that "You cannot escape the responsibility of tomorrow by evading it today."[7] Often we try to evade responsibility by blaming others for situations in our lives. When we do this, we rob ourselves of the opportunity to do anything different in the future. As long as we blame others for our circumstances, we will be caught in a cycle that will continue to produce the same results. When you value responsibility, you see how you have contributed to the problems that exist in your life, and you allow yourself to change the outcome by changing your thoughts and actions. When other students recognize the power and sense of control this value brings to your life, they may be more willing to take control of their own circumstances.

Choice. The power of choice is the power to choose your own responses to things that happen to you. Viktor Frankl wrote about this power to choose in *Man's Search for Meaning*. After relating his deeply moving personal experiences as a prisoner in Auschwitz and other Nazi concentration camps for five years and his struggle to find reasons to live, he concludes: "Everything can be taken from a man or a woman but one thing: the last of human freedoms to choose one's attitude in any given set of circumstances, to choose one's own way."[8] We can choose to give control of our lives to other people or to circumstances and develop the habit of being resigned. But Frankl inspires us to take control of our lives by choosing our responses to our circumstances, no matter how difficult. You can inspire others to do the same.

Independence. The power of independence is the power to detach from debilitating attachments. Attachments can be like addictions. You can be attached to emotions, opinions, expectations, and perceptions. Independence allows you to have a sense of self that is separate from these attachments. Other students will recognize that you have realistic expectations of yourself and that you are unaffected by others' opinions of you. They may begin to reflect on their own thinking and develop more independence.

Service. The power of service is the power to improve the world. The world is full of problems that need to be solved. If you value service, you see problems as opportunities to contribute to the well-being of others and of society as a whole. You look for opportunities that will help you develop skills and talents that will move you toward your purpose. You find that these opportunities bring meaning to your life and provide significant benefits to yourself and others. If you invite your students to do service activities with you, they may experience the same satisfaction.

Dependability. The power of dependability is the power to employ your word. You employ your word by making and keeping agreements. Agreements provide a foundation for many things we often take for granted, such as language and money. The world works because people abide by fundamental agreements. When you make and keep personal agreements, you build relationships that become the foundation for your life and personal well-being. A mentoring relationship, like any other relationship, will grow only if students know that you are dependable.

Positive thinking. The power of positive thinking is the power to choose your thought and conversations. In *The Power of Positive Thinking,* Norman Vincent Peale claims that "The person who sends out positive thoughts activates the world around him positively and draws back to himself positive results."[9] When we choose positive thoughts and conversations, we have the ability to change our past, present, and future. We can look to the past to learn from our experiences. We can focus on what we enjoy about our lives in the present and confidently solve the problems we face. We can look ahead to the goals we want to accomplish and prevent problems that may occur in the future. Your positive attitude will be contagious. Students will begin to see their own lives differently when they see how your attitude affects your whole world.

Humor. The power of humor is the power to risk being a fool and to laugh at your own mistakes. Your sense of humor will give you license to try things you wouldn't otherwise try. You might fail or succeed, but in both cases you will enjoy what you are doing. Others around you will also enjoy your presence because laughter is the most contagious of emotions. Daniel Goleman, author of *Emotional Intelligence,* claims that laughter is more than a sign of friendship; it is also a sign of trust. "Unlike other emotional

signals—especially a smile, which can be feigned—laughter involves highly complex neural systems that are largely involuntary: It's harder to fake."[10] Laughing with your students about your mistakes and theirs will be one of the strongest emotional connections you can make with them.

Balance. The power of balance is the power to surrender control and accept help. If we are willing to admit that we cannot deal with a situation, we open ourselves up to receiving help. By involving others, we avoid becoming entirely consumed by something that is too big for us to handle. We avoid giving in to something that could control our lives. By letting go, we create space for other possibilities. Students are often overwhelmed by the challenges they face. As a mentor, you can help them understand the importance of balance by being open to help and by resisting becoming consumed by your challenges.

Gratitude. The power of gratitude is the power to respect others for the contributions they make to your life. Anne Morrow Lindbergh, the well-known author and wife of famed pilot Charles Lindbergh, believed that gratitude is not something you show by simply expressing appreciation. She said, "One can never pay in gratitude: one can only pay 'in kind' somewhere else in life."[11] If you value gratitude, you will constantly strive to contribute to the lives of others because others have made significant contributions to your own life. For example, you may choose to be a mentor because an important mentor changed your life. You may not be able to adequately express your appreciation to that mentor, but you can show your gratitude by your service "in kind."

Diversity. The power of diversity is the power of understanding and celebrating differences instead of fearing them. Margaret Mead demonstrated her personal commitment to diversity through her work in anthropology. She claimed that "Knowledge for life, sought in reverence of life, can bring life."[12] You can enrich your own life by seeking to understand and appreciate the varied beliefs and perspectives of other people. If you show genuine interest in the unique qualities of each student you work with, you will encourage your students to be more tolerant.

Kindness. The power of kindness is the power of treating others better than they sometimes deserve. If you value kindness, you try to understand how your own emotions affect other people, and you influence other people by effectively managing your emotions. You also recognize the needs of others, and you seek opportunities to satisfy the needs you are qualified to satisfy. Most important, you understand that kindness must be genuine.

Integrity. The power of integrity is the power to be what we want to be. Many people define their lives by what they have or what they do. But integrity is not about external indicators. Integrity is about aligning who we are with the person we want to become. Socrates taught that "The greatest way to live with honor in this world is to be what we pretend to be."[13] The power of this value is the freedom to live without pretense. It involves accepting who you are and what you can do right now and embracing your ability to change. You must understand all of the values that govern your life before you can live with integrity.

Now that you have been introduced to values associated with personal and interpersonal effectiveness, identify the values you consider most important. The values you choose should reflect your deepest commitments and describe the way you see your best self. Activity 6.2 provides an opportunity to do values assessment.

ACTIVITY 6.2   Assessing Values Related to Mentoring

The objective of this activity is to take a good look at the values you possess relative to peer mentoring. Your values will have a strong effect on your success as a mentor. Using the following scale, assess how strongly you agree with the statements about your ability to model the values discussed in the section above.

1—Strongly Disagree   2—Disagree   3—Neutral   4—Agree   5—Strongly Agree

____ I have a clear sense of purpose in both my academic and personal pursuits.

____ I am adaptable to change.

____ I am willing to consider creative and new ideas.

____ I can manage my distractions and focus on the here and now.

____ I see problems as opportunities.

____ I think critically about my own assumptions.

____ I can take responsibility for the circumstances in my life.

____ I carefully choose my responses to all that happens to me.

____ My sense of self is independent of others' opinions and perceptions.

____ I seek opportunities to serve others and improve the world around me.

____ I am dependable.

____ My thoughts and conversations demonstrate positive thinking.

____ I can laugh at myself and risk being a fool.

____ I can balance the need for control and the need for help.

____ I frequently express my gratitude for the contributions others make in my life.

____ I enjoy interacting with people whose perspectives are different than my own.

____ I try to treat people with kindness.

____ I am the person I want to be.

Now that you have completed the assessment, answer the following questions. Seriously reflect on what you view as your greatest strengths and in which areas you would like to improve.

1. Which of the values do you personally think are most important for a peer mentor to model?

    _____

    _____

2. Pick at least three of the values, and clarify them by restating them as "I am . . . /not . . ." statements.

    Example: *"I am responsible, not irresponsible. This means that when someone asks a favor of me and I commit to it, I follow through and get it done."*

    Value: I am _____, not _____.
    Clarification: This means that

    _____.

    Value: I am _____, not _____.
    Clarification: This means that

    _____.

    Value: I am _____, not _____.
    Clarification: This means that

    _____.

3. Which values would you like to work on to help you be a more effective role model to the students you mentor?

    _____

    _____

4. How do you intend to develop those values?

    _____

    _____

    _____

5. Choose at least two people who are close to you, and explain your answers to questions 1 through 4. Friends can help you determine whether you are being too harsh on yourself. They may also be able to help you see your blind spots and hidden strengths. Even more useful, they can give you valuable constructive feedback about how they interpret your values based on what you say and do.

How Will You Help Others Recognize Their Values?

As a mentor, you are in a position to help others recognize their own values. Your role is not to tell them what their values are or to prescribe solutions if they are struggling to be effective. You can ask them to describe their values and discuss how their actions reflect their values. You can share your own experiences with coming to understand your values. You can acknowledge that you are still learning and trying to live by the values you have chosen.

You make life choices—what to do, what to believe, what to buy, how to act—based on your personal values or ideals. Your choice to become a peer mentor, for example, reflects that you value the personal and professional growth that comes from service to others. Being on time for your mentoring responsibilities shows that you value attendance and being punctual. Paying your bills regularly and on time shows that you value financial security. Just as your values play a key role in your drive to achieve important goals, they also play a key role in your students' drive to achieve.

Having carefully clarified values helps your students

- understand what they want out of life. Put simply, human achievements reflect what is valued.

- build a set of rules for life. Values form the basis of their decisions. They will repeatedly consult their values for guidance, wisdom, security, and power, especially in stressful situations.

- find role models who inspire them. Spending time with people who share similar values will help students clarify how they want to pursue their education and will also help them find support as they work toward what's important to them.

Having an idea of how students might use values can assist you as you attempt to help them identify and clarify values they will find useful in their college careers and life in general. Activity 6.3 is designed to provide a values identification and clarification process to use with the students you mentor.

Values can change as a result of circumstances or over time. Life experiences and education give students new perspectives that may alter what they consider important. For example, a fun-loving student who is seriously injured in an auto accident may place greater value on friends and family after the accident than before. Students who have clarified their values often make meaningful choices while in school. As they develop the habits of thinking about their values before they act, they can

- persist in challenging circumstances. Help them clarify their value of education into specific actions. Remind them that actions like turning in papers on time and attending classes are part of how they gain transferable skills from their college coursework.

- choose their majors and career directions. If they have always been concerned about the environment, they may choose to major in ecology.

👥 ACTIVITY 6.3   Helping Others Identify and Clarify Their Values

This activity is designed to help you discuss values with another student. Ask the student to write down the answers to questions 1 through 5 on a piece of paper, and discuss the answers together. Then answer questions 6 and 7 yourself.

1. List five values that are most important to you. Next to each value identify where you learned this value (family, friends, society, media, experience, religion) and why the value is important to you.

2. Choose three values, and explain what each means to you using the "I am . . ./not . . ." model. Example:

   Value: I am an optimist, not a pessimist.

   Clarification: This means that I try to see the good in people instead of focusing on the negative.

3. What values do you live by every day?

4. What do you wish to accomplish in your life?

5. Do you think your values will help you become the person you want to be? Why?

6. What did you learn from doing this activity with another person?

   _____

   _____

   _____

7. As a mentor, when do you think it is appropriate to discuss a person's values with him or her?

   _____

   _____

   _____

If they feel fulfilled when they help people, they may want to consider becoming peer mentors or working toward careers in the behavioral sciences or education.

• choose friends and activities that enrich their lives. Having friends with a desire to succeed in school may increase their own desire as well as reduce their stress level. Joining clubs whose activities support their values can also be a source of strength.

Becoming the person you want to be is an uphill climb. You are going to make mistakes, but wisdom comes when you learn from mistakes. Just don't make the same mistakes over and over again! When you identify the values that describe who you are, you can clarify who you want to become. The most important thing is to be genuinely human. As you become aware of inconsistencies between what you say and what you do, look for ways to make positive changes. This process will build character and help you become a more authentic and effective mentor.

 ## Where are you now?

These questions are designed to help you review the important concepts covered in the chapter. Answering the questions can help you assess your own understanding or prepare for a test.

1. In your own words, describe the differences between a role model and a mentor.
2. Why do you believe it is important for a role model to be positive?
3. Identify and briefly explain the common peer mentor values identified in this chapter.
4. As a mentor, how can you help other students identify and clarify their values?

Case Study Discussion

Review the case study at the beginning of this chapter, and answer the following questions as they relate to the concepts you learned in the chapter. Discuss your answers with other mentors in your program so that you can explore different perspectives and gain greater insight into how to help this person.

Why is Courtney's experience relevant in this chapter?

What would you need to know to help a student like Courtney?

If you had to help Courtney, how would you approach the situation?

If you initial idea didn't work, what else could you do to help Courtney?

 ## Where do you want to be?

Reflect on what you have learned about mentoring in this chapter, and consider how you will apply these ideas to your specific responsibilities as a mentor.

1. What do you consider the most valuable concept in this chapter?

_____

_____

2. Why was it significant to you?

_____

_____

_____

_____

_____

3. How will you apply this concept as a mentor?

_____

_____

_____

_____

_____

Developing Cultural Sensitivity

Case Study: "Hidden Meanings"

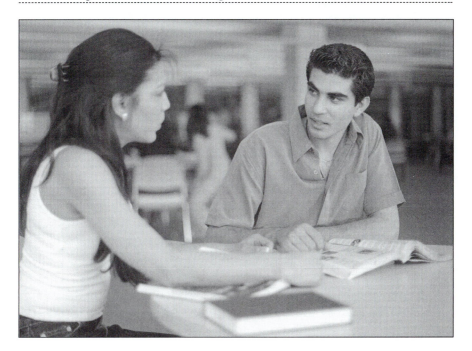

During a get-to-know-you activity at the beginning of the semester, you notice that all of the students but one share several different things about themselves. The lone exception is a young man who introduces himself as Amir and tells you only that he is from Persia. He appears to be relieved that, as he assumed, the other students in the class seem not to know that Persia is now known as Iran.

As the semester continues, you notice that Amir is lagging behind the other students in his assignments and his apparent understanding of the material. You recommend that he meet with a class study group. Amir is concerned about getting too close to other students because he is worried about   105 their reactions to his ethnic and cultural background. He has been called a terrorist on more than one occasion, so he is wary of what other people think of him.

Amir does poorly on the first exam in several classes and continues to miss assignments. He begins to request more and more support from you, and he even asks his instructors to make special accommodations for him.

As you discuss the following questions with other mentors in your program, remember that this case study has been written about a real student facing real challenges. We encourage you to imagine the complexity of the situation and not to oversimplify the issues that the student faces. You may not feel experienced enough to completely answer the questions at this point, but you will have an opportunity to revisit this case study after learning the concepts in this chapter.

As a mentor, how do you demonstrate that you are sensitive to Amir's concerns without allowing him to be too reliant on you?

What are some of the options available on your campus to help Amir?

What don't you know about Amir's culture, and how could you increase your knowledge of it?

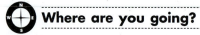 **Where are you going?**

After reading this chapter, you should be familiar with the following concepts related to mentoring.

- Significance of diversity
- ASK model for mentoring diverse students
- Awareness of different cultural perspectives
- Cultural biases and attitudes
- Strategies to skillfully interact with culturally diverse students
- Knowledge of important cultural characteristics

Key Terms

In this chapter, you will encounter the following terms, which appear in bold. You can highlight the definitions as you read or look for them in the glossary at the end of the book.

Assumed similarity	**Ethnicity**
Bias	**Ethnocentrism**
Cultural norms	**Multiculturalism**
Culture	**Prejudice**
Diversity	**Stereotype**
Empathy	**Tolerance**

Why Does Diversity Matter?

Many of today's students have learned to expect differences among their peers, but they have not learned to accept and value those differences. One first-year student said, "I never realized the importance of diversity until I started college. In all my years of school at home I never had a lesson on diversity and I don't recall any teachers stressing it in the classroom. . . . Now that I've finished my first year, I've come to realize how important diversity is. It gives students the opportunity to understand and accept people's differences."[1] Like this student, you must understand the importance of diversity and become aware of your own attitudes toward others. You can be a leader in helping other students understand and accept the diversity on your campus if your attitudes and actions demonstrate the value you see in others.

In a social context, **diversity** refers to people in a community who represent a variety of different ethnic groups, races, languages, religions, genders, sexual orientations, socioeconomic backgrounds, levels of education, political views, ages, and physical or mental abilities. This is a much broader definition of diversity than many people are used to. Your campus may be even more diverse than you realized, but you will not be able to benefit and learn from the different perspectives if you do not get involved in your campus community, engage in real conversations with real people, and learn to work and relax together with a diverse group of students.

Research has shown that students experience many benefits when they interact with diverse student groups, including

- Decreased cultural prejudice and discrimination
- Development of creativity and critical thinking skills
- Improved cultural understanding and tolerance
- Preparation for the challenges of the global society
- Stronger connection to the campus community

These benefits can be realized only if students extend themselves beyond both real and imagined barriers. As a mentor, you can reach out to all students if you approach them as peers and make a sincere effort to develop friendships. Anthony Antonio, a professor at Stanford University, claims that "The most influential experiences with diversity likely involve the development of interracial [and cross-cultural] friendships."[2]

> **EXPERT'S OPINION**
>
> "We all should know that diversity makes for a rich tapestry, and we must understand that all the threads of the tapestry are equal in value no matter what their color."
>
> **Maya Angelou,** *author*

You have already learned that mentoring is based on establishing authentic relationships. You might find it comforting to realize that you do not need to be an anthropologist or a sociologist to effectively mentor diverse students. You simply need to be a sincere friend. This chapter will focus on increasing your awareness of yourself and others so that you are better prepared to recognize and value the differences you encounter. Learning tolerance and respect for the diversity that makes each student unique is one of the most important mentoring skills. By willingly stretching yourself to increase your sensitivity and feel empathy toward others, you will develop personal attributes that will benefit you throughout your life.

How Can You Effectively Mentor Diverse Students?

EXPERT'S OPINION

You will be a more successful mentor if you are aware of three factors that affect your relationship with any student. Joe Wittmer, author of *Valuing Diversity and Similarity,* uses the acronym **ASK** to identify essential aspects of understanding and relating to people with diverse backgrounds.[3]

A   Awareness of self and others

S   Sensitivity through communication skills

K   Knowledge of cultural differences

Awareness begins with understanding your own cultural beliefs and attitudes, including biases and stereotypes. You can show your sensitivity to cultural differences by practicing effective strategies for cross-cultural communication. While you cannot be an expert on every culture you encounter, you can become aware of fundamental differences that affect relationships in different cultures. Figure 7.1 illustrates how these

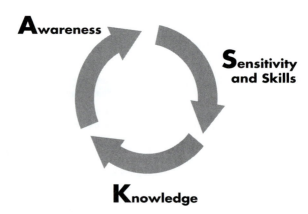

FIGURE 7.1: ASK Model

Source: J. Wittmer, "Valuing Diversity in the Schools: The Counselor's Role," 1992 (ERIC Digest, ED3474575); retrieved September 13, 2006, from http://www.eric.ed.gov/ERICDocs/data/ericdocs2/content_storage_01/0000000b/80/2a/17/04.pdf.

stages are part of a cycle that continues as you build a relationship with each student and gain experience as a mentor.

ASK is an appropriate acronym. The very act of asking yourself whether your beliefs and attitudes are limiting your ability to help another person will make you more aware of the other person's needs. Asking questions and engaging students in meaningful dialogue about themselves and their backgrounds will make you a more effective mentor. Finally, asking for guidance from others with more experience will help you improve your mentoring skills. As you follow the steps suggested by ASK, you will be better prepared to interact with each student in an appropriate manner to meet the student's specific cultural or learning needs.

How Do Cultural Perspectives Affect You?

Before you can appreciate the cultural differences in others, you must recognize the cultural influences in your own life. **Culture** refers to a set of values, behaviors, tastes, knowledge, attitudes, and habits shared by a group of people. In its broadest sense, culture is defined by your ethnic background. **Ethnicity** refers to your association with a particular group based on race, nationality, tribe, religion, or language. An ethnic group can include thousands or millions of people. The definition of *culture* can be only loosely applied to such large groups of people. For example, what is American culture? Can you identify one set of values, behaviors, tastes, and so on that applies to all Americans?

It may be easier to understand the influences of culture in your life by identifying groups that have influenced you, like your family, your friends, or your community. You share similar perspectives with these people because common experiences have influenced how you think and feel and what you do.

Figure 7.2 summarizes the various aspects of diversity introduced in this chapter. You may find these categories helpful as you analyze the cultural influences in your life. You can probably identify a variety of different cultures within each category. For example, different age groups have been identified as baby boomers, Gen X, and millennials. Sociologists have written volumes about the values, behaviors, and attitudes exhibited by each group. As you identify people or groups of people that have influenced you in each area, you will be able to better understand your own cultural perspectives.

Chapter 5 used the idea of the self-system to help you better understand the concept of identity. The Diversity Wheel illustrates how different cultural perspectives surround your self-system. Your experiences and associations in each of these areas have strongly influenced your thoughts and feelings about yourself. Your self-concept, self-esteem, and self-efficacy are defined by beliefs and assumptions that you have acquired through your interaction with others. For example, you may feel pride in the ethnic and racial background you share with your immediate family, but you have developed different views about politics and religion than your parents have.

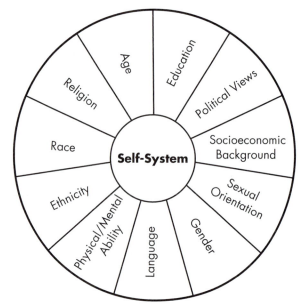

FIGURE 7.2: Diversity Wheel
Source: Adapted from C. Munoz, "Cultural Sensitivity and Diversity Awareness: Bridging the Gap between Families and Providers," *The Source* 6, no. 3 (1996): 1–3; retrieved September 13, 2006, from http://aia.berkeley.edu/media/pdf/source_summer96.pdf.

ACTIVITY 7.1   Defining Cultural Perspectives

The following activity asks you to consider how different cultural perspectives influence your identity and how you will influence others. The objective is to increase your self-awareness, so think carefully about your responses.

1. How would you describe yourself in each of the following areas?

   Ethnicity _____

   Race _____

   Religion _____

   Age _____

   Education _____

   Political views _____

   Socioeconomic background _____

   Sexual orientation _____

   Gender _____

   Language _____

   Physical and mental abilities _____

2. Identify areas that have had the most significant effect on your identity, and explain why.

_____

_____

_____

_____

3. How will your unique attributes help others appreciate the importance of diversity?

_____

_____

_____

_____

How Do Your Cultural Beliefs and Biases Affect Your Attitude?

If you have not had the opportunity to contrast your cultural beliefs and attitudes with differing ideas, you may not realize how you are influenced by them. They may be as difficult to see as the air you breathe. But no matter who you are, you have developed cultural beliefs and assumptions about every aspect of your life. As a college student, these beliefs may be challenged as you interact with people across campus. A professor may question your stand on a certain issue. You may have a roommate whose attitudes about sexual activity differ from your own, or a classmate might lecture you about your food preferences. You soon realize that everyone has *biases*—strong inclinations toward particular perspectives or opinions.

> **EXPERT'S OPINION**
>
> "Everybody has culture, even though some folks think they don't....Culture is how you love and whom you choose to love. It's whether you eat cornbread or pumpernickel. It's how you respond to the dilemmas life offers you and how you celebrate living. It shows itself without you knowing and it tells who you are without you speaking."
>
> **Mona Lake Jones**, *The Color of Culture*

Your biases often reflect significant cultural influences in your life. Many young college students have not analyzed their perspectives and opinions. They tend to believe what they have been taught by authority figures. Experiences with different perspectives in college can help them develop critical thinking skills to evaluate their beliefs and attitudes.

For some, developing cultural awareness can be an overwhelming and uncomfortable process. One student describes his experience:

> I grew up in a small town where everyone was the same race, most belonged to the same religion, and nearly all had the same family values. When I left home to attend the university 200 miles away from my home, I entered a world with so much diversity that I was kind of overwhelmed. It took me months to figure out how I could interact with people who were different than I was and still maintain my own sense of culture. I finally realized that I didn't have to give up parts of myself to gain from them. We were all just people with different points of view, and we were all important.

Becoming culturally aware takes time and patience, but it is worth the effort. Awareness is the basis for understanding the differences between yourself and others and developing meaningful relationships. Your level of cultural awareness will also affect your attitude toward others. Attitudes toward cultural diversity range from prejudice to empathy.

Prejudice is an adverse opinion formed without sufficient knowledge about a person or group of people. It is often based on fear of the unknown, and it can prevent a person from engaging in interaction that might change his or her opinion. As Indira Gandhi said, "You cannot shake hands with a clenched fist."[4] And you cannot learn to understand another person if you allow your prejudice to cloud your judgment.

Ethnocentrism is the belief that your culture is superior to other cultures. It is based on the unrealistic expectation that others should conform to your **cultural norms**—your culture's standards of thinking, feeling, and doing, which you consider to be "normal." A less obvious form of ethnocentrism is **assumed similarity**,[5] the assumption that most people are like you or want to be like you. People with this attitude do not see themselves as intolerant or judgmental; they simply equate their values with basic human values and assume that their point of view is universal. They are likely to argue that race and culture should not matter because we are all human beings.

Tolerance is the acceptance of people whose cultural beliefs and attitudes are different than your own. Helen Keller said, "The highest result of education is tolerance."[6] Through education you become more aware of the value of diversity. You are willing to learn about other cultures, but your understanding is more academic than personal. You learn to acknowledge the differences between cultures without judging or feeling threatened by those differences.

Respect means recognizing the value of individual cultures and raising the level of regard you have for the ideas and traditions of other cultures. Respect helps you enjoy interacting with a variety of different people and helps you actively seek opportunities to learn about other cultures. As a peer mentor, it is important that you actively promote **multiculturalism**, the idea that people should preserve their cultures, allow different cultures to peacefully exist together, and encourage learning about different cultures. You should be aware of multicultural initiatives on your campus. You can do your part to increase respect for others as you befriend students and help them acclimate to dramatic changes in their cultural environment.

Empathy is the ability to identify with and understand another's situation, feelings, and motives.[7] This understanding allows you to experience another culture through the relationship you have with a person from that culture. This attitude represents the highest form of acceptance because instead of measuring another culture against your culture, you understand the other culture as an honorary member of it.

ACTIVITY 7.2   Identifying Cultural Attitudes

The following activity is designed to help you evaluate your attitudes toward differences you encounter in other students. In the first table, mark the column that best describes your attitude toward each of the types of groups, and answer the questions that follow. In the second table, mark the column that best describes your perception of campus-wide attitudes toward each group listed. Answer the final questions after discussing your responses with a group of diverse students.

YOUR ATTITUDES	PREJUDICE	ETHNOCENTRIC (ASSUMED SIMILARITY)	TOLERANCE	RESPECT	EMPATHY
Racial differences					
Ethnic differences					
Language differences					
Religious differences					
Socioeconomic differences					
Gender differences					
Sexual orientation differences					
Age differences					
Physical differences					
Mental differences					

1. Do you feel empathy toward any group listed above? If yes, explain how you developed empathy. If no, identify what may be preventing you from attaining this level of understanding.

   _____

   _____

   _____

2. Do you feel prejudice toward any group listed above? If yes, why?

_____

_____

3. Think about the groups on your campus. Identify one group about which you want to gain more understanding. How will you increase your appreciation of this group?

_____

_____

CAMPUS ATTITUDES	PREJUDICE	ETHNOCENTRIC (ASSUMED SIMILARITY)	TOLERANCE	RESPECT	EMPATHY
Racial differences					
Ethnic differences					
Language differences					
Religious differences					
Socioeconomic differences					
Gender differences					
Sexual orientation differences					
Age differences					
Physical differences					
Mental differences					

4. (Optional) Compare your answers to those of other students or mentors. Did your answers differ significantly from other students' answers? If so, explain.

_____

_____

_____

5. What can you do as a mentor to improve campus attitudes toward different groups?

_____

_____

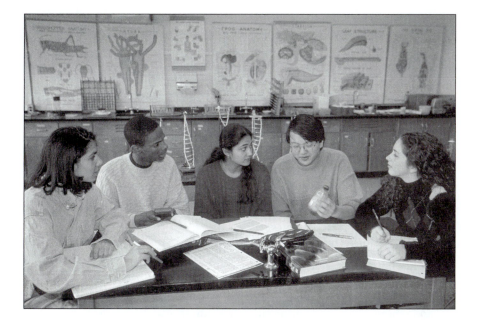

As you consider different perspectives and attitudes about culture, you will learn more by focusing on understanding other points of view rather than defending your own point of view. Part of understanding culture is understanding that your perspective is limited, and part of becoming self-aware is choosing your own response to new and challenging ideas.

What Strategies Will Help You Show Sensitivity toward Culturally Diverse Students?

The following strategies focus on developing sensitivity to the needs and experiences of students whose culture is different than your own.

Acknowledge each individual. One of the most common barriers to effective intercultural interaction is the tendency to see people as part of a group, not as individuals. As a mentor, you can avoid this trap by learning your students' names. People place a high value on their names. Many times a name holds incredible personal value and

MENTOR'S VOICE

The best way to mentor students that are culturally different from me is to withhold judgment. I may never be able to fully understand why they do what they do or everything about their culture but if I accept them for who they are and help them become better students the relationship will be a success.

Albert Mitchell, peer mentor

meaning to the person. Make sure to pronounce the name the way the student does. Don't assume that any pronunciation that comes out of your mouth will be okay. Properly pronouncing names from languages different than your own often takes some effort.

Recognize language barriers. You will quickly recognize obvious language barriers between yourself and some students who speak English as a second language. If you are concerned that a student may not understand you, ask the student to summarize the information so that you can assess understanding. When you approach students with questions or comments, give them time to consider their responses. Some students who are learning English need additional time to translate questions in their minds before feeling comfortable enough to respond.

You may not recognize more subtle differences between your vocabulary and a student's vernacular language, like hip-hop slang. If you are working with a student who frequently uses expressions specific to his or her culture, do not assume that you can use the same terms. They may be offensive when used in a different cultural context. Ask students who use vernacular language to explain what the terms mean to them and when, if ever, it is appropriate for you to use the terms.

Be consistent. Your aspirations for a student's success must demonstrate your desire to be fair. Maintaining equal expectations for all students increases their willingness to put forth the effort needed to understand. Some students face "stereotype threat,"[8] meaning that they cannot escape negative stereotypes associated with their race or ethnic group. The stereotypes have become part of their social identity, and these students tend to perform poorly because their expectations of themselves have been influenced by predominant stereotypes. You can avoid reinforcing the stereotype by building trust, maintaining consistently high expectations, and communicating your confidence in their ability to achieve. If you show students that you believe in them and in their abilities, you can help break down some initial barriers and help them develop specific strategies to deal with both real and perceived stereotypes.

Show respect. You should show the same level of respect for all of your students, no matter what their culture is. As a mentor, you can encourage others to show respect. Don't allow others to make fun of the culture or language of another student. What one person may see as "just teasing" can damage the confidence of another. It can also cause feelings of anger or isolation. Promote inclusion by being observant and demonstrating your respect for all of your students.

Observe interaction carefully. When working with students, keep your eyes as well as your ears open. Cultural differences can manifest themselves through personal interaction. For example, people from different cultures have a wide variety of comfort levels regarding personal space. You can gauge what is appropriate by watching for clues that indicate that a student is uncomfortable or uncertain about the interaction.

Do students seem sure or unsure of your intentions? Do they look like they understand you, or do they look confused? Pay attention to students' nonverbal messages so you can tell when they need reassurance to contribute their ideas.

Encourage interaction. Your students may tend to interact with a limited group of people. Often people of the same culture stick together because they are comfortable with one another. As a mentor, you can create opportunities for students to engage in activities with a variety of students. Some typical group mentoring interactions include study sessions, collaborative classroom presentations, student activities, and service projects. You will be most effective if you remember the following tips.

- Include everyone, and show interest in each person.

- Ask for input from everyone, and endorse each student's ideas.

- Allow all students time to express themselves; don't interrupt.

Suspend judgment. When you judge or criticize another person, you assume that you have sufficient information and that your frame of reference is accurate. In most cases, you do not have the knowledge and experience necessary to understand another person, but a judgmental attitude can prevent you from learning more about her or him. Being willing to suspend judgment means that you are willing to admit that you do not know enough about another person to evaluate or judge. If you suspend judgment and keep an open mind, you will not only be able to learn from other people, but you may also find that others are more open to your ideas.

Show empathy. You show empathy by listening intently to another person. You experience empathy when your perspective changes because you see the world through the other person's eyes for a moment. Dr. Tyrone Holmes, a consultant in intercultural communication, explains that empathy "is a cognitive and psychological state where you truly understand where another person is 'coming from.' *Empathy is the single most important element of multicultural communication.*"[9] If empathy were easy, we would have no problems with multicultural communication. But empathy does not come without effort. If you want to achieve this level of understanding, you need to invest time and energy in the relationship.

> ### EXPERT'S OPINION
>
> "We must suspend our judgment. We should not judge others negatively because they are indirect, or their accents aren't clear, or their tone of voice is tentative, or they avoid eye contact. We must learn patience and suspend judgment long enough to realize these differences don't make one of us right and the other wrong. They simply mean that we approach communication from a different frame of reference and, many times, a different value system."
>
> **Helen Turnbull**, president of Human Facets

Ask for guidance. You will inevitably need to ask for additional information and advice from others. You cannot expect to know everything about working with students from a variety of different cultures. For example, you may not realize that when working with a hearing-impaired student who has an interpreter, you should always look at and speak to the student, not the interpreter. You can learn other important guidelines by talking to your program administrator, a professor, or other mentors, but don't be afraid to talk to the students themselves. If you build a relationship, they will be more willing to share their perspective and give you insight into their culture. Information about characteristics of their culture can often help you solve problems more effectively.

What Cultural Characteristics Should Mentors Know?

Just as it is impossible to know everything, it is equally impossible to present an adequate overview of different cultures. This section presents common cultural characteristics that have been identified in a variety of cultures. Keep in mind that they may or may not be exhibited by students from particular cultures. Beware of the tendency to stereotype students based on popular cultural assumptions.

A **stereotype** is a commonly accepted generalization that is applied to but does not accurately represent individuals within the group. Many times stereotypes are based on limited experience with a certain group and on assumptions that represent oversimplifications or gross exaggerations. A stereotype is not always negative, but it will prevent you from understanding an individual student. Everyone is guilty of accepting and creating stereotypes. Some people quickly accept simplified explanations of why people are the way they are because they do not have sufficient knowledge or experience to know anything different. Others generalize about their own experience with a person and make the inappropriate assumption that this person's attributes and behavior are representative of the entire culture. While people share cultural similarities, each individual is unique in thoughts, feelings, and actions.

The sooner you familiarize yourself with the general characteristics of a student and his or her culture, the sooner you can establish and maintain a successful mentoring relationship. You may recognize many key cultural characteristics in the students you mentor. Some but not all of the common characteristics are listed below.

There are other ways to gain cultural knowledge aside from getting to know individual members of the culture. Chapter 11 discusses student support services on your campus. Many of these services work with multicultural, international, or minority students. By visiting staff members of these resources, you can learn more about how to properly interact with students who are culturally different from you. You can also search for information at your library or on the Internet.

"Cultural Knows": Common Cultural Characteristics

Your culturally diverse students *may*, not *will*, possess some of the following cultural characteristics. Awareness of these characteristics can help a mentor avoid unintentional, damaging, or embarrassing situations.

Eye contact. In many cultures, it is inappropriate to look others directly in the eye when speaking. Students may be showing respect by looking down instead of looking you in the eye.

Hand gestures. Different cultures use hand gestures in different ways. What may appear as "come here" to one student may be viewed as "goodbye" by another. Pointing your finger is a negative gesture in many cultures.

Facial gestures. Some students smile or laugh when they are nervous. This should not be taken to mean that they are not paying attention. It could mean they are feeling uncomfortable with the situation.

Silence. In some cultures, students are told that they should not give opinions or make statements unless they are completely certain they are correct. A student should never be pressured into providing a quick answer.

Religious belief. A student's religious tenets may affect the ability to perform certain tasks. For example, drawing a human face or form is not an accepted practice in some religions.

Cooperation versus competition. In some cultures, positioning yourself as superior to another is considered rude. A student may even perform at a lower level to prevent embarrassing another student.

Loss of face. Some students will not do well when they feel they are being reprimanded by a teacher or mentor. They prefer to be confrontational instead of backing down. Often, providing them with options to choose will remove potential conflicts.

Time. Several cultures view time as flexible rather than linear. When something is done is not as important as the fact that it gets done. People from such cultures might not view being late to class or a study session as a problem.

Physical contact. In some cultures but not in others, people are comfortable shaking hands, hugging, or patting someone on the back. Certain touches that may seem benign to you are completely unacceptable to some students. As a peer mentor, you should avoid touching. You never know what a student's reaction to touch might be.

Recognition. Many cultures have a strong emphasis on the family or group. The student may be uncomfortable receiving praise or recognition as an individual, but may instead prefer the class to be recognized as a whole.

ACTIVITY 7.3   Applying the Ten "Cultural Knows"

The following activity will help you identify the relationship between the general guidelines given in this chapter and specific cultural groups on your campus. To complete this activity, form a group of a least three people who represent various cultural perspectives, and discuss your responses to each question.

1. Identify at least three different cultural groups on your campus. List them below.

_____

_____

2. Which particular "cultural knows" could be most useful to you as you mentor students from those groups? List them below.

_____

_____

3. What are some "cultural knows" you have seen put into action effectively in any of your educational experiences? What was most beneficial about the way they were implemented?

_____

_____

_____

4. What experiences have you had where the "knows" were not used and things did not turn out well as a result? How could the "knows" have been instituted to make a difference?

_____

_____

_____

_____

5. Which, if any, of the "knows" do you hold as a part of your own culture? List them.

_____

_____

6. Where can you go to gather additional information about other cultural characteristics that may be unique to your campus?

_____

_____

Developing cultural perspective is the most important way to improve cultural relations. We have many opportunities to learn new things from people who are different from ourselves. Good peer mentors improve their relationships with students by making concerted efforts to understand them better. Genuine effort empowers you and creates opportunities for your students to empower themselves with richer cultural knowledge. As you attempt to share in the cultural differences of the students around you, you gain a greater appreciation not only for what makes them unique, but also for important contributions of your own cultural characteristics.

 ## Where are you now?

These questions are designed to help you review the important concepts covered in the chapter. Answering these questions can help you assess your own understanding or prepare for a test.

1. Explain why diversity is important.
2. Define the ASK model for mentoring diverse students.
3. What are three significant cultural influences in your life?
4. Discuss ways to develop positive attitudes toward different cultures.
5. Identify three strategies that can improve your mentoring relationship with culturally diverse students.
6. Identify several "cultural knows" you think you may encounter, and explain why they are important for the students you mentor.

Case Study Discussion

Review the case study at the beginning of this chapter, and answer the following questions as they relate to the concepts you learned in the chapter. Discuss your answers with other mentors in your program so that you can explore different perspectives and gain greater insight into how to help this person.

Why is Amir's experience relevant in this chapter?

What would you need to know to help a student like Amir?

If you had to help Amir, how would you approach the situation?

If your initial idea didn't work, what else could you do to help Amir?

 ## Where do you want to be?

Reflect on what you have learned about mentoring in this chapter, and consider how you will apply these ideas to your specific responsibilities as a mentor.

1. What do you consider the most valuable concept in this chapter?

    _____

    _____

2. Why was it significant to you?

    _____

    _____

    _____

    _____

    _____

3. How will you apply this concept as a mentor?

    _____

    _____

    _____

    _____

    _____

Learning Effective Peer Mentoring Skills

Part III guides you through the development and application of practical mentoring skills. Chapter 8 deals with key elements of "Communicating Effectively" in your role as a trusted friend. Chapter 9 provides a model for "Facilitating Learning," and Chapter 10 suggests different strategies for "Planning and Problem Solving." Both chapters help you become a more effective learning coach. Chapter 11, "Utilizing Campus Resources," helps you become more familiar with campus resources so that you can be a strong advocate and connecting link for your students. Chapter 12 focuses on "Continually Improving Your Mentoring Skills" by reevaluating your motives for serving as a mentor and reflecting on your performance.

Communicating Effectively

8

Case Study: "You Didn't Tell Me"

You are assigned to be a peer mentor in a first-year-experience course. Carla, who is registered for the class, doesn't show up during the first week of school. When she finally comes to class, she says that her adviser messed up her schedule and that she had been attending the wrong class. After class, she tells the professor that she can get caught up if she has a copy of the syllabus. The professor tells her that the syllabus is available online and that she can contact you for help with it.

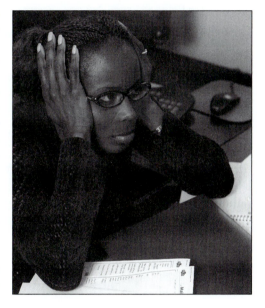

When you see Carla at the next class session, she asks you how to find the syllabus online, but she is distracted by her portable media player while you explain how to access it. She tells you that you won't need to worry about her and that she will be fine. A couple of weeks later, the professor tells you that Carla is falling farther behind and has yet to turn in an assignment.

The problem gets worse when Carla does not show up to take the first exam. The professor tells her that she cannot make up the exam and that she should know that because it is outlined on the syllabus. Carla gets angry and complains that no one told her how to get the syllabus. She demands an opportunity to make up the test since you did not tell her what was going on in the class.

As you discuss the following questions with other mentors in your program, remember that this case study has been written about a real student facing real challenges. We encourage you to imagine the complexity of the situation and not to oversimplify the issues that the student faces. You may not feel experienced enough to completely answer the questions at this point, 125

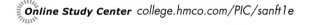

Online Study Center college.hmco.com/PIC/sanft1e

but you will have an opportunity to revisit this case study after learning the concepts in this chapter.

As a mentor, what do you believe your role is in assisting Carla with her problems?

How might you approach Carla about resolving her issues?

What can you do to demonstrate effective student strategies to her?

 **Where are you going?**

After reading this chapter, you should be familiar with the following concepts and terms related to peer mentoring.

- Communicating as a mentor
- Ideas for one-on-one communication
- Ideas for communicating in small groups
- Ideas for large-group presentations
- Giving and receiving feedback
- Other important communication issues

Key Terms

In this chapter, you will encounter the following terms, which appear in bold. You can highlight the definitions as you read or look for them in the glossary at the end of the book.

Active listening
Barriers
Communication
Feedback
"I" messages

Nonverbal communication
Personal space
Q-SPACE
Think/pair/share
Verbal communication

How Is Mentoring Communication Different from Other Communication?

You cannot *not* communicate. As long as you are around or in contact with other people, some form of **communication**—the verbal and nonverbal interaction you have with other people—is taking place. In a given situation, you choose the way you communicate with others. You may choose to listen carefully and respond thoughtfully. Choosing not to respond can send as strong a message as speaking your thoughts outright. Peer mentors are involved in many different interactions with students, program administrators, instructors, and other mentors. You can learn how to communicate well in all of these situations.

In a mentoring relationship, effective communication creates enduring connections that can change the direction of fellow students' lives forever. First, you should realize that communication is a constantly evolving process. To be a successful mentor, you have to be responsive to each student's needs. Ultimately, you recognize and focus on the particular needs of each student or group of students you meet. The following strategies may be useful as you consider how to communicate with your students.

Communicate during transitions. Part of your peer mentoring job is to connect with students when communication is vital to making a successful transition. College students' motivation levels and drive to succeed in school and to graduate are more at risk during certain transitional periods than at other times. These periods include the first six weeks of the freshman year, breaks between semesters, holiday breaks, moves to off-campus housing, and studying abroad. At these times, new students—and even experienced ones—can be more vulnerable and more likely to need student services.

Encourage students to be independent. You will most likely develop comfortable and friendly relationships with the students, but you will be more than their friend. Many students will see you as an authority figure and will expect you to take charge and direct their interactions with you. A student's overreliance on you to direct situations is what makes communication in a mentoring relationship most challenging. Especially at the beginning of your mentor interactions, you will have to put forth more effort to make things successful, but you want to gradually help your students to take on more responsibility and become more independent.

Keep your students' best interests at heart. As mentioned in Chapter 6, college students value authentic people. They immediately sense hype and do not accept people they consider fake. If you are not genuine, students will not listen no matter what you say. Through word and action, you can communicate what it takes to be a successful student, but they have to recognize that you are sincere in your effort to be a mentor.

Let the program speak for itself. As a mentor, you represent more than just yourself; you are part of a larger program. Students associate what you do and say with your mentoring program. Because of this, you will often be responsible for any communication that takes place. Students don't want to be forced, overtly sold, or pitched into joining. They usually prefer to be educated about what you do as a mentor and given options about how to participate.

Another aspect of communication that is different in peer mentoring than in other relationships is that, depending on the structure of your program, you might be mentoring students individually, meeting with study groups, or presenting to a whole class. You will not facilitate a small group study session the same way you will give a presentation to an entire class or meet with a student on a one-on-one basis. This chapter offers guidelines to help you prepare to effectively meet the needs of each unique situation in which you find yourself.

What Are Useful One-on-One Communication Guidelines?

You probably have never seen a bumper sticker that says "Communication Happens!" It's just not that simple. Although communication happens constantly, it takes effort from all parties involved to be successful. Peer mentors have plenty of opportunities to work at it with their students. You are already aware of many good communication strategies. This section mainly addresses important one-on-one communication skills: appropriate use of personal space, active listening, and verbal and nonverbal communication.

Personal Space

Each student you encounter has a unique comfort zone when it comes to **personal space** and physical contact. Typically, students are used to sitting near one another in a classroom and are likely to be comfortable if you occupy a seat next to a student you wish to talk with. Don't assume, however, that the student will be comfortable if you sit down next to him or her on a couch or if you pat him or her on the back. Respecting the wishes of your students is crucial. You also need to protect yourself from potential misperception about your intentions.

Physical contact can be a powerful way of expressing yourself, but it is also the most misunderstood form of nonverbal expression. It often can be misconstrued, especially when you are first getting to know someone. The acceptability of touching differs from one culture to another, and North America is generally a no-contact culture. North Americans tend to touch their pets more than they touch close friends and family members. Touching can be perceived as sexual harassment. Although a touch on the arm, shoulder, or the top of the hand is generally "safe," the best practice, especially on first meetings, is a handshake or no touching or physical contact at all.

Take your time before entering another's personal space. Look for clues that indicate how comfortable the other person is with you. Some students make friends quickly and are comfortable with you the first time you meet. Others like to take their time to make sure they want to be in the relationship and to develop trust. Be prepared to adjust your style accordingly.

Active Listening

Henry David Thoreau said, "It takes two to speak the truth—one to speak, and another to hear."[1] When communicating with others, it is as important to listen as it is to speak. You may have been told "You have two ears and one mouth. Use them proportionally!" If you are a passive listener, you will be hearing but not listening. Try to suspend personal thoughts and needs, and consciously concentrate on the speaker.

Active listening requires intentional thought and understanding. It does not happen accidentally. Think of a boring lecture at which you were physically present, but your thoughts were somewhere else. How much did you get from the lecture? Probably not much learning occurred. Your students will often want to use you as a sounding board because you were recently in their shoes as a new student. They see you as someone in a position to help, and they will be anticipating your full attention to what they are communicating.

In their 2005 book *Contacts*,[2] Michael and Teri Gamble identify both ineffective and effective listening techniques:

Ineffective

Apprehensive. You become defensive because you are afraid of what the other person will say.

Burned-out. Your mind shuts down because you cannot deal with any more information.

Distracted. You may stop listening to another person because you become distracted or lose focus.

Lazy. You do not want to put effort into trying to understand the other person.

Out-of-control. You allow your emotions to distort the person's message, and you overreact to what the other person has said.

Selfish. You focus more on yourself and what you want to say than on what the other person is saying.

Fake listening. You nod your head and try to look interested in what the person is saying.

Effective

Appreciative listening. You listen for enjoyment, such as to music or TV. As a mentor, you engage in this type of listening when you hang out with students to share a few laughs.

Comprehensive listening. You listen to gain knowledge. You may listen to a student describe his struggle in math, or you may visit with an instructor about her plans for next week's class. If you want to be effective at this type of listening, suspend judgment and delay evaluating what you hear until you have all the information.

Critical listening. You analyze the truth or validity of what the other person is saying. After listening to understand, you may begin to ask yourself whether you accept or reject what you have heard.

ACTIVITY 8.1   Identifying Your Listening Habits

This activity will help you identify your listening habits and reflect on what they mean to you as a mentor. Complete the assessment, and answer the questions about your listening skills.

Do you ever find yourself . . .	NEVER		SOMETIMES		ALWAYS
1. apprehensive about what the other person is saying?	4	3	2	1	0
2. burned out when listening to another person?	4	3	2	1	0
3. distracted by your thoughts or surroundings?	4	3	2	1	0
4. unwilling to put effort into listening?	4	3	2	1	0
5. overreacting to what the other person is saying?	4	3	2	1	0
6. focused on your own response or ideas?	4	3	2	1	0
7. nodding when you're not really listening?	4	3	2	1	0
8. enjoying the conversation?	0	1	2	3	4
9. listening to understand important information?	0	1	2	3	4
10. evaluating or judging *before* the other person is finished?	4	3	2	1	0
11. waiting until the other person is finished to evaluate?	0	1	2	3	4
12. listening and understanding the other person's point of view?	0	1	2	3	4

If your score is between 32 and 48, you are an excellent listener.

If your score is between 16 and 32, you are doing well, but you should identify specific areas where you want to improve.

If your score is below 16, you can improve by focusing on the areas where you scored the lowest.

Total _____

1. Describe your strengths as a listener.

_____

_____

2. Describe your weaknesses as a listener.

_____

_____

3. How can ineffective listening affect your mentoring relationships?

_____

_____

4. How can effective listening affect your mentoring relationships?

_____

_____

5. Why is it important to be aware of your own listening habits?

_____

_____

Empathic listening. When you listen empathically, you understand another person's dilemma from his or her point of view. According to Daniel Goleman, author of *Emotional Intelligence,* "Being able to put aside one's self-centered focus and impulses . . . opens the way to empathy, to real listening, to taking another's perspective."[3] This type of listening allows you to understand another person the way he or she wants to be understood.

As you spend time with your students, you will soon realize that the ways you communicate with each other will vary. Some will want to spend their time with you on the phone or face-to-face. Others will prefer less personal approaches such as e-mail or text messaging. Any of these ways can either work for you or against you as you interact with each other.

Verbal and Nonverbal Messages

Another piece of the communication puzzle is how your ***verbal*** and ***nonverbal*** messages affect your conversations. The following verbal and nonverbal guidelines come from Dave Ellis's *Becoming a Master Student.*[4]

Be quiet. Take the time to develop your response after the student has completed his or her message. If the student still has more to say, do not cut him or her off. This also allows you to get the entire message that is sent.

Maintain eye contact. Looking at the speaker lets the person know

> ### MENTOR'S VOICE
>
> *I've met with several students outside of class and been able to listen to them. I think that it's so rewarding when students feel that they can confide in me, or come to me for help.*
>
> **Whitney Shaw**, peer mentor

that you are present. It also provides you with an opportunity to evaluate body language and behavior. Direct eye contact is not encouraged in all cultures. Take your cues about eye contact from the student.

Display openness. Face the person, and keep the space between you clear. Don't look off in other directions. Crossing your arms gives the appearance of not being open to the person.

Send acknowledgments. Periodically do something that shows that you are still in the conversation. Nod your head, and say "OK" or "Uh-huh." Doing so does not necessarily mean that you agree, just that you are listening.

Paraphrase. Repeat what the speaker said to make sure you understand it. Say something like "so what you are saying is . . ." The speaker will tell you whether you are getting it or not.

Listen beyond words. Watch and listen for nonverbal cues, such as someone who claims to be excited but sounds bored. It is important to listen to the emotion and tone behind the words.

Take care of yourself. If you can't join a conversation with one of your students, tell the truth. Saying something like "I'd love to talk to you, but I need to get to class right now. Can I call you later?" is fine as long as you are being honest. Don't pretend to listen if you can't do it at the time.

Listen for requests. When a student complains "I don't get anything out of the class," he or she may mean "I don't know how to take good notes." Watch for requests that may be hiding behind a complaint.

Replace "You" messages with "I" messages. Using "You" messages sets you up for painful interactions. When you say "You are so lazy. Why don't you come to class?" to a student, the typical defensive response is "Why should I come? The class is a waste of time!" "You" messages are not always accurate. They are packed with emotion and often do not accomplish anything positive. Using **"I" messages** can completely change a relationship. "I" messages take the heat out of the conversation. When you say "I worry when you miss class. Is there something I can do to help you get there?" the other person is less likely to feel pressure and become defensive.

Notice barriers to sending messages. Barriers are obstacles that get in the way of effective communication. They can be technical, physical, social, emotional, or mental. For example, your cell phone might keep cutting out on you when you try to call people, or the person with whom you are communicating could be so upset that your message never gets through. Words may have different meanings to another person than they do to you, or you may not understand the tone of a written message.

No matter what type of communicating you do, you will occasionally run into barriers. These barriers may be a result of the attitudes of those involved, or

⚐ ⚐⚐ ACTIVITY 8.2 Identifying Communication Barriers

This activity is designed to provide you with an opportunity to recognize barriers you may run into and to come up with potential solutions to avoid or deal with them.

Part 1. Work independently. Think of different communication interactions in the categories listed below. Identify some of the barriers that got in the way of making those interactions work. List potential solutions you could implement to avoid the barrier or make it less likely to happen in the future. Be specific. The idea is to come up with practical solutions that might be useful in the future. For example, if you identified a barrier for e-mail as the possibility of misinterpreting the tone of the message, you might list using an emoticon or naming the intended tone as potential solutions.

FORM OF COMMUNICATION	POSSIBLE BARRIERS	POTENTIAL SOLUTIONS
Face to face		
Telephone		
Text messaging		
E-mail		
Internet postings (Facebook, MySpace)		

Part 2. Role-play. Find a partner, and role-play. Imagine that you are a peer mentor who needs to give constructive criticism about a class assignment to a student. First, come up with a specific message to deliver to the student. In a role-play format, act out the scenario using the different communication forms above.

1. Which forms of communication would be most effective, and why?

_____

_____

2. Which forms of communication would be least effective, and why?

_____

_____

3. Can you think of forms of communication interactions other than the ones listed above? If so, what are they?

_____

_____

4. Which types of interactions do you think you will most likely use as a peer mentor, and what will you personally try to do to make them effective?

_____

_____

_____

they may occur for other reasons. Different types of communication tend to have different types of obstacles.

What Are Some Useful Communication Ideas You Can Use When Working with Small Groups?

Mentors often work in small groups in a variety of settings. These groups might have different purposes, including in-class discussions or presentations, service-learning activities, study groups, or connecting with campus activities. There are some common communication tools to employ to help the groups be effective. In addition to making a personal connection, as discussed in Chapter 4, tools for effective group communication include seeking participation, clarifying meanings, offering ideas, facilitating outcomes, and evaluating processes.

Seeking participation. Contribution is necessary. Each member of the group needs to feel like part of the team's success. Encourage positive interactions that lead to a feeling of safety. If someone is not participating, perhaps you can ask for the person's opinion about something that is nonthreatening. For example, answering questions about the format of a coming test or presentation is typically a safe contribution. Expressing thanks for involvement can also help generate more involvement.

Clarifying group roles. Students in any group with which you are involved may assume that you are the leader and that you are responsible for the group's success. Explain your mentoring role in relation to the group, and listen carefully to make sure the members understand their roles as well. Suggest stopping now and then to be certain everyone is up to date on what is happening. Some impatient or strong-willed students may take over and start making too many decisions based on limited perspective, stifling group effectiveness. Students who do not feel involved may tune out. No student's ideas should be dismissed without due consideration, nor should any student be made to feel uncomfortable just because she or he has not understood the discussion.

Offering ideas. As the peer mentor, you are likely to have pertinent experience that would help the group successfully complete the learning objectives. You may want to suggest plans or ideas for the group's consideration. Don't offer ideas too quickly, because an inexperienced group is likely to agree to anything you suggest. The group members view it as a way to avoid coming up with their own ideas. Some members may feel that their ideas will not be as accepted as being as good as yours. The best ideas for the group may come from the members. You may want to feed off of something someone else has said and credit that person for the idea.

Facilitating outcomes. Just as you do not want to offer your ideas too quickly, you need to be careful to facilitate without controlling the outcome. You may need to gently guide the discussion to keep it on track. Encourage participants to follow their own leads and utilize their own skills. Incorporate your ideas if doing so can enrich the overall experience. You may need to say "I think you were headed in the right direction with that comment. What other ideas does that bring to mind?" Using questions is a great way to lead without controlling.

> ## MENTOR'S VOICE
>
> *While meeting with various groups in and out of class, I was able to get to know some of the students better and on a more personal basis. I was able to ask questions about them specifically so that I could relate to them and what they are going through.*
> **Jessica Dollar**, peer mentor

Evaluating processes. As a mentor, you can help students recognize the value of working and learning in small groups. Once again, asking questions can be a great way to facilitate this. Avoid telling students how you think they did and what improvements they should make. Let them come up with their own thoughts about the process. If they feel like they are effective, they will be more likely to create their own groups in the future.

What Are Some Useful Communication Ideas for Presenting to Large Groups?

If your mentor program requires presentations in class, you will need to utilize yet another set of skills to interact with a larger group of students. A public speaking class can be a wonderful resource for a presenter, and you might

consider taking a course if you have not done so. However, presenting to a class requires more than good public speaking skills. You want to maintain an interactive atmosphere as you present your ideas. One of the best ways to do that is to ask your audience questions and have the audience members discuss ideas or teach each other at key points during the discussion. Chapter 9 presents more information on facilitating the learning of your students.

Think/Pair/Share

The **think/pair/share** strategy is one of the most successful models for getting large groups involved in a presentation. In its simplest form, it provides students with time to (1) think about the topic of discussion, (2) pair up with one or more other students, and (3) share thoughts or understanding about the topic. Using this model helps students recognize the value of paying attention and participating in class. Students who think about what they are learning and teach it to others are more likely to remember the material.

Think/pair/share is a great way to get your students involved in the presentation without putting them on the spot in front of the entire class. When students interact with just one or two other people, they tend to feel more comfortable sharing what they understand about the subject. It also allows them to have an experience of doing more than just listening to a presenter talk. The more students use their own senses and get involved in the learning process, the better. They can hear something, look at presentation props, write notes, process their thoughts, and express concepts in their own words. If you use this strategy often, try to get your students to form different pairings each time. They will benefit from the different perspectives and be less likely to socialize instead of staying on task.

Q-SPACE

Q-SPACE is an acronym for a strategy to help you present to a group by way of using questions. The letters stand for *question, silence/selection/sample/ survey, probe, accept, clarify*, and *explain*.

Utilizing questions in presentations requires students to engage in thought and to be involved. You want to keep them interested in the topic, perhaps even have them lead the discussion in response to your questions. A potential problem with using questions is that the students may not know what to reply or don't want to reply. Lack of response can unnerve even the most experienced mentor.

The idea behind this strategy is that you learn how to carefully and effectively utilize questions as you make your presentation. You don't just think of the questions you will use, but you also determine whom you will ask.

Question. Begin with carefully thought-out questions that will generate the desired responses.

Silence. Prepare yourself to accept the silence that may follow your question. Depending on learning styles, some students need at least ten or twenty seconds to think about and develop an answer to a question. Don't be afraid to allow them that time.

Selection. Think about whom to ask. Sometimes anyone in the room can answer what you are asking. Other times you will use your previous experience to determine ahead of time which student to ask. It may even be appropriate to ask students in advance or to give them the question ahead of time. Call the student by name before asking the question, and remember to allow time for the student to think about the answer.

Sample. Ask two or three students to generate more possible answers and viewpoints. Never respond to the first answer by saying "Right." That kills possible responses from other students. They stop thinking if they believe the desired answer was given.

Survey. Sometimes you may not understand the response, or you want to find out what the class thinks about a response. Ask the class to respond to student's answers. For example, you may ask "What are your thoughts on that?" or "Does someone else have a different perspective about it?" or "How many agree with _____?"

Probe for details. Ask for more information if you feel students are unclear about their answers. Ask why they responded the way they did or what they can add to support or clarify their answer. Asking for evidence from the text or an example will often strengthen the student's response.

Accept and value the response. Let students know that you value responses and the thinking behind them, especially if they are not correct. You could say "Thank you; that is a very interesting idea—anything more? Does anyone else have an idea you would like to add?"

Clarify. You may have to ask another student to restate the answer or explain how to know that the response is correct. Determine what sources show that the answer is accurate. Try to connect the answer to readings or lectures. Ask the student who has responded if you can ask other students to add to the answer.

Explain by extrapolating. Take the answer one step farther by asking for application examples from the students. Get them thinking about how this has been or could be applied to them. Asking how an idea might relate to another situation is a key reason for this step.

The more prepared you are to give presentations, the more effective you will be at handling curves that come your way—and they will come your way! It takes a lot of time and effort to become a good presenter and even

MENTOR'S VOICE

Class preparation is challenging and requires time. Every day I want to review and be prepared so that I am a good example of a successful student. The nice thing about my position is that I am where they all want to be in a couple of years. I've been in their shoes and succeeded.

Marc Palmer, peer mentor

ACTIVITY 8.3   Implementing Questioning Techniques

The purpose of this activity is to provide you with an opportunity to practice the Q-SPACE technique. Do the first question on your own, and do the second question as an activity in class or with a study group. After discussing your answers with other students, complete questions 3 through 5 on your own.

1. Prepare five questions from this or any other chapter of this book that would generate an appropriate class discussion.

_____

_____

_____

_____

_____

2. Choose your best questions, and ask a group of people to respond to them.

3. After the group discussion, answer the following questions.

Did you ask more than one person to respond?	Yes	No
Did you ask for more details when they responded?	Yes	No
Did you ask the person to clarify if you did understand his or her response?	Yes	No
Did you elaborate on the person's answer by sharing your own thoughts?	Yes	No
Did your questions generate a beneficial discussion?	Yes	No

4. How did the questioning techniques you used affect your discussion?

_____

_____

_____

_____

5. What would you do differently next time you are asked to facilitate a discussion?

_____

_____

_____

more time to be a good questioner. Paying attention to details of the presentation, recognizing your own strengths and limitations, and learning from past presentation experiences will ultimately help you become a more effective presenter. You will learn how to read your audience and know who can help you get your message across. By taking advantage of resources, even the most hesitant presenter can gain more and more comfort with each presenting experience. Always rehearse your presentation out loud with your instructor or friends before class. The students will recognize your preparation, or lack thereof, almost immediately.

How Do You Give and Receive Feedback?

Feedback can be positive or negative, or anywhere between these two extremes. Most people usually don't have problems with giving and receiving the positives. Because of that, this section mainly deals with the not-so-positives.

As a mentor, you will experience feedback on a regular basis. You will often need to provide feedback to students, instructors, and/or program coordinators. You will be the recipient of feedback from the same people. Following are some helpful ideas to guide you as you strive to successfully deal with feedback. As you look through them, you will see that there are many similarities with what you can do in both giving and receiving feedback.

Giving Feedback

Before phase. Before you give feedback, make sure you are aware of the situation, the purpose of your feedback, your plan of action, and the potential reaction of the person.

Think about the purpose of the feedback and how it may be received. Be clear about the particulars of the situation. Use your listening skills as you pay attention to the person's responses and ask for clarification if needed.

Ask yourself: Am I doing it to offer praise, to provide constructive criticism, or to generate alternative solutions? Is what I have to say specifically related to my mentoring stewardship?

Someone who has asked you to provide feedback is more likely to listen if the feedback is not all positive. In this case, some constructive criticism may be most helpful.

Ask yourself: Was the feedback solicited or unsolicited?

Take a moment to assess your awareness of what the person may be thinking and/or feeling about the situation.

Ask yourself: Do I understand the situation? Does the other person understand the situation? Have any misconceptions occurred?

If you are unclear about the answers to any of the questions, you may not be ready to proceed. Make sure you are prepared to move forward before offering the feedback.

During phase. As you go through the process of providing feedback, consistently evaluate what is happening. You need to take care not only of the other person, but of yourself as well. Do what you can to keep the experience effective and appropriate.

If the feedback addresses a negative behavior or perception, be certain that you have the student's permission to comment. Remain focused on the issue that is causing the problem; avoid attacking the person's self-esteem or self-concept. Talk about self-efficacy, the person's confidence in her or his ability to accomplish certain things (see Chapter 5).

Keep control of yourself during the process. No matter what you do, you cannot determine the student's response. If you are talking about a positive, the person will probably be fine with what you have to say. If the feedback will be difficult for the person to hear, give it in a calm, cool manner. Don't raise your voice or use language that could be viewed as abusive. Avoid any type of emotional or physical manipulation or intimidation.

A common mistake is to openly criticize or complain without offering alternatives. If you give feedback about something that is not working well, you should also give ideas about how to change the behavior. For example, if the student is constantly late to class, you might recommend meeting to walk to class together or arriving five minutes early to conduct a review.

When you meet with a student outside of the classroom, maintain an appropriate relationship. Meet in a place that is both neutral and public. Avoid any possible impropriety.

After phase. Find a way to wrap things up in an effective manner. Focus on encouragement, expectations, and taking the needed time.

Let people know that you brought the problem to their attention because you care about them and the program. Your motivation is to make things run more smoothly in the future, and you have confidence that it can happen.

Do whatever is necessary to make sure all parties understand what you plan to do with the feedback. Determine how to proceed.

If the feedback is difficult for someone to receive, allow the person the time to respond to or think about it. You don't want to rush things just so you can get it over with.

Receiving Feedback

As a peer mentor, you are destined to have many opportunities to receive feedback. It can come from students, peers, program administrators, and others. If you stay open-minded about the expressed opinions and listen carefully, you can take advantage of chances for personal growth and development.

Before phase. Prepare yourself by suspending judgments about your-self, your mentor or adviser, or the student. Take time to carefully listen. Remember that a suggestion for change doesn't mean that the service you are providing is not valuable. It may mean that, with a little alter-ation, you could do even greater things. Keep an open mind.

Organize yourself so you have everything you need for the feedback session. That includes something to write on and write with to help you keep track of questions or take notes.

During phase. The most important thing you can do while someone is giving you feedback is simply listen. Utilize the skills mentioned earlier in this chapter. When you carefully listen and follow a procedure, you are less likely to give in to an emotional reaction.

During the session, make sure you are watching and listening for ver-bal and nonverbal cues. Pay attention to body language.

Let the person get all the way through what he or she has to say before responding. This is not the time to shoot back a quick response, make excuses for your behavior, or even apologize.

Before you respond, carefully evaluate the criticism and try to under-stand where the person is coming from. If you are unsure about anything that was expressed, ask for clarification.

Respond to the feedback without letting your emotions get in the way. Don't raise your voice, and be careful about the words you use. The motivation for giving you feedback is probably to help you make adjust-ments to be more successful. In other words, the person giving you the feedback most likely has your best interests, as well as the success of the program, at heart.

After phase. What you do after receiving feedback is important to how the relationship will continue in the future. You usually don't need to provide an immediate response. You also need to make known how you will utilize the feedback.

Sometimes putting a little distance between the feedback and the response can be useful. Even ten or fifteen minutes can make a significant difference by giving you time to talk the feedback over with someone else. This doesn't mean holding a complaint session. If you really want to make things work, try to get an objective point of view. If you feel like you need more time, don't be afraid to ask for it.

All parties should ultimately know what the outcomes of the feed-back will be. Ask for suggestions on how to proceed, or provide others with information about the direction you plan to take.

Even though you decide how to respond to the feedback, you may not have a say in the final outcome. Peer mentors are under the direction of a program and must abide by the program's policies and procedures.

Peer mentors may be tempted to soften their feedback to students so as not to sound too harsh. They may not want to jeopardize the relationship. For example, you may not want to tell a student that she is failing a class, but you can work with her on identifying areas where she can improve her grade. Learning how to give negative feedback without adversely affecting a relationship is an important skill to master.

What Are Other Important Communication Issues to Remember?

Do no harm. Whatever channel or method of communication you choose, use care with the things you can control. As the sender of the communication, be sure that what you express is appropriate and useful. Don't do anything that will hurt another person. Like a doctor with patients, a mentor always should do no harm when interacting with students.

This is especially the case when contacting the class as a whole, such as with e-mail. Be certain not to put anyone on the spot or send anything that might be deemed offensive. A tip-off is what you feel as you prepare to send the message. If you are wondering whether there may be a problem with the content, stop and talk to someone in a position of authority. If you question the appropriateness of the communication even the slightest, don't send it. There is too much potential damage to the mentoring relationship or the mentor program if something goes wrong and a student is hurt or upset. No peer mentor goes into a relationship looking for ways to sabotage it, but it does happen on occasion, and it is a painful experience for everyone involved.

Keep confidences. Another important thing to do is to maintain confidentiality. A student may disclose private information to you. You must make sure that information stays between you and the student. The only time you should share it is if the student is in danger of doing harm to self or others. At such times, it is entirely appropriate to attempt an intervention by referring the student to resources that can help. (See Chapter 11 for appropriate steps in making a referral.) It is also imperative to keep an open line of communication with a program administrator to ask about the proper policies and procedures.

Watch your writing. E-mail, instant messaging, and other Web resources like MySpace and Facebook are great ways to contact students, to dispense such information as changes in a study group meeting place or announcements

> **MENTOR'S VOICE**
>
> *I feel like I can ask anyone in our mentor program for help if I am having a problem with a student or just need advice. No matter what, no matter where, there is always someone you can turn to and ask for an opinion.*
>
> **Alissa Walcott**, peer mentor

Table 8.1: Contact List

NAME	POSITION	PHONE	E-MAIL	OFFICE/ADDRESS
Bill Johnson	Program Director	555–1284 (work)	billj@univ.edu	AD 101
Nancy Ortega	Class Instructor	555–9678 (work)	nancyo@univ.edu	LA 206
David Pierce	Peer Mentor	555–3468 (home)	dpierce@univ.edu	337 Oak Lane
Chanda Wells	Peer Mentor	555–3965 (cell)	cwells@univ.edu	#21 Dodd Apts.
Lee Kwan	Peer Mentor	555–1862 (cell)	lkwan@univ.edu	#14 West Hall

about a campus activity, and just to chat. They are not, however, a forum for all personal interactions. Information sent via e-mail is not confidential, so you should not send confidential information in e-mail. Make sure to meet face-to-face with students on issues that might be "hot," such as critiquing a performance or discussing missing class. Sometimes, people are more critical in writing than in speaking because there is no threat of immediate response. Beware of getting too personal with your students' feelings—especially when using electronic communication.

Create contact lists. Use a list or spreadsheet to keep track of important contact information for people involved with your mentoring program. It will come in handy if you run into problems, want advice, or just want to visit with another mentor. You might try something as simple as Table 8.1, which is a quick reference on how to contact others in your program.

One of the great things about being involved in a peer mentor program is the support system in place to help you succeed. You will interact with other mentors, instructors, and program staff. Open and effective communication with these people can be a strong support for you. They all want you to succeed. Just as you were once in your students' shoes, the support people have likely been where you are. Let them mentor you as you gain experience.

 Where are you now?

After reading this chapter, consider what you have learned about the following concepts.

1. Describe the differences between mentoring communication and other communication.

2. Identify the most important one-on-one communication guideline, and explain why you believe it to be most important.

3. What are the five small-group communication guidelines mentioned in this chapter?

4. Explain why question preparation is so important when presenting to large groups.

5. List one idea found in each of the before, during, and after sections on giving and receiving feedback.

6. In your own words, explain the "do no harm" philosophy mentioned in the chapter.

Case Study Discussion

Review the case study at the beginning of this chapter, and answer the following questions as they relate to the concepts you learned in the chapter. Discuss your answers with other mentors in your program so that you can explore different perspectives and gain greater insight into how to help this person.

Why is Carla's experience relevant in this chapter?

What would you need to know to help a student like Carla?

If you had to help Carla, how would you approach the situation?

If your initial idea didn't work, what else could you do to help Carla?

 ## Where do you want to be?

Reflect on what you have learned about mentoring in this chapter, and consider how you will apply these ideas to your specific responsibilities as a mentor.

1. What do you consider the most valuable concept in this chapter?

_____

_____

2. Why was it significant to you?

_____

_____

_____

_____

_____

3. How will you apply this concept as a mentor?

   _____

   _____

   _____

   _____

   _____

9 Facilitating Learning

Case Study: "Walk the Talk"

Sophia has always seen herself as an independent spirit who does not conform to society's expectations. As a college student, she believes that other people's ideas about studying and learning are basically useless to her because she is not interested in learning anything that does not agree with her personal philosophy. You overheard her telling a classmate, "The best way to do anything is your own way. Why go about doing things any other way if all you get out of it is the monotonous headache of conformity?"

Sophia is on academic probation and was required to enroll in a study skills class. She views it as just another unnecessary class. When different ideas about taking tests, taking notes, doing reading, and other topics are presented, Sophia sighs and even laughs. She does not attempt to apply any of the ideas to her own studying. When Sophia participates in a study group session with you, she voices her negative opinions about new study strategies to the other group members, and she appears to enjoy making them feel uncomfortable.

As you discuss the following questions with other mentors in your program, remember that this case study has been written about a real student facing real challenges. We encourage you to imagine the complexity of the situation and not to oversimplify the issues that the student faces. You may not feel experienced enough to completely answer the questions at this point, but you will have an opportunity to revisit this case study after learning the concepts in this chapter.

In your opinion, what are the greatest problems Sophia is facing?

As a mentor, how do you demonstrate that you are sensitive to Sophia's opinions?

What can you do to help Sophia recognize that there may be value in other ideas?

How are you able to demonstrate that you have learned to use diverse study strategies?

 Where are you going?

After reading this chapter, you should be familiar with the following concepts related to mentoring.

- Definition of *facilitating*
- Differences between pedagogy and andragogy
- Significance of metacognition
- Basic processes in the brain
- Multiple intelligences and learning
- A-I model for active learning
- Value of peer-to-peer teaching

Key Terms

In this chapter, you will encounter the following terms, which appear in bold. You can highlight the definitions as you read or look for them in the glossary at the end of the book.

Abstract conceptualization
Active experimentation
Active learning
Andragogy
Application
Concrete experience
Dendrites
Facilitate
Intelligence

Interpretation
Metacognition
Multiple intelligences
Neural networks
Pedagogy
Reflective observation
Schema
Triune theory

What Does It Mean to Facilitate Learning?

Facilitate means to make something happen or to make something easier. As a mentor, you facilitate learning when you help students learn how to learn. Chapter 3 introduced the concept of learning coach. A coach is a facilitator. The coach creates opportunities for the team to learn skills through practice and teaches strategies to help team members succeed. The coach also motivates the team to work toward its goals. Most important, the coach does not do what students must do for themselves—play the game.

Legendary UCLA basketball coach John Wooden, who holds the all-time record for NCAA championships, described what it means to facilitate: "If I did my job right, most of my work was done before the game ever started." The same thing can be said of a peer mentor and facilitating learning. It is not what *you* do that helps your students succeed or fail, but what you empower them to do for themselves—they are in their own game.

Effective facilitation actively involves both the mentor and the student. You are more likely to motivate your students to participate in study groups or try new study strategies when you have a personal relationship

> ### EXPERT'S OPINION
>
> "Students who are actively involved in learning, that is, who spend more time on task, *especially with others*, are more likely to learn and, in turn, more likely to stay and graduate."
>
> **Vincent Tinto**, "Enhancing Student Persistence: Connecting the Dots"

ACTIVITY 9.1   An Effective Facilitator

Complete the following activity to help you recognize what qualities in a facilitator are important to you. Discuss these questions with another student to understand what he or she values in a facilitator.

1. Think of someone who helped you learn a particular skill or concept. Describe what this person helped you learn and how he or she helped facilitate your learning experience.

- Your answer:

_____

_____

- Student's answer:

_____

_____

2. Did you recognize this person as "real"? Do you believe that being real is an important quality for a facilitator? Why?

- Your answer:

_____

_____

- Student's answer:

_____

_____

3. Did this person accept your contribution? Do you believe that such acceptance is an important quality for a facilitator? Why?
- Your answer:

_____

_____

- Student's answer:

_____

_____

4. Did this person understand what made you unique as a student? Do you believe that seeing each student as unique is an important quality for a facilitator? Why?
- Your answer:

_____

_____

- Student's answer:

_____

_____

with them. Carl Rogers, who is well known for his work in psychology, identified three "core conditions" that must exist for facilitation to be effective.[1] These core conditions will help you establish credibility and influence your students.

1. **Realness.** As a mentor, you must be a real student and a genuine person. After all, you are still playing the game. If you try to be the know-it-all expert, you will be too focused on your knowledge to create an appropriate learning setting to empower your students.

2. **Acceptance.** If you accept your students as unique individuals with valuable insights, they will be more willing to contribute. As they contribute, they will engage more effectively in the learning process.

3. **Understanding.** By connecting with your students and understanding the essential elements of learning, you can understand how each student learns best. You can also help students increase their awareness of their

learning process, of what sparks their interest, and of what frustrates them so that they can learn more effectively.

Learning is a personal experience, and realness, acceptance, and understanding are crucial conditions that reinforce the importance of being aware of yourself and others. You can be a more effective facilitator when you understand your own learning process and are genuinely interested in understanding how your students learn. When students sense that you have confidence in their ability to learn, they will be more likely to trust you as a learning coach. This chapter focuses on different aspects of learning that will help you gain the understanding that Rogers identifies as a core condition.

How Does Maturity Affect Students' Approach to Learning?

As important as it is to be a skilled facilitator, maturity is another important consideration that affects students' involvement in the learning process. If you can recognize how your students' attitudes toward learning are changing, you can be a more effective mentor.

Table 9.1: Different Approaches to Learning

	PEDAGOGY	ANDRAGOGY
Self-concept	Students depend on the teacher to determine what, when, and how to learn a new subject.	Students are independent learners who make their own decisions about what, when, and how to learn a new subject.
Experience	Students lack experience so they look to the teacher as an expert who can provide knowledge.	Students create knowledge by relating new concepts to their experience through discussion, reflection, and problem-solving activities.
Choice	Students learn what they are expected to learn.	Students' roles and responsibilities in life guide what they choose to learn.
Application	Students do not recognize how new concepts apply in their lives.	Students immediately apply new concepts to situations in their lives.
Motivation	Students are motivated by external rewards or punishments like grades.	Students are motivated by an internal desire to learn.

Source: Adapted from M. K. Smith, "Andragogy," *The Encyclopaedia of Informal Education* (1996; 1999); retrieved September 15, 2006, from http://www.infed.org/lifelonglearning/b-andra.htm.

Students who are making the transition to college are also making significant transitions into adulthood and, consequently, in the way they view education. Malcolm Knowles, an expert in adult learning, identified five areas in which an adult's approach to learning differs from a child's approach. He uses the terms **andragogy** (teaching adults) and **pedagogy** (teaching children) to explain the different approaches.

Your students will come across many different approaches to learning and teaching in their college experience, and they face two very different challenges. First, they will have to understand their own approaches to learning and their purposes for getting a college education. Second, they will have to deal

MENTOR'S VOICE

We need to be instilling in our students the desire to learn, the desire to search out knowledge in all facets of their lives so they can be lifelong students, not because they have to be, but because they want to be. Once we show them what is possible when it comes to gaining knowledge and wisdom, the other aspects of what we teach will become second nature to them.

Ben Duffy, peer mentor

ACTIVITY 9.2   Defining Your Approach to Learning

Complete the following activity to help you recognize your own approach to learning. Then ask another student the same questions. Consider how your approaches differ and why it is important to define your approach to learning.

1. Do you see yourself as a self-directed learner, or do you rely on the teacher's direction? Explain.

- Your answer:

_____

_____

- Student's answer:

_____

_____

2. Do you view your life experience as relevant to your education? Explain.

- Your answer:

_____

_____

- Student's answer:

_____

_____

3. Are you content taking general education courses, or are you ready to pursue your interest in specific subjects? Explain.

- Your answer:

_____

_____

- Student's answer:

_____

4. Do you believe that your education is important to your future career, or is it important in your life now? Explain.

- Your answer:

_____

_____

- Student's answer:

_____

5. Are you more motivated by grades or by the desire to learn? Explain.

- Your answer:

_____

_____

- Student's answer:

_____

6. Why is it important to understand your approach to learning? Explain.

- Your answer:

_____

_____

- Student's answer:

_____

_____

with professors whose approaches may not meet their expectations. Some professors present a standardized curriculum and expect students to master the material they present. Other professors want their students to be self-directed learners. These professors expect students to contribute to class discussions, to gain personal insights, and to make real-life applications. As a mentor, you can help your students understand their own expectations and adjust to the different learning experiences they will have in each type of classroom.

What Is Metacognition?

Meta means beyond or above, and *cognition* refers to all the things that go on inside your brain—thinking, perceiving, and learning. **Metacognition** is thinking *about* thinking and learning *about* learning. It's your ability to stand above your mental processes, observe them, and take conscious control of them.

A simple way to experience metacognition is to use the bug-on-the-wall technique. By consciously imagining that you can see yourself and your learning situation from the perspective of a bug on the wall, you will notice factors that you would otherwise overlook. Being in metacognitive control of your own learning is a powerful skill. With it, your odds of success in anything you choose to do increase dramatically.

Students who master metacognition can

- Choose and apply various strategies for reading, writing, speaking, listening, managing time, and doing related tasks
- Describe their preferred learning styles and develop new ones
- Make accurate assessments of their current abilities
- Modify strategies so that they work in several contexts
- Monitor their behavior and change their habits
- Recognize the ways that they will benefit from learning a subject

With metacognition, you can become your own best teacher. When you recognize how metacognition affects your ability to learn, you can coach other students as they develop metacognition and realize the power it has to improve their education.[2]

How Can You Stimulate Learning in the Brain?

One important approach to being a metacognitive learner is to understand the basic processes that occur in your brain as you learn. Knowledge of the natural process of learning will help you be a more effective mentor.

The brain is an organ in the body, and all organs know what to do and how to do it. Research on newborns and infants shows that people are born with brains that already know how to learn, think, and remember. These abilities are retained and strengthened as we grow. Even though learning is a natural process,

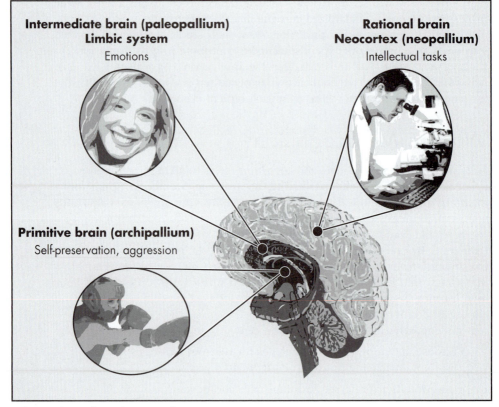

**Intermediate brain (paleopallium)
Limbic system**

Emotions

**Rational brain
Neocortex (neopallium)**

Intellectual tasks

Primitive brain (archipallium)

Self-preservation, aggression

FIGURE 9.1: The Triune Brain

some students lack confidence in their brains' ability to function correctly. Some have been told enough times that they cannot learn that they actually believe it. If you understand how learning happens naturally, you can help other students gain confidence in their ability to learn.

Knowledge about the brain and about how learning occurs is advancing at a rapid pace. Learning involves three basic processes—doing, feeling, and thinking. In Chapter 5 you learned about these processes as three basic aspects of self-awareness. Each process relates to a specific region of the brain, and everything you learn involves the interaction of these three regions.

The **triune theory**, developed by Paul MacLean, former director of the Laboratory of the Brain and Behavior at the United States National Institute of Mental Health, explains that the brain is made up of three connected layers of increasingly sophisticated tissues.[3] Physically, it almost looks like a brain within a brain within a brain.

> **Primal brain.** The first layer begins in the cord of nerves and threads at the bottom of your spine and continues into a fist-sized structure near the base of your skull. It is also known as the reptilian complex and primitive brain. It governs physical survival, maintenance of the body,

and instinctive actions and reactions. Some of the instinctive behaviors are imprinting (first impressions), dominance (competition), territoriality ("my space," "my room"), and imitation (fashions, fads). You may be able to help students recognize how these instinctive behaviors affect their ability to function. If a negative impression of a professor is imprinted in their minds, they may be preventing themselves from learning in that class, or they may be imitating ineffective behaviors of other students. While many of the functions of the primal brain are automatic, they can be influenced by the higher levels in the brain. The primal brain is literally the *doing* processor, and it can be regulated by the brain's feeling and thinking processors.

Limbic brain. The next layer, called the limbic structure, wraps around the top of the primal brain structure. The structure is located just below your ears. Emotions are located in the limbic brain, which governs and processes feelings. It processes your attitudes about life and your relationship to others. The emotional middle brain is also the gatekeeper between different parts of the brain and has the ability to control the instincts of the primitive brain to some extent. The intensity of the human drive to learn and seek meaningful connections and patterns is firmly centered within this middle layer.

Neocortex. The final layer, the neocortex, emerges out of the connecting tissue of the limbic structure into the right and left hemispheres and folds neatly inside the top of your skull like the hood on a sweatshirt. It is nearest to the top of your head and comes down below your eyes and behind your nose. It gives the brain its bumpy sponge-like appearance, but more important, it is the thinking processor; it is where most thinking and reasoning take place. The neocortex makes it possible for you to recognize the consequences of your actions and analyze your feelings. It allows you to develop self-awareness and metacognitive skills, which can help you make reasonable decisions. The neocortex interacts with the other parts of the brain through the limbic structure.

When you understand the importance of these three distinct processors, you can help students become aware of how the three processes naturally interact to make learning possible. When students develop awareness of their thoughts and feelings, they can change their behavior and make decisions that will improve their ability to learn. You will not be explaining the brain in this much detail to new students, but understanding the process can help you facilitate learning with confidence in the strategies you recommend.

The brain develops cognitive neural structures similar to computer networks. These structures consist of **dendrites** that look like trees with branches that grow and connect with each other as you learn. The branch-like extensions allow neurons to interconnect and form **neural networks** that represent knowledge. Figure 9.2 shows how dendrites grow from the neuron, and Figure 9.3 shows how complex the networks can become.

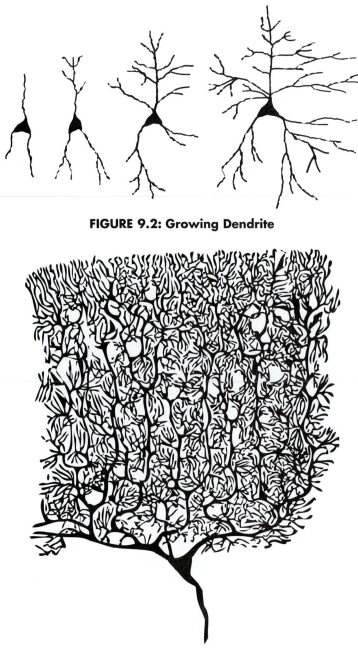

FIGURE 9.2: Growing Dendrite

FIGURE 9.3: Neural Network

How the Brain Learns

Rita Smilkstein, author of *We're Born to Learn*, identified five rules of how the brain learns and develops neural networks.[4] These rules can serve as guidelines as you help students improve their study habits and enhance their ability to learn.

1. **Schema.** You learn by connecting new information to what you already know. Background knowledge is known as *schema*, and our schema is like the trunk of the tree in our neural networks. We cannot grow new branches unless they are attached to a base of knowledge that already exists in our brains.

   Schema means structured framework. The neural network in your brain is a framework of knowledge, and you can comprehend new concepts only if you understand how they fit in an existing framework. For example, you learn new vocabulary based on words you already know. If you cannot connect a new word to a word you already know, you do not comprehend the meaning of the new word. As a mentor, you can help students make connections between new concepts they are studying and the knowledge they already have.

2. **Practice.** You learn from what you actively practice. As you practice and review new skills and concepts, the branches of your knowledge develop and grow stronger. Practice includes making mistakes, correcting mistakes, learning from mistakes, and trying over and over again. Making mistakes is a natural and necessary part of learning.

   As you actively practice new skills, your brain cells are growing. Learning takes time because you need time to grow neural networks. You can help students understand this concept by encouraging them to spend time working with the concepts they are learning. If they struggle with math, they should spend more time, not less, working through practice problems.

3. **Stimulating experiences.** You learn by stimulating the different processors in your brain. A stimulating experience causes chemical and electrical reactions in the brain that cause neural structures to grow. Learning often becomes more stimulating when students share ideas with other students. You can facilitate study groups and encourage discussions that give students opportunities to get more involved in learning new ideas.

4. **Use it or lose it.** If you do not use your knowledge, you lose it. The brain actually begins to prune the unused branches of your neural networks. Anyone who learned a foreign language but has not spoken it for years knows firsthand how you can lose the ability to speak fluently. As a mentor, you can help students prepare for tests or final exams by encouraging them to review the material often so that the neural networks in their brains continue to grow.

5. **Emotions.** Your emotions affect your ability to learn. Emotions produce chemicals that affect the brain's ability to learn, think, and remember. Fear and doubt produce chemicals that prevent learning; the chemicals produced by confidence and interest—including endorphins, the so-called pleasure hormones—enhance the ability to learn.

 Online Study Center *college.hmco.com/PIC/sanft1e*

👤 👥 ACTIVITY 9.3   **Understanding How Your Brain Learns**

Complete the following activity to help you recognize the significance of Smilkstein's rules in your own learning experiences. Then ask another student the same questions. Consider how you can help other students understand how these rules affect their ability to learn.

1. What happened when you tried to learn something new without any background knowledge in that subject? Why is schema important?
   - Your answer:

   _____

   _____

   - Student's answer:

   _____

   _____

2. Describe something you learned to do through practice. Why is practice important in learning?
   - Your answer:

   _____

   _____

   - Student's answer:

   _____

   _____

3. Describe a time when you were excited about something you learned. Why is it easier to learn a new skill when you are stimulated by the experience?
   - Your answer:

   _____

   _____

   - Student's answer:

   _____

   _____

4. Describe a skill you have lost because you didn't practice it regularly.
   - Your answer:

   _____

   _____

• Student's answer:

_____

_____

5. Identify a positive or a negative emotion that is currently affecting your ability to learn. How do emotions affect your ability to learn?

• Your answer:

_____

_____

• Student's answer:

_____

_____

If you are concerned that a student's negative emotions are preventing his or her ability to learn, you can help that student process the emotions or connect with a professional who can help. You can also help establish a sense of community among the students you mentor. Students who are comfortable and enjoy being together are more likely to learn together.

How Is Intelligence Related to Learning?

Everyone is intelligent. **Intelligence** can be described as "the capacity to acquire and apply knowledge."[5] Howard Gardner introduced his theory of **multiple intelligences** in 1983; more recently, he published *Intelligence Reframed: Multiple Intelligences for the 21st Century.*[6] Gardner believes that people have different aptitudes for learning and applying concepts in different areas. While someone may be good at math, that same person may not understand the importance of social skills. Math and social skills represent different types of intelligence, according to Gardner. He has identified eight different intelligences. Table 9.2 briefly introduces each intelligence.

Table 9.2: Multiple Intelligences

DEFINITION	METACOGNITIVE AWARENESS	STUDY TIPS
Bodily/kinesthetic intelligence involves physical motion and understanding your body.	Ask students if they are aware of their • Conscious control of movement • Connection between mind and body • Ability to learn or mimic physical movement	If students want to develop this area, encourage them to • Be physically active while studying—for example, to pace as they read • Create hands-on activities or games based on specific concepts
Interpersonal intelligence includes person-to-person relationships and communication.	Ask students if they have • Awareness of verbal and nonverbal communication • Sensitivity to others' moods and feelings • Ability to discern others' intentions	If students want to develop this area, encourage them to • Form and conduct study groups early in the term • Create flash cards and use them when studying with a partner • Teach the topic they're studying to someone else
Intrapersonal intelligence relates to understanding your self-system and increasing self-awareness.	Ask students if they have • Awareness of different emotions • Tendency to reflect • Ability to feel empathy	If students want to develop this area, encourage them to • Connect course content to personal values • Keep a journal that relates coursework to everyday life

Table 9.2: (Continued)

DEFINITION	METACOGNITIVE AWARENESS	STUDY TIPS
Logical/mathematical intelligence deals with inductive and deductive reasoning skills, abstract patterns, and numbers.	Ask students if they have • Ability to perform complex calculations • Ability to reason and recognize abstract patterns	If students want to develop this area, encourage them to • Convert text into tables, charts, and graphs • Express ideas in numerical terms • Group concepts into categories and look for underlying patterns
Musical/rhythmic intelligence involves recognition of tonal patterns and sensitivity to rhythm and beat.	Ask students if they have • Sensitivity to sound • Ability to recognize, create, and recreate melodies and rhythms	If students want to develop this area, encourage them to • Find music that illustrates the concept they are learning • Put on background music that enhances concentration
Naturalist/adventurer intelligence relies on being outside and connecting with the complex dynamics in natural settings.	Ask students if they are aware of their • Apparent restlessness indoors • Intuitive understanding of outdoor activities	If students want to develop this area, encourage them to • Take a walk outside during a study break • Find an appropriate place to study outdoors
Verbal/linguistic intelligence deals with written and spoken words.	Ask students if they are aware of their • Ability to comprehend the meaning and structure of language • Tendency to develop detailed explanations	If students want to develop this area, encourage them to • Highlight, underline, or write notes in the textbook • Recite new ideas in their own words • Talk to others about what they are studying

(continued)

Table 9.2: (Continued)

DEFINITION	METACOGNITIVE AWARENESS	STUDY TIPS
Visual/spatial intelligence includes the ability to create mental pictures and comprehend multidimensional images.	Ask students if they are aware of their • Active imagination • Ability to graphically represent ideas • Ability to recognize the relationship between different objects	If students want to develop this area, encourage them to • Draw, sketch, or visualize the concepts they are learning • Use different colors for different topics in their notes • Refocus when their attention wanders by drawing or sketching

Source: Adapted from D. Ellis, *Becoming a Master Student,* 11th ed. (Boston: Houghton-Mifflin, 2006), 38–39.

When students can identify their intelligences, they can begin to recognize their natural abilities and the types of learning experiences that stimulate their brains. They can also identify areas in which they want to increase their intelligence through conscious effort and practice. As a mentor, you can help build students' self-esteem and confidence in their learning abilities by encouraging them to inventory their intelligences. Greater awareness of their intelligences will allow your students to develop learning strategies that help them study and learn best.

What Is Active Learning?

As students begin to recognize how learning and intelligence relate to them, they will be more likely to get involved in learning. **Active learning** is engaging in the learning process through active participation in a variety of learning activities. Studies have shown that we learn the most when we use a variety of different approaches to learning. If you read, hear,

---

EXPERT'S OPINION

"Learning is not a spectator sport. Students do not learn much just by sitting in class listening to teachers, memorizing prepackaged assignments, and spitting out answers. They must talk about what they are learning, write about it, relate it to past experiences, apply it to their daily lives. They must make what they learn part of themselves."

Arthur W. Chickering and **Zelda F. Gamson,** "Seven Principles of Good Practice"

see, discuss, and do something related to a topic, you are more likely to find significance in and remember it.

David Kolb, author of *Experiential Learning: Experience as the Source of Learning and Development*, defined a model of learning based on how people perceive and process information. First, he described how you perceive information or how you associate meaning with the things you are learning. You use the thinking and feeling processors in your brain when you develop your perceptions of concepts. Kolb defined **concrete experience** as your initial response to actual experiences. It involves your feelings or reactions in a learning situation. He used the term **abstract conceptualization** to describe how you think about and analyze a situation to develop concepts, ideas, and theories about your experiences. Next, he described how you process information or apply the knowledge. You apply new knowledge by watching to see how it works or by doing something with it. He used the terms **reflective observation** to describe what you see and **active experimentation** to describe what you do.

Kolb's model defines learning as a process that involves all four modes of learning—feeling, thinking, watching, and doing. You are already familiar with doing, feeling, and thinking as processes in the brain. Using this model, we can define active learning more specifically as learning that engages all four modes of learning—feeling, thinking, watching, and doing. According to Kolb, "Knowledge results from the combination of grasping experience and transforming it."[7] As a mentor, you can provide a learning experience by creating opportunities for your students to both watch and do, and you can let them transform the experience by encouraging them to share their thoughts and feelings.

A-I Mentoring Model

The A-I mentoring model is not about creating artificial intelligence, as the acronym might imply, but rather about learning through application and interpretation. Similar to Kolb's experiential learning model, it suggests that all learning experiences should incorporate application and an opportunity for interpretation. As a mentor, you can prepare learning activities that incorporate both aspects of learning, and you can teach your students to improve their study habits by doing both application and interpretation activities.

For example, if you want to help students improve test-taking skills, you will have to do more than talk about taking tests. You can begin with an interpretation activity by asking the students to describe what they did to prepare for the last test they took. You can then identify a specific strategy that will help them be better prepared for the next test. You might choose an application activity like preparing a practice exam. After the students have prepared and taken the practice exam, you can ask them to consider what they learned

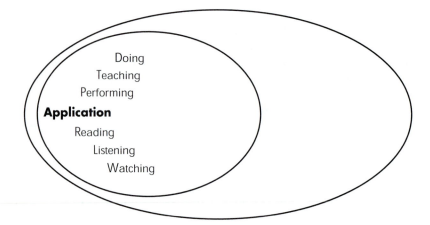

FIGURE 9.4: Student's Schema: Application

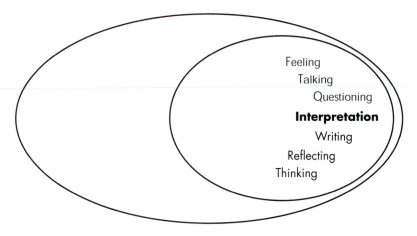

FIGURE 9.5: Student's Schema: Interpretation

from the process. Finally, you can help them modify the process to fit their own personal strengths and preferences.

The student's schema defines the context for this learning model. The large oval in Figures 9.4 and 9.5 represents the student's schema. Learning cannot take place outside the context of what the student knows because new knowledge has to relate to something the student understands. You should always begin a learning activity by assessing the student's existing knowledge. You can use a few thoughtful questions to help you assess the student's schema, such as "What do you know about this subject?" and "Do you enjoy learning about this subject? Why?" You will then have a better sense of where the student is coming from, which will allow you to relate the new information to what the student already knows.

Application incorporates activities that help students process new information. A few of many possible application activities are shown in Figure 9.4. This stage of the model is what Kolb describes as "grasping experience." You can work with an instructor or other mentors to create application experiences that will be beneficial for your students. It is important to be aware that some students prefer hands-on activities, while other students prefer to observe. As the facilitator, you can help students identify their own learning preferences, and you can encourage them to move out of their comfort zones and try something new. You should also try new activities yourself. Your ability to effectively facilitate learning will be limited if you always approach learning the same way.

Though interpretation follows application in this model, learning does not necessarily happen in a specific order. Some students need to understand the personal significance of a topic before they are motivated to apply their knowledge. **Interpretation** allows students to clarify their own perceptions of what they are learning and consider alternative points of view. Figure 9.5 identifies different methods of interpretation. As a facilitator, you should allow ample time for students to discuss their own reactions and ideas. This process provides them with an opportunity to not only reinforce what they have learned, but also, as Kolb put it, to transform their knowledge.

Application and interpretation combine to create an environment in which students are engaged in learning, as shown in Figure 9.6. As a facilitator, it is your responsibility to come up with different combinations of appropriate activities. The possibilities are endless. You could ask a student to apply specific memory techniques and then discuss the benefits of those techniques. You could ask another student to take notes in a class and then

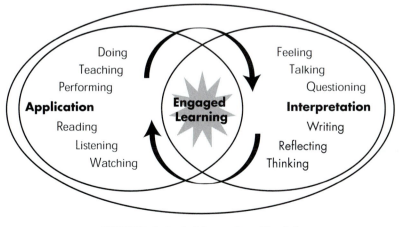

FIGURE 9.6: A-I Learning Model

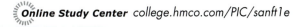

analyze the notes together to identify areas that could be improved. Whatever your approach, remember that learning involves doing, watching, thinking, and feeling.

You may realize that these two principles of learning apply in a variety of situations. An athlete needs to practice skills and analyze his or her performance to improve those skills. In Activity 9.4, practice is an example of application, and the analysis that follows is an example of interpretation. As a mentor, you will be working with students in a variety of different settings. The A-I model applies whether you are working one-on-one or with a large class. If you want your students to learn the concepts you are trying to teach, you need to create opportunities for them to apply the concepts and to interpret what those concepts mean to them.

ᛜᛜᛜ ACTIVITY 9.4　Application and Interpretation Examples

Discuss the following learning situations with a small group of students. Consider why application and interpretation are important in each of the following learning experiences.

Activity	Why Is Application Important? (Identify a specific application activity that works well in this situation.)	Why Is Interpretation Important? (Identify a specific interpretation activity that works well in this situation.)
1. Learning to play a sport	Application is important because you cannot fully learn to play a sport without doing it. You can learn from watching other people, but you must also practice regularly.	Interpretation is important because you cannot improve your skills if you do not reflect on your performance. Talking with a coach or keeping a workout journal would help you measure your progress.
2. Preparing to play a dramatic character		
3. Solving math equations		
4. Studying history		
5. Giving a presentation		

How Can You Be an Effective Facilitator?

Whether you are facilitating a session one-on-one, with a small group, or with an entire class, Figure 9.7 lists helpful tips on how to facilitate it. Some of the tips are suitable for use in all three types of sessions, while others lend themselves better to particular settings.

1	**Have a purpose.** One important ethical obligation is to not waste your students' time. You must genuinely care about your students and that must be why you are helping them. If you are teaching a concept in a classroom setting, make sure to keep within the time allotted by the instructor.
2	**Relate to your students.** Taking a look at the students you are mentoring is one of the first steps in creating a good mentoring plan. Try to identify something about the culture and sense of community of the person or group. You have the advantage of having been in their shoes. They are likely to trust your point of view if you can show that you know what they are going through. Give examples from your own experience to which they can relate.
3	**Know what you are talking about.** One of the quickest ways to establish credibility is to demonstrate that you know what you are talking about. Having all necessary information to answer most questions the students ask will make you seem trustworthy. If you are not sure about something, don't guess. Giving students incorrect information will make them less likely to trust you in the future. Take the time to get correct information from someone who knows.
4	**Be honest.** Demonstrating truthfulness by example is critical. If you are not prepared to meet with a student or to give a presentation, be honest about it. Most people can tell whether someone is being honest with them. In today's society, too many students cheat or plagiarize to get ahead. You can model the way an honest effort and good organizational skills will serve students better than dishonesty in their academic careers.
5	**Have a conversation.** Learning sessions do not have to be difficult. They can be as simple as communicating with people you know well; hopefully, you will get to know your students well. You don't need to always be the expert or to lecture when you talk to students. Relax and be genuine, as if you are having an everyday conversation with a friend or coworker. Remember that one of your roles is to be the trusted friend.
6	**Involve others.** Don't take responsibility for doing all the talking or for doing all the planning for your mentoring session or presentation. Your students will rely on you a lot in the beginning, but allow them to start doing for themselves early on. The more they are involved,

continues on next page

FIGURE 9.7: Facilitating Checklist

	the more they will learn. Evaluate their readiness, and give them assignments accordingly. Teach them how to help themselves and others.
7	**Respect your students**. As discussed in Chapter 7, your students will have diverse knowledge, cultures, gender, religious beliefs, values, physical abilities, and more. No matter how much you think you know about them, you will never know everything. Respect your students, and avoid saying anything that may insult them. If you do offend a class member for any reason, take responsibility and attempt to mend the situation as quickly as possible.
8	**Be organized.** When giving a presentation, have a clear introduction, an organized body, and a solid conclusion. In the introduction, grab listeners attention and then show, tell, or act out what you are going to teach. In the body of the lesson, teach your important points using the A-I model. When concluding, summarize your key points. Then have students discuss the information with one another. Students remember more when they discuss information with each other.
9	**Use visual aids and handouts to add meaning.** Think about the different learning preferences your students have, and generate visual aids and handouts accordingly. The material should appeal to them as much as possible. Visual aids should be easily viewable by all students and ought to add understanding or credibility to your teaching. Handouts should be simple and to the point.
10	**Practice, practice, practice.** Rehearse your presentation at least twice before delivering it. Use an outline or note cards, with full details of statistics and quotations, but don't rely on memory aids completely. In Western cultures, eye contact is a measure of honesty and trustworthiness. Lift your eyes; don't just read to the students. You are conversing with them because you have something valuable to teach them, and you are the right person to do it.

FIGURE 9.7: Facilitating Checklist (Continued)

Make sure to do advance planning. Your students will expect you to be prepared. Take time for the final touches that will help you facilitate. You don't have to fear being the expert or speaking in public. You are working with students with whom you have a relationship. You have developed trust and respect for each other. You can be confident that the students are likely to listen to and follow advice from another student on important educational matters. Use Figure 9.7 as a checklist, and you will be excited to step up to the challenges you face.

If you care about your students and focus on them rather than on your performance, facilitating learning can be fun and rewarding. You will come away from the experience with the same endorphins that a good workout gives you. You can make a contribution to your students in ways that their instructors cannot hope to match. That is why you are in the important position of peer mentor.

Why Is Peer-to-Peer Teaching Effective?

Mentors can coach new college students through the process of becoming mature learners. As mentioned in Chapter 2, students are more likely to accept and apply certain strategies from a peer than from an instructor. Most students will respect what the teacher has to say, but as a peer mentor you are able to teach concepts to your students in a way the faculty member cannot. Your students view you as one of them. They believe you when you speak because you can relate to their lives. You also have the benefit of having learned the material as a student, and you can teach it with that student perspective in mind. Facilitating another's learning might seem daunting, but who can understand a student better than another student?

MENTOR'S VOICE

Sure, the same information can be learned by the students from any teacher. But having the bonus of being able to learn things like study skills, time management, note taking, and test taking strategies from a peer that has used those same skills is very valuable. The mentor is able to put new insights on these topics. I feel that students are able to relate to peer mentors more and by doing so will have a strong desire to try and continue to use the skills that are taught.

Seth Mathers, peer mentor

 Where are you now?

These questions are designed to help you review the important concepts covered in the chapter. Answering these questions can help you assess your own understanding or prepare for a test.

1. What does it mean to facilitate learning?
2. Explain the difference between pedagogy and andragogy.
3. Define *metacognition*, and explain why it is necessary to enhance your learning.
4. Identify the three basic processes in the brain.
5. Describe each of the eight intelligences.
6. Explain how you can use the A-I mentoring model to encourage active learning.
7. Why is peer-to-peer teaching effective?

Case Study Discussion

Review the case study at the beginning of this chapter, and answer the following questions as they relate to the concepts you learned in the chapter. Discuss your answers with other mentors in your program so that you can explore different perspectives and gain greater insight into how to help this person.

Why is Sophia's experience relevant in this chapter?

What do you need to know to help a student like Sophia?

If you had to help Sophia, how would you approach the situation?

If your initial idea didn't work, what else could you do to help Sophia?

 Where do you want to be?

Reflect on what you have learned about mentoring in this chapter, and consider how you will apply these ideas to your specific responsibilities as a mentor.

1. What do you consider the most valuable concept in this chapter?

    _____

    _____

2. Why was it significant to you?

    _____

    _____

    _____

    _____

    _____

3. How will you apply this concept as a mentor?

    _____

    _____

    _____

    _____

    _____

Planning and Problem Solving

Case Study: "The Single Mom"

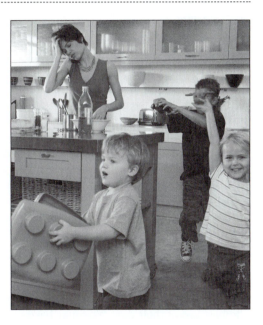

Anna feels that she is being pulled in too many directions at once. Her life feels out of balance. A single mother of two sons, she is trying to make it through college on her own and is dealing with a deadbeat ex-husband. She gets limited help from her parents while she works twenty-four hours a week and goes to school full time.

Trying to manage her household and social life and meeting her children's needs leave Anna feeling overwhelmed. She worries about losing her temper with her sons and constantly disrupting their routine, as well as "abandoning" her friends. These worries lead to incredible feelings of guilt.

Sometimes Anna misses classes or arrives late because she needs to take a child to the doctor or run some other errand she believes cannot wait. Missing out on information from classes creates a problem with getting homework submitted or even completed. She wants to do well in school and maintain her personal life, but she is becoming overwhelmed with feelings of inadequacy.

As you discuss the following questions with other mentors in your program, remember that this case study has been written about a real student facing real challenges. We encourage you to imagine the complexity of the situation and not to oversimplify the issues that the student faces. You may not feel experienced enough to completely answer the questions at this point, but you will have an opportunity to revisit this case study after learning the concepts in this chapter. 171

As a mentor, what do you believe your role is in assisting Anna with her problems?

How might you approach Anna about resolving her issues?

What can you do to demonstrate effective student strategies to her?

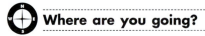 **Where are you going?**

After reading this chapter, you should be familiar with the following concepts related to peer mentoring.

- Personal planning methods
- Semester planning strategies
- Goal-setting ideas
- Decision-making styles
- Problem-solving processes

Key Terms

In this chapter, you will encounter the following terms, which appear in bold. You can highlight the definitions as you read or look for them in the glossary at the end of the book.

Decision-making styles
Four Ms

Problem-solving components
SMART goals

What Do You Need to Know about Planning?

If you fail to plan, you plan to fail.

Students in transition often do not know how to organize themselves and make the best use of their time. You may have experienced the same difficulties when you first entered college. As a peer mentor, you have the opportunity to help your students learn how to recognize problems with planning and how to plan successfully. You do this in both words and actions. That is, your ability to demonstrate the benefits of planning in your own life will be as influential as anything you say about the importance of planning. As you work through the activities in this chapter, consider what you can do to improve your own planning techniques and how you can demonstrate each strategy for the students you mentor.

Some students are masters at generating endless excuses for their lack of planning. They will tell you they forgot about an assignment, a study group, or even an exam. Do you exhibit any of these behaviors? If so, now is the time to commit to making changes. You cannot risk modeling irresponsibility as a peer mentor. You should be in a position to help students realize that they are responsible for their own decisions and that playing a blame game or excusing their conduct suggests a lack of responsibility.

As you have learned from the case studies in this book, you can identify problems that students have and develop potential solutions. But it is a much different challenge to work through those problems with real students. For example, you may conclude that Anna could benefit from a few time-management strategies, but you must also remember to be sensitive to Anna's situation. If you have never been a single mother, you cannot completely comprehend the challenges she faces, and your solution may not be as effective as you think it will be. As a mentor, you will be more effective if you try to understand students' problems from their points of view before you try to solve the problems (see the discussions on empathy in Chapters 7 and 8).

ACTIVITY 10.1   My Planning Experiences

This activity asks you to look at times when you have planned well and not so well. As you answer the questions, be honest about your planning strengths and weaknesses.

1. Identify times when you succeeded as a result of good planning. What strategies did you utilize to make your plans effective?

_____

_____

2. Which of the planning strategies identified in question 1 have you continued to use?

_____

_____

3. Think of times you were not prepared because of poor planning. What excuses did you make?

_____

_____

4. In those instances, if you were unwilling to accept responsibility, what did you learn about responsibility?

_____

_____

5. What might you do in the future to demonstrate more responsible behavior?

_____

_____

Planning can be overwhelming. College students have to plan for this week, this month, this semester, and next semester while also thinking about life and career goals after college. You may also be balancing a full class load with an active social life and a part-time job. As a peer mentor, you have additional responsibilities.

- Scheduling study groups and activities with students while allowing for personal study time

- Prioritizing goals to follow through with mentor duties and personal responsibilities

- Making effective decisions as they apply to your various responsibilities

- Solving problems effectively

This chapter addresses all four planning elements. Another integral part of planning is taking time to review and evaluate what is working and where you can improve. You should do this on a regular basis either on your own or as part of a regular program evaluation. Chapter 12 goes into more detail about reflection and evaluation.

How Can You Help Students Plan for the Semester?

You can model effective planning if you become a good planner yourself, particularly when it comes to study time. Write down the things you need to do and when you need to do them. Many tools are available to help you, including notebooks, calendars, PDAs, and desk or daily planners. Find the one that best fits your needs, and become proficient at using it. *Use it* is the key phrase. If you take the time to organize yourself, you can teach that skill to someone else. The activities in this chapter provide effective tools and strategies. Try them out for yourself, and then show others how to use them.

To successfully manage study time, one good idea is to create a semester timeline or semester calendar. Thousands of students have utilized and benefited from such timelines and calendars. These planning tools lay out an entire semester in one place so the student can readily see the overall picture. Incorporate information from each syllabus you have for the semester. Figures 10.1 and 10.2 show what a semester timeline and a semester calendar look like. Refer to them as you complete Activity 10.2.

To create a semester timeline, draw a line and divide it according to the months in the semester. On the timeline, mark the due dates of exams, papers, projects, and other important things. Some students prefer to use a timeline rather than a calendar because they can see the entire semester at a glance, and major assignments stand out more than they do on a calendar.

The semester calendar includes the same information as the timeline. The calendar format allows you to include more detail for each month. In the example below, a student can see that nothing is due during the week of March 20–26, but that the following week is packed with two exams and a presentation. This view

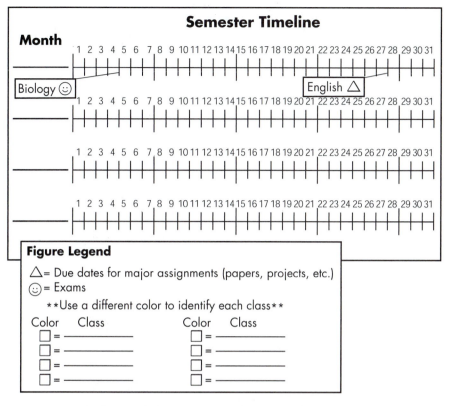

FIGURE 10.1: Semester Timeline with Legend

ACTIVITY 10.2   Semester Planning

Now that you know how to create a timeline and a calendar, select one of the two, and create your own for the current semester.

1. Explain which format works better for you and why.

_____

_____

2. Find a student, and explain what you do to plan for the semester and why it works for you. What did you learn about being a mentor when you did this activity with another person?

_____

_____

MARCH						
Sun	**Mon**	**Tue**	**Wed**	**Thurs**	**Fri**	**Sat**
		1 BIOL 101 chap 5 quiz	2	3 MATH 101 chap 7 quiz	4	5
6	7	8	9 ENGL 101 research paper	10 UNIV 101 exam#2	11	12
13	14	15 BIOL 101 chap 6 quiz	16	17 MATH 101 chap 8 quiz	18	19
20	21	22	23	24	25	26
27	28	29 UNIV 101 presentation BIOL 101 exam #3	30	31		

FIGURE 10.2: Semester Calendar

makes it apparent that the student should get the presentation ready the week before. That allows more time to study for biology and math. (It's a good idea to use different colors for each class so everything doesn't just blend together.)

How Can You Demonstrate Effective Goal Setting?

Planning helps with the achievement of academic goals. In the words of famed University of Kentucky basketball coach Adolph Rupp, "If you see a man on top of a mountain, he didn't just light there!" It takes planning and effort to get to the top of a mountain. The same can be said for achieving goals in higher education. Planning and goal setting go hand in hand. As you spend time with your students, you will learn about their goals and desires. The more you know about goal setting, the better prepared you will be to help them reach their goals.

A goal not written is only a wish.

ThinkTQ.com, a publisher of virtual personal and professional training products, recently announced the results of its 2005 Goals Study.[1] According to the study, fewer than 15 percent of people surveyed wrote down their goals. This means that more than 85 percent of people don't put their goals where they can see or review them. The chance of achieving a goal goes down if the goal is not written.

When writing goals, make them **SMART**:

Specific

Measurable

Attainable

Relevant

Time-limited

When a goal is specific, it is clear and concise. You know what it is and can easily explain it to yourself and others. A measurable goal can be monitored for progress. It will have steps that can be accounted for. An attainable goal is one that you can achieve. You don't want to make it so easy that you need not try, but it also should not be impossible to reach, leading to frustration and disappointment. Making sure the goal is important to you makes it relevant. It must be your goal, not someone else's goal for you. Finally, the goal must be time-limited. This means that you must set deadlines for completing it and be able to determine when it is completed.

The **Four Ms** are a powerful yet simple method for setting goals that was developed by peer mentors at Utah Valley State College.

Motivation. Why do you want to achieve the goal or solve the problem?

Make commitments. Who can help you commit to reaching the goal?

Modify environment. What do you need to do differently to make the goal possible?

Monitor actions. How will you track your progress?

Both SMART goals and the Four Ms will help you remember specific steps to set effective goals. Each method of setting goals employs different strategies that might appeal to different types of people. It is wise to have a number of different strategies so you can meet the individual needs of the students you mentor. One method may appeal to one student but not work for another student.

After completing Activities 10.3 and 10.4, facilitate the activities with another student. The more you practice, the more comfortable you will be, and you will be better able to facilitate effectively.

ACTIVITY 10.3   Identifying Life Goals

This activity will take you through a series of questions about your goals and will prepare you to do a similar activity as a peer mentor. The activity creates an opportunity to do some brainstorming with your students about what they want from education and life. Educational goals will certainly be something you want to help new students develop, but it is important to remember that goals can be related to careers, relationships, leisure, and so on.

Answer these questions for yourself, and then discuss them with another student.

1. What are some goals that you would like to accomplish by the end of your life?

   _____

   _____

   _____

2. What are some goals that you would like to achieve in the next ten or twenty years?

   _____

   _____

   _____

3. What are your goals for the next three to five years?

   _____

   _____

   _____

4. What goals do you have for this academic year?

   _____

   _____

   _____

5. What are some things you need to do in order to accomplish this year's goals?

   _____

   _____

   _____

6. List the things you will do this week and the things you will do today that relate to your goals for this year. These may be specific course assignments, talking to a professor, or starting volunteer work. Add anything else you want to accomplish during the day or week to this list. You now have a to-do list!

_____

_____

_____

7. Which of these activities do you really enjoy doing? Which do you find difficult? Which do you avoid doing? How many of the difficult things relate to your lifetime goals? Think about it.

_____

_____

_____

8. When you have finished this activity on your own, take another student through the process of answering the questions listed above.

_____

_____

_____

9. What did you learn about being a mentor when you did this activity with another person?

_____

_____

_____

ACTIVITY 10.4 Setting Effective Goals

In this activity, you will choose one goal you identified in Activity 10.3 and develop a plan to accomplish it. You can use either the SMART or Four M goal-setting method. Once you have selected a goal, this activity helps you dissect it and look at the achievement process in a way that gets to the specifics of the goal, including what will be required to complete it and what roadblocks you may encounter along the way. The activity pushes you to plan what needs to happen in order to accomplish your goal. Complete the activity for yourself, and then discuss it with another student.

Option 1. SMART Goal Setting

1. Write down your goal.

_____

_____

2. Fill in the following table to show how your goal meets the criteria of SMART goal setting.

IS IT . . . ?	YES	NO	EXPLAIN
Specific			
Measurable			
Attainable			
Relevant			
Time-limited			

3. What will be your reward when you reach the goal? In other words, how will reaching the goal benefit you?

_____

_____

4. Rewrite your goal to include pertinent information from questions 2 and 3.

_____

_____

_____

5. What actions do you need to take to reach your goal? For example, do you need to gather information, obtain money, learn new skills, or make special arrangements? How much time will you need to accomplish each action? When should you have completed each action?

	ACTION	ESTIMATED TIME	DUE DATE
1.			
2.			
3.			
4.			
5.			

6. List at least three possible barriers you might face as you strive to achieve your goal.

_____

_____

7. Take another student through the process of completing this activity for one of her or his goals. What did you learn about being a mentor when you did this activity with another person?

_____

_____

Option 2. Four Ms Goal Setting

In this option, you will outline a goal on an index card that you can carry with you to remind you to follow through on the steps necessary to achieve the goal. All you need is a 3 x 5 inch index card for each goal you want to accomplish, a pen or pencil, and a little imagination. Complete one card for yourself, and then teach at least one other student how to make a Four Ms card. Refer to Figure 10.3 as a guide.

1. In the center of the card, write _Goal_, and under it write what you wish to accomplish or the habit you want to break.

2. In the upper left corner, write _Motivation_. Beneath it list your reasons for wanting to achieve the goal.

Motivation

Qualify for scholarship
Feel better about myself
Get into first-choice master's program

Make Commitments

Myself
Roommates
Faculty advisor

Goal

Improve my GPA to 3.5 by graduation through
use of better study habits

Modify

Use library and labs
Study comes before play
Complete readings and
  assignments before class

Monitor

Plan and track study sessions
Grade updates from instructors
Regular appointments with advisor

FIGURE 10.3: Four Ms Goal Card

 Online Study Center _college.hmco.com/PIC/sanft1e_

3. In the upper right corner, write *Make Commitments* and list people who will help as you work to reach your goal.

4. In the bottom left corner, write *Modify.* Under it list the things you will change as you work on the goal.

5. In the bottom right corner, write *Monitor.* Below list the ways you will be able to track your progress.

6. Teach at least one other student how to create a Four Ms card. What did you learn about being a mentor when you did this activity with another person?

_____

_____

How Can You Demonstrate Effective Decision Making?

Think about the way you made decisions as a new student. There were likely times when you jumped into something without giving it much thought. There were also likely times when you carefully considered every angle before making

> **EXPERT'S OPINION**
>
> "In any moment of decision, the best thing you can do is the right thing. The worst thing you can do is nothing."
>
> **Teddy Roosevelt**

the decision. Like many people, you probably make most of your decisions following certain styles—and you may not even be aware of doing so. But as a peer mentor, you will find it useful to be aware of the ways students commonly make decisions. You will be able to help your students determine whether they are thinking things through clearly or jumping in without taking enough time to make solid decisions.

Following are some common **decision-making styles** that people use depending on the situation and the type of decision to be made. They will help you become aware of your own decision-making processes and allow you to talk about different types of decision making with the students you mentor. Some decisions are the result of a combination of styles, while others clearly demonstrate a single style.

Rational. Reflects the thorough search and evaluation of alternatives

Intuitive. Reflects the tendency to rely on hunches and feelings

Dependent. Reflects a search for advice, input, and direction from others

Avoidant. Reflects procrastination or unwillingness to decide

Spontaneous. Reflects the tendency to make snap, spur-of-the-moment decisions

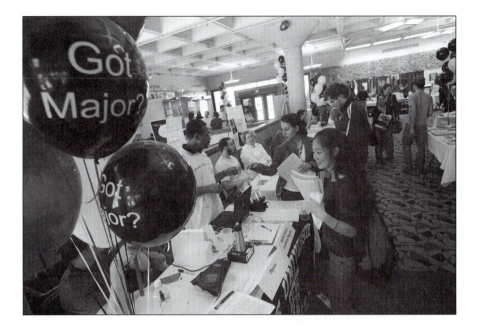

👤 ACTIVITY 10.5   General Decision-Making Style Assessment

This assessment will help you identify the extent to which you tend to employ rational, intuitive, dependent, avoidant, and spontaneous decision-making styles. In the grid below, circle the number that corresponds with how strongly you agree or disagree with each statement.

	Strongly Disagree	Somewhat Disagree	Neither Agree Nor Disagree	Somewhat Agree	Strongly Agree
a. I plan my important decisions carefully.	1	2	3	4	5
b. I double-check my information sources to be sure I have the right facts before making decisions.	1	2	3	4	5
c. I make decisions in a logical and systematic way.	1	2	3	4	5
d. My decision-making requires careful thought.	1	2	3	4	5
e. When making a decision, I consider various options in terms of a specific goal.	1	2	3	4	5

		Strongly Disagree	Somewhat Disagree	Neither Agree Nor Disagree	Somewhat Agree	Strongly Agree
f.	When making decisions, I rely on instinct.	1	2	3	4	5
g.	When I make decisions, I rely on intuition.	1	2	3	4	5
h.	I generally make that feel right to me. decisions	1	2	3	4	5
i.	When I make a decision, it is more important for me to feel the decision is right than to have a rational reason for it.	1	2	3	4	5
j.	When I make a decision, I trust my inner feelings and reactions.	1	2	3	4	5
k.	I need the assistance of others when making important decisions.	1	2	3	4	5
l.	I rarely make important decisions without consulting other people.	1	2	3	4	5
m.	If I have the support of others, it is easier for me to make important decisions.	1	2	3	4	5
n.	I use the advice of other people in making my important decisions.	1	2	3	4	5
o.	I like to have someone to steer me in the right direction when I am faced with important decisions.	1	2	3	4	5
p.	I avoid making important decisions until the pressure is on.	1	2	3	4	5
q.	I postpone decision making whenever possible.	1	2	3	4	5
r.	I often procrastinate when it comes to making important decisions.	1	2	3	4	5
s.	I generally make important decisions at the last minute.	1	2	3	4	5

	Strongly Disagree	Somewhat Disagree	Neither Agree Nor Disagree	Somewhat Agree	Strongly Agree
t. I put off making decisions because thinking about them makes me uneasy.	1	2	3	4	5
u. I generally make snap decisions.	1	2	3	4	5
v. I often make decisions on the spur of the moment.	1	2	3	4	5
w. I make quick decisions.	1	2	3	4	5
x. I often make impulsive decisions.	1	2	3	4	5
y. When making decisions, I do what seems natural at the moment.	1	2	3	4	5

Compute a total score for each decision-making style by adding the numbers of your answers for each group. Scores of 18 or higher in any category indicate a high propensity to make decisions in the particular style measured. Scores of 8 or less in any category suggest you typically do not make decisions in the particular style measured.

Rational decision making (**a** thru **e**)   _____

Intuitive decision making (**f** thru **j**)   _____

Dependent decision making (**k** thru **o**)   _____

Avoidant decision making (**p** thru **t**)   _____

Spontaneous decision making (**u** thru **y**)   _____

Source: S. G. Scott and R. A. Bruce. "Decision Making Style: The Development of a New Measure," *Educational and Psychological Measurements* 55 (1995): 818–831. Face validity and logical content validity; alpha's from .68 to .94.

Describe your own decision-making style, and discuss at least three different ways that decision making applies to your role as a mentor.

_____

_____

_____

_____

_____

One thing you may have realized is that, like you, students use certain decision-making styles based on the importance and type of decision to be made. For example, when deciding what to order at a restaurant, they may be spontaneous or seek advice from someone else. If the decision is highly personal, they may choose to make the decision intuitively. In most cases, they will not go wrong if they utilize a rational decision-making process because that means they have thought about possible outcomes and done some critical thinking. Typically, the avoidant style is the one you don't want your students to use because it can lead to additional problems and painful consequences.

How Can You Demonstrate Effective Problem Solving?

As a peer mentor, you might encounter problems with students, fellow mentors, program administrators, faculty members, or aspects of your own life. The real problems with which you are dealing will test your ability to apply the techniques you have learned in everyday situations. They will also provide you with great, often humorous mentoring stories to use when you help new students deal with their realities. This section introduces **problem-solving components**. Utilize the ones that will be most useful according to the type of decision to be made.

Tips for Effective Problem Solving

Figure 10.4 illustrates tips for effective problem solving. The arrows suggest that the stages of problem solving may not follow a particular sequence. Being effective at solving problems includes having the flexibility to move between the stages as more information becomes available or as the situation changes.

> **Defining the problem.** Just what is the problem you are trying to solve? Sometimes people waste a lot of time because they are not clear about what they want to happen. Get specific, and determine what the decision is about. For example, a student named Eric confides that he cannot continue attending college. Further discussion identifies the problem as his not earning enough money to pay for his education.

> **Generating possible solutions.** Brainstorm or meditate about potential solutions to the dilemma. There is usually more than one possible solution. More often than not, you will be able to come up with a good list of options to review. In the example, you and Eric brainstorm the following ideas: Eric could find a better-paying job or seek advancement with his current employer; he could quit school, work full-time for a year, and save his money; he could apply for grants, loans, or scholarships; or he could ask his family for additional support.

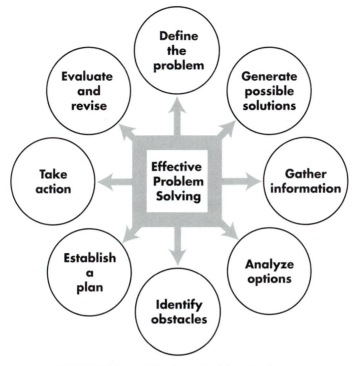

FIGURE 10.4: Effective Problem Solving

Gathering information. To come up with a good solution, you need to collect as much data about the decision as possible. After you determine possible solutions, find out as much as you can about each outcome. As his mentor, you encourage Eric to ask for a raise, check the want-ads, and use the college's career center to search for employment opportunities. You take him to a financial aid adviser to collect information about available options. He speaks with family members about the possibility of their helping to support him.

Analyzing options. Based on the information you gathered, which outcomes can you discard, and which can you pursue? Look at all of the possibilities, even those that are not currently appealing. Eric determines that his family is unable to assist him, so that option is dropped. He begins to weigh the pros and cons of paying back student loans and of working more and not attending school the following year. He finds that he will be eligible for a grant and/or scholarship the next academic year if he applies in time.

Identifying obstacles. What problems might you face with each decision? This is not a stage you want to leave out; if you do, you could end up getting blindsided. You and Eric identify obstacles. If he drops out now, he may never return. If he gets a loan, he may have difficulty paying it back. If he applies for a grant or scholarship, it will not be awarded until the following school year. If he changes his current job, he may not enjoy the new one.

Establishing a plan. You don't want to do things in an arbitrary manner. Keep the Boy Scout motto—"Be Prepared"—in mind as you determine how to make your solution the best it can be. Eric determines that by taking a better paying position at work that requires a few more hours and attending school part-time for a semester, he can stay in school. He will qualify for financial assistance from a scholarship or grant by the following year, and things should work out. You encourage him as best you can.

Taking action. Some people need help with following through. If you have used these tips for problem solving, you can be more confident with the choice. Taking action can be scary, but you just need to jump in and do it. Eric fills out the applications for financial aid and meets the deadlines. He works more hours the next semester while attending college part-time. He saves as much money as he can.

Evaluating and revising. When you evaluate your choices, you know when something is working and when it is not. Sometimes decisions need to be altered to come up with a more effective solution. The evaluation process will probably be Eric's sole responsibility, since he will likely not be in your mentoring program after the current semester. He will need to determine whether things are working. If you are still available to him, you may want to discuss how things are going and help him brainstorm new ideas, if needed.

These ideas will work no matter whom you are dealing with, and especially with the students you mentor. Your students will have a vast array of personal difficulties, attitudes, and motivations. One size does not fit all when it comes to students. If the problem involves course material, you can help by setting up a study session or getting students connected with classmates. If a student shares a personal problem with you, you may be able to provide some referrals. Your awareness of campus resources and connections to professionals will be a huge asset for students.

If the problem is of a sensitive nature, do not attempt to address it on your own. Avoid putting yourself in a position where you are in over your head. You must honor confidences, but do not try to become a counselor for a student. Refer the student to the instructor, campus counseling services, or another appropriate resource. Campus resources are discussed in more detail in Chapter 11.

At times you may feel that you have to direct a student's attention to a problem because the student does not seem to recognize it. Be careful. Students will not hesitate to create a scene and cast blame on you if you say something they don't want to hear or do something they don't agree with. Ask for time to prepare yourself before you respond to the student. Get input from someone in a position of authority to make sure you respond appropriately. An instructor or adviser may know something about the student's situation that you do not.

Being prepared with good strategies for planning, goal setting, decision making, and problem solving will make it easier to mentor your students. The nice thing about using these strategies is that they also benefit you. To get the full effect, you must practice them. As the Greek philosopher Epictetus said, "First say to yourself what you would be; and then do what you have to do."

⊕ Where are you now?

These questions are designed to help you review the important concepts covered in the chapter. Answering these questions can help you assess your own understanding or prepare for a test.

1. Describe tools you currently use in your personal planning. What could you do to be more effective?

2. Of the semester timeline and the semester calendar, which would be most valuable to you, and why?

3. What are the five components of setting SMART goals?

4. Describe the different decision-making styles, and explain why you defer to your preferred style(s).

5. Which tips for effective decision making and problem solving are most important to implement as you solve problems?

Case Study Discussion

Review the case study at the beginning of this chapter, and answer the following questions as they relate to the concepts you learned in the chapter. Discuss your answers with other mentors in your program so that you can explore different perspectives and gain greater insight into how to help this person.

Why is Anna's experience relevant in this chapter?

What would you need to know to help a student like Anna?

If you had to help Anna, how would you approach the situation?

If your initial idea didn't work, what else could you do to help Anna?

⊕ Where do you want to be?

Reflect on what you have learned about mentoring in this chapter, and consider how you will apply these ideas to your specific responsibilities as a mentor.

1. What do you consider to be the most valuable concept in this chapter?

_____

_____

2. Why was it significant to you?

_____

_____

_____

_____

3. How will you apply this concept as a mentor?

_____

_____

_____

_____

Utilizing Campus Resources

Case Study: "Feeling Lost"

Kim is an extremely shy freshman who has moved away from his few close personal friends for the first time in his life to attend college. He feels lonely and lost. He attends every class but always sits on the outer edge of the room, away from other students. When he is called on in class, he gets nervous and fumbles over his words.

One day you see Kim sitting alone in the cafeteria, and you ask if you can sit with him. After you and he find and discuss some common interests, he begins to open up to you. He tells you that he doesn't know why he is so shy and that his shyness annoys him. He says he can't think straight in class, so he makes mistakes that embarrass him. He tells you that he is kind of used to it, but that he would like to know how to act and what to say around people.

You also discover that Kim is eligible for several of the college's assistance programs, but he is too afraid or unsure about making the contacts to get the help.

191

As you discuss the following questions with other mentors in your program, remember that this case study has been written about a real student facing real challenges. We encourage you to imagine the complexity of the situation and not to oversimplify the issues that the student faces. You may not feel experienced enough to completely answer the questions at this point, but you will have an opportunity to revisit this case study after learning the concepts in this chapter.

As a mentor, how do you respond when someone suddenly opens up to you?

What campus resources do you know of that could help Kim resolve some of his problems?

What do you think you should do to help him, and where do you draw your boundaries?

 Where are you going?

After reading this chapter, you should be familiar with the following concepts related to mentoring.

- Importance of campus resources
- Academic resources
- Student support services
- Resources for stress management

Key Terms

In this chapter, you will encounter the following terms, which appear in bold. You can highlight the definitions as you read or look for the terms in the glossary at the end of the book.

Academic resources
Campus resources
Digital divide
Distress

Eustress
Information literacy
Student support services

Why Is It Important to Know Your Campus Resources?

This chapter provides an overview of resources that will be valuable as you mentor other students. Since each campus has different resources, you are encouraged to identify resources particular to your own institution that are not discussed here.

Campus resources are programs and departments designed to relieve college-student stress and provide opportunities for learning. However, as in

Kim's case, many of these services aren't used by the students who need them because the students don't know about them or aren't comfortable about accessing them. When students need help, their anxiety can decrease the likelihood of their investigating needed resources. If you simply send a student to a resource, he or she often won't go. But if you say "I know _____ in the _____ office, who can help. Let me walk you over and introduce you," your helpfulness in connecting the student to the resource will relieve some of the anxiety.

As a peer mentor, you can help students overcome their natural resistance about seeking help by knowing more than what services are available. Knowing who in those programs or departments can help students and how they can help is more important than knowing what they do. Mentoring is about developing successful relationships; your knowledge of campus resources will be most helpful when it is based on personal relationships and experience. When you intentionally get to know the faculty and student service personnel on your campus and understand how they can help your students, you will develop a powerful network of human resources.

Students' problems can range from finding a short-term loan to pay tuition to getting treatment for an eating disorder. Your students are not likely to come up to you and say, "I have a problem that I'm facing right now or anticipate facing in the future that I don't know how to handle by myself." They are more likely to drop hints about their problems. If you are a trusted friend who is prepared to make a personal recommendation, you can connect them with people who can help them solve the problems. Often, problems will be time-sensitive, so having both knowledge of what the potential problems are and the ability to make connections quickly is in everyone's best interests.

As a mentor, you are a valuable resource for first-year students. You may work with them in an orientation group, a residence hall, a learning community, or a first-year-experience course. You have been selected because you can relate to them as a peer and you have the experience to help them make a successful transition. It is important to consider your knowledge and experience as a resource and to reflect on how you can improve your campus community through the service you provide. One of the best ways to be a great resource for students is to become as familiar as possible with potential problems college students face and the services your institution offers to help solve them.

MENTOR'S VOICE

When I first came to college I had a belief that I only had time to go to class, do my work, and get home. Once I began applying for different programs and getting to know people I started liking my school experience, and now I want to help other students make connections. I feel very comfortable with helping others become a part of our institution and know there is something here for everyone. I think as mentors—if we really try—we can help each student feel connected. There are opportunities all around us and resources available. All we need to do is connect students with the right resources. I didn't want to be connected at first, but now you couldn't disconnect me, even if you tried.
Shirley Rosser, peer mentor

What Academic Resources Are Available to You?

Academic resources are services on a campus that directly relate to helping students achieve their academic goals. The key academic resources we discuss are academic advising, faculty, the library, and technology.

Academic advising may be a student's first contact on campus, but an advisor is more than a gatekeeper. Students often fail to recognize the importance of working closely with their advisers. Research on the first-year experience emphasizes that "effective advising is clearly much more than scheduling and registration. It is a developmental process in which course selection and registration take place within the broader context of the student's life and career plan."[1] Students who return to their advisers each semester receive valuable guidance that will help them progress through their college years.

As a peer mentor, you are not a trained adviser, but you can help students find the information they need about courses and registration. You should know the important deadlines for registration and tuition payments. You can also show students how to access the online class schedule and official course catalog. These resources provide information about departments, majors, courses, and graduation requirements.

Every college student understands that registration and tuition go hand in hand. Most students could benefit from meeting with a financial aid adviser as well as an academic adviser. Students who cannot finance their education do not continue their education. As a mentor, you can direct them to the financial aid office, but you could also assist them with the basic steps of applying for scholarships, grants, or loans if you have done it yourself. Your experience can provide students with assurance that the financial aid bureaucracy is manageable.

You may not typically identify faculty members as a resource, but they can provide services beyond teaching when students make the effort to get to know them. After taking several upper-division courses from a professor, a college student went to his office to turn in a term paper. The professor asked, "Did you have trouble finding my office?" The student replied, "No, not particularly," to which the professor responded, "Why haven't you been here before?" The student had never considered visiting with her professor, and as a result she failed to take advantage of all he had to offer.

Most professors will work one-on-one with students who have questions about what they are learning in class. They can also offer valuable career counseling and professional networking. They have a broad range of professional experience and contacts, and they are usually involved in scholarly and creative activities. Often, they will involve students in their activities, providing the students with significant learning experiences and preparation for graduate or professional school. A faculty mentor can help students gain a thorough and rigorous understanding of various scholarship opportunities and/or creative outlets by introducing them to publications,

ACTIVITY 11.1   *Critical Registration Information*

This activity helps you prepare for questions about basic information that any peer mentor should know. If you know where the information is and how to access it, you will be ready to provide correct information when needed.

1. Where can students find their academic advisers? Is there a general listing somewhere? If so, how do students access it?

   _____

   _____

2. Where can students find the official course catalog? Is it available online? If so, what is the URL?

   _____

   _____

3. Where can students find the class schedule for the upcoming semester? Is it available online? If so, what is the URL?

   _____

   _____

4. What are the registration and tuition payment deadlines for the upcoming semester? Is this information available online? If so, what is the URL?

   _____

   _____

5. Are you familiar with the FAFSA, scholarship, grant, and loan applications? If not, how can you get information about them?

   _____

   _____

research, grant applications, exhibits, and performances that will enhance their studies.

Faculty members often sponsor cultural and educational opportunities on campus, such as study-abroad programs, honors programs, and performing arts groups. Study-abroad programs can provide such diverse opportunities as studying health-related issues in Ghana or Shakespeare in London. They increase your cultural awareness and add an unforgettable dimension to your college studies. These programs typically offer credit that can be applied to most majors. Honors programs provide an enriched educational experience within a community of engaged students and faculty. They often offer courses with enriched curricula, small classes, and outstanding, handpicked faculty members who mentor students on preparing for graduate school, building career opportunities, or designing and conducting original projects. Performing arts and exhibits can include on-campus theatrical productions, concerts, museums, art galleries, observatories, and special collections at the library.

Your students will likely ask about your experience in certain courses and your recommendation regarding faculty. You can be one of the most reliable sources of information about the faculty and programs because you can relate your feedback to the students' preferred learning styles. For example, saying "The professor requires a lot of assignments, but will give you time in class to discuss what was assigned. She was positive and always encouraged us, so I didn't mind the workload" is more helpful than saying "You should take her

---

ACTIVITY 11.2   Connecting with Faculty

Reflect on your own experiences with faculty members. Answer the questions based on those experiences.

1. How did you perceive your professors when you first came to college?

_____

_____

2. How has your perspective changed as you have gained more experience?

_____

_____

3. Have you had experience with a professor who has provided a service for you beyond his or her expected teaching role? If so, explain.

_____

_____

4. How can the students you mentor take advantage of the resources their professors can offer?

_____

_____

5. As a mentor, how can you help students improve their interactions with their professors?

_____

_____

class because she is nice." Encourage students to get feedback from several other students and to consider their own learning preferences when they are making decisions about courses and instructors.

The library makes some first-year college students uncomfortable. Some say it is too quiet. Others say it is confusing and not helpful. One student said, "A library is a place that is cold and kind of scary. It is freezing and rather easy to get lost in, especially the first few times. The library holds a lot of information but none of it will you find because it's hidden and categorized in weird ways. The only ones who truly understand the library are the librarians."[2] You may be able to relate to this student's feelings.

In the twenty-first century, learning to use the library involves learning to access information from a variety of sources. Your library probably provides a tutorial on general library use and on techniques for locating information resources. Library instruction enhances a student's ability to locate appropriate research materials and improve the quality of academic research for term papers. These skills are known as **information literacy**. As a mentor, you should be familiar with your library's tutorial program and be able to demonstrate basic information literacy skills.

The questions in the following checklist are based on standards for information literacy established by the Association of College and Research Librarians. They deal with the basic skills college students need to be successful with research and writing.

Table 11.1: Information Literacy Checklist

	YES	NO
1. Can you determine the type of information you need for a specific assignment?		
2. Can you access the information you need quickly and effectively?		
3. Can you evaluate information and its source critically and select the most appropriate information for the assignment?		
4. Can you use information effectively in completing an assignment?		
5. Do you use information ethically and legally because you understand the economic, legal, and social issues surrounding the use of information?		
6. Do you consider yourself to be "information literate"?		

Source: Adapted from Association of College and Research Librarians, *Information and Literacy Competency Standards for Higher Education.* Quoted in M. M. Watts, "The Place of the Library versus the Library as Place," in *Challenging and Supporting the First-Year Student,* ed. M. Lee Upcraft, John N. Gardner, Betsy O. Barefoot, and Associates, 339–355 (San Francisco: Jossey-Bass, 2005).

If you can answer "yes" to the questions, think back to how you learned skills and who helped you learn them. If you cannot answer "yes" to some of the questions, meet with the people in your library, and learn how to improve your information literacy.

Technology can be a major obstacle for students. As a mentor, you should be sensitive to the **digital divide**—the cultural and socioeconomic factors that influence a student's access to and comfort with technology. You can help bridge the divide by determining your students' level of comfort and skill with technology and considering strategies to help individual students meet the campus standard.

Academic information about your campus is at students' fingertips. Many visit the institution's website before they come to campus, but they may not be aware of the breadth of available information. Surf your campus website to identify links that would be useful for first-year students, such as registration deadlines and the campus activity calendar. Many courses offer online components that use tools like Blackboard and WebCT, and some courses are conducted entirely online. If you mentor students in a freshman seminar, work with the instructor to incorporate an online component. This will provide a nonthreatening opportunity for students to explore the tools available to them. You can also encourage your students to take the initiative and to seek help with their technical concerns from a knowledgeable source, whether that is the campus IT staff or the instructor of an online course.

Many students have their own computers, but all students should know where to find computers they can use. If a student has not been to a campus computer

lab, offer to go with him or her the first time. Another important resource for students is e-mail. This is sometimes a preferred mode of communication with instructors. Ask students if they know how to access their campus e-mail accounts. If they are in the habit of using personal accounts, show them how to forward their messages to their main account.

What Student Support Services Are Available to You?

Student support services are services on a campus that support students through the process of completing their college experience. They often focus on areas that help meet the personal interests and needs of the student.

Many students are unfamiliar with the broad range of available services. Orientation programs and first-year seminars are designed to make students aware of resources, but most of the time students are overwhelmed by the amount of information they receive. As a mentor, you can help students identify the resources that are most relevant to them.

As an experienced student, you know not only where the resources are but also some of the quirks or unwritten rules related to them. For example, you may know that the advisement center provides one-on-one attention for students who are determining their class schedules for the following semester— and that it is not busy in the mornings or that certain advisers are more inclined to help newer students. Mentoring students through the process of utilizing campus resources is not just about knowing where to send them. It also takes the ability to completely explain and help the student feel comfortable with accessing a resource.

College campuses have a plethora of support services for students. They don't always include a direct link to academic services, but they are just as important. Some of the most common student support services are listed below. Think about what you know about the resources as you read through the list. You will then be asked to complete Activity 11.3, which will help you document what you know and develop connections to these or similar offices or departments.

College Unions or Student Unions are services and facilities designed for students and other members of the campus community.

- Food services (food court, catering)
- Student government (activities, councils)
- Student media (newspaper, TV)
- Student clubs and organizations (academic, personal interest)
- Service facilities (bank, post office)
- Social facilities (auditorium, ballroom, conference rooms)
- Recreation facilities (game room, theater)

Student employment helps students seeking job opportunities on and off campus to offset the cost of their education.

Recreation programs include a variety of activities, such as personal fitness, intramural, club sports, and outdoor recreation equipment rental.

Career services offer career counseling and job planning and placement for both students and graduates.

Financial aid services provide students with information and assistance in paying for their education through grants, loans, and scholarships.

Peer tutoring centers may include tutors, a math lab, a writing center, and other discipline-specific assistance programs.

Adult learner programs provide support for students over age twenty-four who often work full-time to support their dependents.

Women's programs support women through traditional social, academic, and professional barriers as they pursue college education.

Student athlete services assist student athletes with their academic success, compliance, and progress toward graduation.

Service-learning engages students in real applications of the concepts they are learning in the classroom by providing service opportunities that also meet identified community needs.

Lesbian, gay, bisexual, and transgender student services provide support to students with issues related to sexual orientation, who often are not protected against discrimination.

Services for students with disabilities provide assistance to students with learning disabilities, health-related disabilities, and hearing, sight, or physical impairment.

International student services offer compliance and academic counseling for students unfamiliar with American higher education practices.

Minority student services offer minority students community with students of the same racial, ethnic, or cultural background.

Health and wellness services provide services for both physical and mental health as well as programs like smoking cessation and Alcoholics Anonymous.

Religious and faith-based services allow students to learn about and participate in on-campus faith-based organizations that promote tolerance and support spiritual development.

Add other services your institution offers to this list.

_____

_____

ACTIVITY 11.3 Identifying Campus Resources

What you know and who you know will be of great value as you refer students to resources. This activity helps you learn about available services and also develop personal connections with them. Find a partner, and visit the resources listed above. Fill in the following table with the resource name, campus location, contact person's name, phone number, and/or e-mail address of someone you have personally met who is connected with that resource.

RESOURCE	LOCATION	CONTACT PERSON	PHONE OR E-MAIL

How Can Campus Resources Help Students Deal with Stress?

Today on many campuses an overwhelming number of students experience physical and mental health issues related to stress. A 1998 article in the *Philadelphia Inquirer* began with this grim claim:

> "Warning: Attending college can cause headaches, nausea, sleeplessness, irritability and eating disorders." You are not likely to see that kind of label on those glossy college brochures

that feature photos of perfect lawns, impressive stone buildings and happy students. But all those maladies are symptoms of stress, and all, according to campus officials and counselors, are being found in increasing numbers of students. In the last decade, they say, more students have arrived at college barely able to cope when the pressure builds.[3]

EXPERT'S OPINION

"Understanding the source of a student's stress may assist you in offering appropriate help. A mentor who believes in the student, who knows how to teach the student to use his or her strengths, and who recognizes the value of taking one step at a time can be a major positive influence."

Wilbert J. McKeachie, *McKeachie's Teaching Tips, Strategies, Research, and Theory for College and University Teachers*

As a mentor, you will likely encounter students with these or similar issues. At times you may be enough of a resource to help, but other times you will not be able to deal with them completely on your own. You want to be familiar with the resources your campus has to help students cope with difficult issues and be prepared to refer your students to professional experts.

Understanding Stress Management

There are two types of stress. **Eustress** is the good, or positive, stress you encounter when getting married, buying a home, or starting a new job. **Distress** is the bad, or negative, stress caused by such factors as a debilitating injury, the death of a loved one, or loss of employment.

Your institution's health and counseling centers will help students deal with the pressures of school life, usually at no or low cost. Many offer information about alcohol, tobacco, and drug abuse and addiction, as well as wellness and stress management workshops and programs. Rather than waiting to access these resources until a need arises, take the time now to familiarize yourself with the specific offerings on your campus so you will be prepared when your students face stress-related problems.

The stressors that you and your students are likely to experience are listed in Table 11.1 and are typically related to your or their personal life (roommates, family), professional life (work, school), and health (physical, mental). How you choose to deal with them will often determine how successful you are as a student. If you have developed effective stress management skills, you can share them with students who are struggling with similar issues.

Your personal attempts at managing stress can be positive or negative. Be careful not to carry any of them too far. For example, you might try to relieve a stressful situation by having a beer. But drinking more and more to relieve stress may create a new set of stressors. Some basic strategies usually help in dealing with stress. These effective stress fighters include nutrition, exercise, relaxation, breathing techniques, preventive maintenance, and humor.

Table 11.2: Common Stressors of College Students

Having enough money	Car trouble	Dealing with illness
Relationship problems	Finding and keeping a job	Making life decisions
Managing time		Responsibility for self
Problem roommates	Taking tests	Speaking in front of others
Lack of sleep	Feelings of loneliness	
Meeting deadlines	Achieving high expectations	
Family pressures		
Being a perfectionist	Amount of homework	

They can help students strike a good balance in their physical and mental well-being.

Nutrition. It is not uncommon to see students having diet soda and pastry for breakfast, high-fat fast food for lunch and dinner, and candy between meals. Changing a poor diet to proper nutrition will properly fuel the student's system and better prepare it to fight stress.

Exercise. Students "burn off" things that are bothering them by doing something that is physically active. Exercise releases endorphins, which create feelings like euphoria and serenity.

Relaxation. When things are stressful, going for a walk, listening to music, taking a bath, and watching a movie are ways that people relax.

Breathing techniques. Paying attention to breathing is crucial to managing stress. A simple exercise like breathing in through the nose, holding the air for a few seconds, and exhaling through the mouth can have a remarkably calming effect when repeated several times.

Preventive maintenance. Many stressful situations would not exist if people took measures to prevent them. Turning assignments in on time, reading before class, and scheduling study sessions automatically relieve a lot of stress related to homework. It's like putting oil in the car to prevent ruining the engine.

Humor. People often look back at stressful situations and find humor in their reactions. Though it is not always easy to do, trying to find the humor as a situation develops can reduce stress. Laughing relaxes muscles, gets more oxygen into the system, and lowers blood pressure.

Making a Referral

When helping students, ask for permission before consulting with others. Maintaining confidentiality is a top priority for both you and your students. The only time you don't need to ask permission is when a student might harm him or

ACTIVITY 11.4   *Stress Management*

This activity is designed to help you look at your perceptions of how stress affects you and other college students. After you answer the questions on your own, discuss them with other peer mentors.

1. What evidence have you witnessed that indicates that stress is a major cause of health problems for college students? Explain.

_____

_____

_____

2. What are the major stressors in your life?

_____

_____

3. What do you do to manage your stress? Which strategies are positive, and which are negative?

_____

_____

_____

4. Have you or has a friend had to deal with major physical or emotional reactions to stress? Why is it important to seek professional help?

_____

_____

5. As a mentor, how can you see yourself helping another student deal with stress?

_____

_____

_____

herself or others. If you are working with students who are struggling with serious emotional problems, walk with them to the counseling center or another appropriate resource on your campus, and assist with the initial contact. If you don't already know the receptionist, make introductions. Willingness to personally go with students to a professional vastly increases the likelihood that they will follow through and get the help they need.

The following steps may be helpful in making a referral.

Step 1. Identify the need for additional help.
- Listen to the person.
- Watch for signs of distress.
- Know the limits of what you can do to help.

Step 2. Ask questions to clarify the student's need.
- Ask the student to describe the situation or problem.
- Ask the student if he or she has considered additional help.
- Ask for the student's permission if you want to consult with another person.

Step 3. Make appropriate connections.
- Consult with an appropriate person who is familiar with resources and options available to help the student.
- Check out recommended resources to confirm their ability to help.
- Personalize the referral by giving the student the name of someone who can help.
- Provide specific information about where to go and how to contact the resource.
- Allow the student to decide how and when to make contact with the resource.
- Be patient.

Step 4. Follow up and maintain confidentiality.
- Encourage the student to follow up with you after making the first contact.
- Check on the student yourself if you do not hear from him or her.
- Find out whether the referral was helpful.
- Never share private information with others unless the student is suicidal or poses a threat to others. In such a case, contact your program coordinator immediately.

Many services are available on campus to help students achieve academic and personal success. Try to set a goal to become as familiar with as many of these resources as possible. By doing so, not only will you enhance your own college experience, but you will also enhance the experiences of the students you mentor. It's not just what you know, but whom you know. Your understanding of where to find a service and of the ins and outs of that service will make you a great resource for your students.

 Where are you now?

These questions are designed to help you review the important concepts covered in the chapter. Answering these questions can help you assess your own understanding or prepare for a test.

1. In your own words, describe why it is important to have a working knowledge of the resources available on your campus.

Online Study Center college.hmco.com/PIC/sanft1e

2. What are the key functions of the academic resources of advising, faculty, library, and technology?

3. Identify student support services you need to learn more about. What are your plans to become more familiar with them?

4. Describe personal examples of how you effectively utilize stress management strategies.

Case Study Discussion

Review the case study at the beginning of this chapter, and answer the following questions as they relate to the concepts you learned in the chapter. Discuss your answers with other mentors in your program so that you can explore different perspectives and gain greater insight into how to help this person.

Why is Kim's experience relevant in this chapter?

What would you need to know to help a student like Kim?

If you had to help Kim, how would you approach the situation?

If your initial idea didn't work, what else could you do to help Kim?

 ## Where do you want to be?

Reflect on what you have learned about mentoring in this chapter, and consider how you will apply these ideas to your specific responsibilities as a mentor.

1. What do you consider the most valuable concept in this chapter?

_____

_____

2. Why was it significant to you?

_____

_____

_____

_____

3. How will you apply this concept as a mentor?

_____

_____

_____

_____

Continually Improving Your Mentoring Skills

Case Study: "What's the Point?"

Peter has been involved with your university's peer mentor program for nearly two years. Because he considers himself experienced, he feels that he does not need to participate in ongoing training or complete required reports for the program. He seems to feel that the effort is a waste of his time. At this point, he is basically going through the motions of mentoring.

Peter's program requires a weekly Internet journal entry that is designed to help him be a more effective mentor by reflecting on his mentoring interactions, prioritizing the needs of the students, and setting goals to meet those needs. Peter has not only avoided the weekly reports for the last few weeks; he also missed the last training meeting for peer mentors. When asked about his journal entries and meeting attendance, he always has an excuse for not following through.

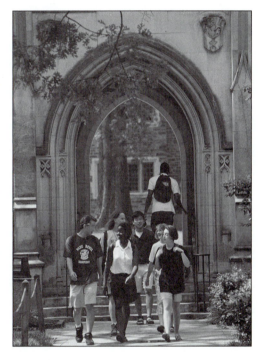

When the students Peter mentors are asked about his performance, they seem hesitant to say anything negative about him. They say they are fine and that he is "okay" as a mentor. It is fairly obvious that they don't want to get him in trouble. You have hung out with Peter, so your program administrator asks you to see what you can do to help motivate him.

As you discuss the following questions with other mentors in your program, remember that this case study has been written about a real student facing   207 *real challenges. We encourage you to imagine the complexity of the situation and not to oversimplify the issues that the student faces. You may not feel experienced enough to completely answer the questions at this point, but you will have an opportunity to revisit this case study after learning the concepts in this chapter.*

In your opinion, why is it important for Peter to engage in ongoing reporting and evaluation of his mentoring activity and to chronicle his goal setting and reflection?

What approach could you take as a friend that would not turn Peter off or cause him to withdraw even further and resent the requirements of the program even more?

How can you help a fellow mentor improve?

What can you do to avoid becoming complacent about your own mentoring activities?

 Where are you going?

After reading this chapter, you should be familiar with the following concepts related to peer mentoring.

- Motivation in your role as a peer mentor
- Confidence in your mentoring abilities

- Definition of critical reflection
- Purpose of evaluation
- Improving your performance

Key Terms

In this chapter, you will encounter the following terms, which appear in bold. You can highlight the definitions as you read or look for them in the glossary at the end of the book.

Availability bias
Critical reflection
Evaluation

Experiential learning
Johari window

How Does Your Motivation Affect Your Mentoring?

Chapter 1 asked you to consider the source of your motivation to be a mentor and discussed the importance of maintaining a balance between being self-focused and other-focused. At that point, you had little experience of being a mentor. Now you have more experience, and you will have to find the motivation to continue to improve. Like Peter, you may become complacent as time passes.

You will find more satisfaction in your role if you make an effort to maintain the quality of your mentoring. In the case study, the quality of Peter's mentoring had deteriorated, and he lacked energy to maintain quality interaction with his students or his peers. He had become so self-focused that he felt that his experience justified a mediocre effort. He had forgotten that mentoring is about recognizing each person as a unique individual and developing a relationship with that person. Regardless of how many students Peter mentored before, he never mentored this particular group of students. You can avoid finding yourself in Peter's situation if you remember the following guidelines.

Each experience is a learning experience. An experienced educator once said, "The great thing about teaching is there is always more to learn."[1] The same is true of mentoring. If you regularly reflect on your experiences, you will find countless opportunities to learn about yourself and others and the new ideas you are grappling with in your college courses. If you are simply going through the motions, you may not realize how interesting and stimulating your everyday experiences can be.

Every individual faces unique and interesting challenges. You may have been motivated to become a mentor because you are a people-person. If that is the case, you are more likely to enjoy your responsibilities if you focus on the people. As you gain experience, you can spend less time worrying about your skills and more time enjoying your relationships. You may develop lasting friendships with the students, mentors, and administrators in your program.

You can mentor students and other mentors. You may be formally assigned to work with a particular group of students, but you could be an informal mentor to others with whom you work on a regular basis. You can also maintain the quality of your mentoring as you build a sense of community with other mentors and support one another.

Your program administrators can help you. Program administrators are there for you. They can listen, offer advice, and empathize with what you are going through. You will gain more from your experience as a mentor if you develop a relationship with the administrators and faculty members in your program. They can support you in ways that other students cannot.

You have an impact on the success of your whole program. You will find the motivation to continue to give your best effort if you understand the bigger picture. Initially, your focus is on understanding your responsibilities and improving your skills. As you become more confident in your abilities, you can focus more on developing relationships with your peers and the professionals on campus. As your network of relationships grows, you see how your program contributes to the campus community. You can be a leader among your peers and help others see new ways of contributing and connecting to campus.

How Confident of Your Mentoring Abilities Have You Become?

As you have worked through the activities and readings in this book, your concept of what it means to be a mentor has changed. Your experiences with students and mentors have helped you better understand how you interact with other people. You have also had the opportunity to increase your awareness of yourself, including the attitudes and assumptions that influence your interaction with others. Considering what you have learned and identifying areas where you want to learn more will help you acquire a sense of perspective about where you have been and where you want to go in your own development as a mentor. At the beginning of this book, you were asked to rate your confidence in all the areas covered. Rate yourself again to see how you have changed.

👤 ACTIVITY 12.1   Mentoring Confidence Inventory

Use the following scale to rate your confidence in each of the following areas.

0 Not Confident
1 Slightly Confident
2 Somewhat Confident
3 Fairly Confident
4 Quite Confident
5 Completely Confident

Then consider how the activities and information in this book have affected your confidence by comparing your scores now (postassessment) with the scores you gave yourself in Chapter 1 (preassessment).

Postassessment	Becoming a Peer Mentor	Preassessment
0 1 2 3 4 5	1. I know what it means to be a mentor.	0 1 2 3 4 5
0 1 2 3 4 5	2. I know the difference between mentoring and tutoring.	0 1 2 3 4 5
0 1 2 3 4 5	3. I know why I want to become a peer mentor.	0 1 2 3 4 5
0 1 2 3 4 5	4. I understand how my motivation affects my performance.	0 1 2 3 4 5
0 1 2 3 4 5	5. I am prepared to balance peer mentoring responsibilities with my other life responsibilities.	0 1 2 3 4 5
Total __ /25		Total __ /25

Helping Students Make the Transition to College

0 1 2 3 4 5   1. I can explain why college students need peer mentors.   0 1 2 3 4 5

0 1 2 3 4 5   2. I understand the differences between high school and college.   0 1 2 3 4 5

0 1 2 3 4 5   3. I am aware of how peer mentors can help students make the transition to college.   0 1 2 3 4 5

0 1 2 3 4 5   4. I am aware of the objectives of the first-year-experience program on my campus.   0 1 2 3 4 5

0 1 2 3 4 5   5. I understand how involvement can affect my development as a student.   0 1 2 3 4 5

Total __ /25   Total __ /25

Defining Roles

0 1 2 3 4 5   1. I understand my role within the mentor program.   0 1 2 3 4 5

0 1 2 3 4 5   2. I know the different roles I have with the students I mentor.   0 1 2 3 4 5

0 1 2 3 4 5   3. I understand the student's role in the mentoring relationship.   0 1 2 3 4 5

0 1 2 3 4 5   4. I am capable of fulfilling the different roles of a peer mentor.   0 1 2 3 4 5

0 1 2 3 4 5   5. I know how to develop my mentoring skills in each of the different roles I have as a mentor.   0 1 2 3 4 5

Total __ /25   Total __ /25

Establishing and Maintaining Relationships

0 1 2 3 4 5   1. I can explain what makes a mentoring relationship different from other relationships.   0 1 2 3 4 5

0 1 2 3 4 5   2. I know what students are looking for in a mentoring relationship.   0 1 2 3 4 5

0 1 2 3 4 5   3. I know how to establish an effective mentoring relationship.   0 1 2 3 4 5

0 1 2 3 4 5   4. I know what to do to maintain a good mentoring relationship.   0 1 2 3 4 5

0 1 2 3 4 5   5. I know how to end a mentoring relationship in a positive way.   0 1 2 3 4 5

Total __ /25   Total __ /25

Understanding Self-Awareness

0 1 2 3 4 5   1. I understand why self-awareness is necessary to a mentor.   0 1 2 3 4 5

0 1 2 3 4 5   2. I know the difference between self-concept, self-esteem, and self-efficacy.   0 1 2 3 4 5

0 1 2 3 4 5   3. I understand how self-efficacy affects agency.   0 1 2 3 4 5

0 1 2 3 4 5   4. I am aware of my thoughts, feelings, and actions.   0 1 2 3 4 5

0 1 2 3 4 5   5. I know the different types of awareness essential for college students.   0 1 2 3 4 5

Total __ /25   Total __ /25

Becoming a Role Model

0 1 2 3 4 5   1. I understand the differences between being a peer mentor and being a role model.   0 1 2 3 4 5

0 1 2 3 4 5   2. I am comfortable being honest about my strengths and weaknesses.   0 1 2 3 4 5

0 1 2 3 4 5   3. I can identify my own personal values.   0 1 2 3 4 5

0 1 2 3 4 5   4. I am aware of how my choices and actions reflect my values.   0 1 2 3 4 5

0 1 2 3 4 5   5. I am confident in my ability to help others recognize their own values.   0 1 2 3 4 5

Total __ /25   Total __ /25

Developing Cultural Sensitivity

0 1 2 3 4 5   1. I understand the benefits of diversity on a college campus.   0 1 2 3 4 5

0 1 2 3 4 5   2. I respect and value the diversity of the students I mentor.   0 1 2 3 4 5

0 1 2 3 4 5   3. I recognize how cultural influences affect my perspective.   0 1 2 3 4 5

0 1 2 3 4 5   4. I am aware of my own attitude toward cultural differences.   0 1 2 3 4 5

0 1 2 3 4 5   5. I employ effective strategies for cross-cultural interaction.   0 1 2 3 4 5

Total __ /25   Total __ /25

Communicating Effectively

0 1 2 3 4 5   1. I understand how communicating as a mentor is different than communicating in other relationships I have.   0 1 2 3 4 5

0 1 2 3 4 5   2. I have effective listening skills.   0 1 2 3 4 5

0 1 2 3 4 5   3. I am aware of my verbal and nonverbal messages.   0 1 2 3 4 5

0 1 2 3 4 5   4. I am confident in my presentation and group discussion skills.   0 1 2 3 4 5

0 1 2 3 4 5   5. I understand how to effectively give and receive feedback.   0 1 2 3 4 5

Total __ /25   Total __ /25

Facilitating Learning

0 1 2 3 4 5   1. I know what it means to facilitate learning.   0 1 2 3 4 5

0 1 2 3 4 5   2. I know the differences between adolescent learners and adult learners.   0 1 2 3 4 5

0 1 2 3 4 5   3. I understand that I must use different facilitation techniques for different types of learners.   0 1 2 3 4 5

0 1 2 3 4 5   4. I can incorporate active learning techniques in my teaching.   0 1 2 3 4 5

0 1 2 3 4 5   5. I can explain the value of peer-to-peer teaching.   0 1 2 3 4 5

Total __ /25   Total __ /25

Planning and Problem Solving

0 1 2 3 4 5   1. I know how to plan to be an effective mentor.   0 1 2 3 4 5

0 1 2 3 4 5   2. I could help other students plan for the semester.   0 1 2 3 4 5

0 1 2 3 4 5   3. I can demonstrate effective goal setting for other students.   0 1 2 3 4 5

0 1 2 3 4 5   4. I understand different decision-making styles.   0 1 2 3 4 5

0 1 2 3 4 5   5. I know what skills are required to conduct effective problem solving.   0 1 2 3 4 5

Total __ /25   Total __ /25

Online Study Center college.hmco.com/PIC/sanft1e

Utilizing Campus Resources

0 1 2 3 4 5   1. I can explain to students why it is important to be aware of campus resources.   0 1 2 3 4 5

0 1 2 3 4 5   2. I am familiar with academic resources available on campus.   0 1 2 3 4 5

0 1 2 3 4 5   3. I am familiar with student support services available on campus.   0 1 2 3 4 5

0 1 2 3 4 5   4. I have a network of people to whom I can refer students who need help.   0 1 2 3 4 5

0 1 2 3 4 5   5. I can recognize the signs of stress and help students identify the resources that can help them manage their stress.   0 1 2 3 4 5

Total __ /25   Total __ /25

Evaluating Your Mentoring Skills

0 1 2 3 4 5   1. I understand the importance of critical reflection.   0 1 2 3 4 5

0 1 2 3 4 5   2. I know how to evaluate my skills and performance.   0 1 2 3 4 5

0 1 2 3 4 5   3. I am comfortable asking others for feedback.   0 1 2 3 4 5

0 1 2 3 4 5   4. I understand the benefits of reflective journaling.   0 1 2 3 4 5

0 1 2 3 4 5   5. I am aware of how my motivation can change.   0 1 2 3 4 5

Total __ /25   Total __ /25

Consider your total score in each area to assess your confidence in your mentoring knowledge and skills.

0–5   Not Confident
6–10   Slightly Confident
11–15 Somewhat Confident
16–20 Fairly Confident
21–24 Quite Confident
25   Completely Confident

1. In which areas have you made the most improvement? Explain what you learned in each area that made the most significant difference in your confidence level.

_____

_____

_____

_____

2. In which areas would you like to see more improvement? Explain what you will you do to improve in these areas.

_____

_____

_____

_____

3. Why do you want to continue to be a peer mentor?

_____

_____

_____

_____

4. Why would students want you to be their mentor?

_____

_____

_____

_____

What Is Critical Reflection?

Reflection will help you view each experience as a learning experience. *Reflection* can be simply defined as the reproduction of a thing or image, like the reflection of an object in a mirror. In terms of your involvement as a mentor, reflection offers the opportunity to hold a mirror to your contribution and view your actions and interactions as if you were a somewhat objective observer. The practice of reflection lets you better understand the reasons for what happened and why they are significant.

Critical reflection is more than casual reminiscing. John Dewey, author of *How We Think*, was the first to identify the connection between reflection and critical thinking. He defined reflection as "active, persistent, and careful consideration of any belief or supposed form of knowledge."[2] He claimed that reflection involves complex thinking skills such as problem solving, hypothesis testing, inference, and imaginative action planning. If you intend to learn from your experience and improve your performance

Online Study Center college.hmco.com/PIC/sanft1e

as a mentor, you must be "active, persistent, and careful" as you consider how your beliefs and assumptions affect your experiences.

You may have spent a couple of hours preparing a presentation for your students, but they did not respond well when you gave the presentation. As you reflect, you could consider the assumptions you made about your students or the assumptions you made about your presentation abilities. Or you may unexpectedly meet one of your students and find that she needs someone to listen as she shares things you would not have otherwise known. You can now be more helpful to her than you could have been before, but first you should consider what assumptions she made about you when she shared such personal information. Reflection allows you to turn everyday experiences into lessons learned.

EXPERT'S OPINION

"Without reflection, we go blindly on our way, creating more unintended consequences, and failing to achieve anything useful."

Margaret Wheatley, "It's An Interconnected World"

Why Is Evaluating Your Skills and Performance Important?

Critical reflection is a form of evaluation; but as it has been defined so far, it is limited by your personal perspective and knowledge. **Evaluation**, as used here, involves more than individual reflection. It is the ability to assess the level of your performance by understanding your program's expectations and seeking feedback from others. While reflection is the first step in learning from experience, evaluation provides a basis of comparison that will allow you to determine your strengths and weaknesses.

Feedback from others is essential to understanding your performance as a mentor. Chapter 8 included basic guidelines for giving and receiving feedback. This chapter focuses on why seeking feedback is important. You will not know how other people perceive or interpret your words and actions if you are not open to feedback. Students and others you work with give both implicit and explicit feedback. You will have to recognize implicit feedback in nonverbal responses and in offhand suggestions in casual conversation. You can ask for explicit feedback, and some students will tell you what they think. But you will have a better idea of how you are doing if you provide opportunities for all your students to share their opinions in a nonconfrontational setting, like an anonymous survey. Work with your program administrators and faculty to develop a system for administering a formal evaluation like the one in Figure 12.1 each semester, and also conduct informal surveys when you feel they would be useful. You can give students 3 x 5 inch index cards and ask them to write feedback about what you are doing well and what you can improve.

Your feedback can help your mentor identify his or her own strengths and weaknesses. Using the following scale, honestly evaluate your mentor's performance this semester.

1—Strongly Disagree
2—Disagree
3—Neutral
4—Agree
5—Strongly Agree

	Strongly Disagree	Disagree	Neutral	Agree	Strongly Agree	Not Applicable
My mentor is motivated to help me succeed.	1	2	3	4	5	na
My mentor helps me meet the challenges of making the transition to college.	1	2	3	4	5	na
My mentor is a trusted friend.	1	2	3	4	5	na
My mentor helps me connect to the campus.	1	2	3	4	5	na
My mentor helps me learn new study strategies.	1	2	3	4	5	na
My mentor helps me understand my rights and responsibilities as a student.	1	2	3	4	5	na
My mentor leads by example.	1	2	3	4	5	na
My mentor helps me become more self-aware.	1	2	3	4	5	na
My mentor has established and maintained an effective relationship with me.	1	2	3	4	5	na
My mentor demonstrates effective communication skills.	1	2	3	4	5	na
My mentor helps me better understand how to learn and study.	1	2	3	4	5	na
My mentor demonstrates effective planning.	1	2	3	4	5	na
My mentor demonstrates effective problem solving.	1	2	3	4	5	na
My mentor helps me become familiar with campus resources to meet my needs.	1	2	3	4	5	na
My mentor is sensitive to cultural differences.	1	2	3	4	5	na

What has your mentor done that has been most helpful to you?

_____

_____

_____

What could your mentor do to be more helpful to you?

_____

_____

_____

FIGURE 12.1: Student Evaluation

The most valuable feedback may come from someone who is a mentor to you. This person could be another mentor or a program administrator. You can ask her or him to observe your interactions with other students, or you could discuss your frustrations. A mentor in the program will understand your expectations and challenges. Because of your relationship with this person, he or she will be more comfortable openly discussing feedback.

One reason it is important to evaluate your performance through feedback from others can be explained by the **Johari window**, which is illustrated in Figure 12.2.[3] The shaded area represents your self. *Open area* represents things about you that are obvious to both you and others. *Hidden area* represents things you know about yourself that you are unwilling to reveal to others. *Blind area* represents things that other people know about you that you do not realize. Such "blind spots" can limit your ability to relate well to others. You should seek feedback to help you identify and address your blind spots. *Unknown area* represents all the things you still have to learn about yourself, including unknown fears or undiscovered talents.

If, as a student and a mentor, you are willing to step out of your comfort zone and experience new things, you will learn things about yourself that currently lie in that unknown area. If you make a genuine effort to increase your self-awareness by understanding how others see you, your open area will grow, and the other areas will begin to shrink.

One caution about feedback is to avoid **availability bias**, also known as the fallacy of generalization. In other words, just because two or three students are willing to offer their opinions, do not assume that the opinions represent the opinion of the entire group. We all tend to generalize based on information that is readily available to us. Unfortunately, this tendency often leads to inaccurate conclusions and poor decision making.

Feedback will give you insight into what your students think about you as a mentor, and it will also help you assess whether you are meeting your program's requirements and expectations. Your impact as a mentor cannot

	Known to Self	Not Known to Self
Known to Others	**Open area**	**Blind area**
Not Known to Others	**Hidden area**	**Unknown area**

FIGURE 12.2: The Johari Window

ACTIVITY 12.2   Seeking Feedback

Discuss your performance as a mentor with students and/or a program administrator. Answer the following questions based on the feedback you receive.

1. What did you learn from the feedback?

_____

_____

2. What do you want to continue doing?

_____

_____

3. What would you like to do differently?

_____

_____

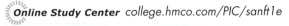

be measured by a popularity poll. Instead, you have to consider how your performance supports your program's goals and the needs of first-year students.

How Can I Improve My Performance?

You will need to seek feedback from others and engage in critical reflection to assess your performance. Journal writing can be an effective way to improve your performance if you reflect on your experiences, explore your insights, process feedback, and track your progress toward goals that you set for yourself. Keeping a journal is a common practice in **experiential learning** or hands-on learning. As a mentor, you are learning from experience. You learn teaching techniques and interpersonal skills, among other things, as you work with students. You learn from your own observations, interactions, decisions, and insights. A journal allows you to record your activities, track your goals, and document your accomplishments over an extended period of time. You will be able to look back and see the challenges and obstacles you helped yourself and your students overcome, as well as the lessons you learned along the way.

You will gain the most from journal writing if you write about your experiences with the intent of learning from them and better understanding yourself as a mentor. If you view the journal as busy work imposed on you by others, your writing will be superficial and meaningless. If you are trying to satisfy someone else's expectations, you may be overly dramatic. Stephen Brookfield, author of *Becoming a Critically Reflective Teacher*, warns that "Journals . . . have the potential to become ritualistic and mandated confessionals—the educational equivalent of the tabloid-like, sensationalistic outpourings of talk-show participants."[4] In other words, you may be tempted to sensationalize your experiences if you are too concerned about what others will think. Your journal does not need to document the greatest mentoring insights of all time. You simply need to record and reflect on your everyday experiences. You are the only one who can measure the value of your experiences and the degree to which they affected you.

At the end of each chapter, you have been asked to reflect on what you have learned about mentoring and to consider how you would apply those concepts. Review your comments and reflect on what you have learned and how well you have integrated the ideas into your own mentoring. Now that you have reached the end of this book, you will want to develop your own method of recording your experiences and reflecting on your insights. The following assignment will help you get started. You should do this activity consistently.

MENTOR'S VOICE

Our weekly journals are important. They are great for having the mentors personally evaluate the past week, tracking the hours we spent mentoring, and reflecting on what we did well and what we can improve on. They are great for maintaining and improving our skills.

Darren Tintle, peer mentor

ACTIVITY 12.3   Weekly Journal

This assignment will be most effective if you employ it in the future to chronicle your growth and experiences as a peer mentor. Your journal can become a vital part of your mentoring program.

1. Write a paragraph describing what you did as a mentor this week. The purpose of this assignment is to reflect on your performance as a mentor. Consider what is going well and what you need to work on.

2. What goals or assignments do you have for this coming week?

Where are you now?

These questions are designed to help you review the important concepts covered in the chapter. Answering these questions can help you assess your own understanding or prepare for a test.

1. Discuss how your motivation as a mentor can change over time.

2. Discuss how your confidence in your mentoring abilities has changed.

3. What is critical reflection? Why is it important?

4. Why is it important to evaluate your performance?

5. How can you improve your performance by keeping a journal?

Case Study Discussion

Review the case study at the beginning of this chapter, and answer the following questions as they relate to the concepts you learned in the chapter. Discuss your answers with other mentors in your program so that you can explore different perspectives and gain greater insight into how to help this person.

Why is Peter's experience relevant in this chapter?

What would you need to know to help a student like Peter?

If you had to help Peter, how would you approach the situation?

If your initial idea didn't work, what else could you do to help Peter?

 ## Where do you want to be?

Reflect on what you have learned about mentoring in this chapter, and consider how you will apply these ideas to your specific responsibilities as a mentor.

1. What do you consider the most valuable concept in this chapter?

_____

_____

2. Why was it significant to you?

    _____

    _____

    _____

    _____

3. How will you apply this concept as a mentor?

    _____

    _____

    _____

    _____

Notes

Chapter 2

1. N. K. Schlossberg, E. B. Waters, and J. Goodman, *Counseling Adults in Transition,* 2nd ed. (New York: Springer, 1995). Quoted in Nancy J. Evans, Deanna S. Forney, and Florence Guido-DiBrito, *Student Development in College* (San Francisco: Jossey-Bass, 1998), 111.
2. Evans, Forney, and Guido-DiBritto, *Student Development in College.*
3. ACT News Release, "Many U.S. Colleges Overlooking a Potential Cure for College Dropouts," June 23, 2004.
4. J. Hoyt and M. Lundell, "Why Students Drop Out: A Retention Study at Utah Valley State College," *National Association for Developmental Education (NADE)* (Fall 1999).
5. J. Hoyt and M. Lundell, "The Effect of Risk Factors and Student Service Interventions on College Retention," juried paper for the National Student Affairs Administrators in Higher Education (NASPA), Denver, CO, 2004. http://www.uvsc.edu/ir/research/Retentionwriteup.pdf.
6. M. Lee Upcraft, John N. Gardner, Betsy O. Barefoot and Associates, eds., *Challenging and Supporting the First-Year Student* (San Francisco: Jossey-Bass, 2005), 1-14.
7. National Center for Education Statistics, *Trends in Academic Progress* (NAEP, 2004).
8. H. Boylan, L. Bliss, and B. Bonham, "Program Components and Their Relationship to Student Performance," *Journal of Developmental Education* 20 (1997): 2-9.
9. National Center for Education Statistics, *Survey Report: College Level Remediation in the Fall of 1999* (Washington, DC: U.S. Department of Education, Office of Educational Research and Improvement, 2004).
10. V. Tinto, "Reconstructing the First Year of College," *Planning for Higher Education* 25, no. 1: (1996): 1-7.
11. A. W. Astin, "Student Involvement: A Developmental Theory for Higher Education," *Journal of College Student Personnel* 25 (1984): 297-308.
12. Mark J. Chidister, Frank H. Bell, Jr., and Kurt M. Earnest, "Lessons from Peers: The Design Exchange," in *Student-Assisted Teaching: A Guide to Faculty-Student Teamwork,* ed. Judith E. Miller, James E. Groccia, Marilyn S. Miller (Bolton, MA: Anker Publishing, 2001), 8-14; Cheryl Golden and Calverta McMorris, "Student-Directed Instruction in an Undergraduate Psychopathology Course," in *Student Assisted Teaching,* 140-44.
13. V. Tinto, "Enhancing Student Persistence: Connecting the Dots" (presented at the University of Wisconsin–Madison, October 23-25, 2002).

Chapter 3

1. A. W. Astin, *What Matters in College: Four Critical Years Revisited* (San Francisco: Jossey-Bass, 1993).
2. Attributed to William James. Retrieved February 2, 2007, from http://en.wikiquote.org/wiki/William James.

Chapter 4

1. Rey Carr, *What Makes Mentoring Different from Other Business Roles?* Peer Resources Net Papers, 2001.

2. Madeleine L'Engle, *Walking on Water: Reflections on Faith and Art* (New York: Bantam Books, 1980), 193.

Chapter 5

1. Johann Diaz, "Why Self Awareness/Emotional Intelligence Is So Important," 2003. Retrieved September 11, 2006, from http://www.mbamatch.com/Knowledge_Base/Leadership/EI%20SA%20and%20the%20Enneagram.htm.
2. Retrieved September 11, 2006, from http://education.yahoo.com/reference/dictionary/entry/efficacy.
3. Albert Bandura, "Social Cognitive Theory: An Agentic Perspective," *Annual Review of Psychology* 52 (2001): 1–26.
4. John Dewey, *How We Think* (Lexington, MA: D.C. Heath, 1910).
5. Retrieved January 23, 2007 from http://www.brainyquote.com/quotes/quotes/a/alberteins121993.html.

Chapter 6

1. C. Ende and F. Newton, *Students Helping Students* (San Francisco: Jossey-Bass, 2000).
2. Henry David Thoreau, *Walden, or Life in the Woods*, "Where I Lived, and What I Lived For," (1854). Retrieved January 26, 2007 from http://thoreau.eserver.org/walden02.html.
3. Attributed to Edward R. Murrow. Retrieved February 2, 2007 from http://en.wikiquote.org/wiki/Edward_R._Murrow.
4. Albert Einstein, "What Life Means to Einstein," Interview with George Sylvester Viereck in *The Saturday Evening Post* (26 October 1929). Retrieved January 30, 7007 from http://en.wikiquote.org/wiki/Albert_Einstein.
5. Wayne Dyer, *The Power of Intention*, 2004, published and distributed in the United States by Hay House, Inc., P.O. Box 5100, Carlsbad, CA.
6. William Glasser, *Take Effective Control of Your Life* (New York: Harper & Row, 1984).
7. Abraham Lincoln, attributed to *The Collected Works of Abraham Lincoln*, ed. Roy P. Basler (New Brunswick, NJ: Rutgers University Press, 1953).
8. Viktor E. Frankl, *Man's Search for Meaning* (Boston: Beacon Press, 1959), 66.
9. Norman Vincent Peale, *The Power of Positive Thinking* (New York: Ballantine Books, 1996).
10. D. Goleman, R. Boyatzis, and A. McKee, *Primal Leadership: Realizing the Power of Emotional Intelligence* (Boston: Harvard Business School Press, 2002), 10.
11. Ann Morrow Lindbergh, *Listen! The Wind* (New York: Harcourt, Brace and Company, 1938).
12. Margaret Mead, *Blackberry Winter: My Earlier Years* (New York: William Morrow and Company, 1972), 296.
13. Attributed to Socrates. Retrieved January 30, 2007 from http://en.wikiquote.org/wiki/Socrates.

Chapter 7

1. W. T. Jones, "The Realities of Diversity and the Campus Climate for First-Year Students," in *Challenging and Supporting the First-Year Student*, ed. M. Lee Upcraft, John N. Gardner, Betsy O. Barefoot, and Associates.
2. A. L. Antonio, "When Does Race Matter in College Friendships? Exploring Men's Diverse and Homogeneous Friendship Groups," *The Review of Higher Education* 27, no. 4 (2004): 553–75.

3. J. Wittmer, "Valuing Diversity in the Schools: The Counselor's Role," 1992 (ERIC Digest ED3474575); retrieved September 13, 2006, from http://www.eric.ed.gov/ERICDocs/data/ericdocs2/content_storage_01/0000000b/80/2a/17/04.pdf.

4. Indira Gandhi, quoted in *Christian Science Monitor*, 17 May 1982. Retrieved January 29, 2007 from http://www.bartleby.com/63/12/112.html.

5. Wittmer, "Valuing Diversity."

6. Helen Keller. Retrieved January 29, 2007 from http://www.cultureofpeace.org/quotes/tolerance-quotes.htm

7. Retrieved September 13, 2006, from http://education.yahoo.com/reference/dictionary/entry/empathy

8. C. M. Steele, "Thin Ice: 'Stereotype Threat' and Black College Students," *About Campus* 5, no. 2 (2000): 2-5.

9. T. A. Holmes, "Removing the Barriers to Effective Multicultural Communication," *Connections: Communicating in Culturally Diverse Environments* 2, no. 3 (2005): 1-2; retrieved September 13, 2006, from http://www.doctorholmes.net/CONNECTIONS%20Newsletter%20Volume%202-3.pdf.

Chapter 8

1. Henry David Thoreau. Retrieved January 29, 2007 from http://www.bartleby.com/66/71/58571.html. "A Week on the Concord and Merrimack Rivers" (1849), in *The Writings of Henry David Thoreau*, vol. 1 (Boston: Houghton Mifflin, 1906), 283.

2. T. K. Gamble and M. W. Gamble, *Contacts: Interpersonal Communication in Theory, Practice, and Context* (Boston: Houghton Mifflin, 2005), 109-10, 117-21.

3. D. Goleman,. *Emotional Intelligence* (New York: Bantam, 1995), 285.

4. D. Ellis, *Becoming a Master Student,* 11th ed. (Boston: Houghton Mifflin, 2006), 249-51.

Chapter 9

1. M. K. Smith, "Carl Rogers," *The Encyclopedia of Informal Education,* 1997. Retrieved September 15, 2006, from http://www.infed.org/thinkers/et-rogers.htm.

2. Adapted from D. Ellis, *Becoming a Master Student,* 11th ed. (Boston: Houghton Mifflin, 2006), 42.

3. Renate Nummela Caine and Geoffrey Caine, "Making Connections: Teaching and the Human Brain" (Nashville, TN: Incentive Publications, 1990). Retrieved September 15, 2006, from http://www.buffalostate.edu/orgs/bcp/brainbasics/triune.html.

4. R. Smilkstein, *We're Born to Learn,* (Thousand Oaks, CA: Corwin Press, 2003).

5. Retrieved September 15, 2006, from http://education.yahoo.com/reference/dictionary/entry/intelligence;_ylt=AmUFP1H3S5WSQ0k_i.slcZmsgMMF.

6. H. Gardner, *Intelligence Reframed: Multiple Intelligences for the 21st Century* (New York: Basic Books, 1999).

7. D. A. Kolb, *Experiential Learning* (Englewood Cliffs, NJ: Prentice Hall, 1984), 41.

Chapter 10

1. These results are based on a sample size of 32,896 ThinkTQ.com registered users in the United States. Results indicate a 95 percent confidence level and a margin of error of +/−1.5 percent. (Theoretically, with a sample of this size, one can say with 95 percent certainty that the results have a statistical precision of ±1.5 percentage points of what they would be if the entire adult population had been polled with

complete accuracy. For "statistics gurus," this translates into two standard deviations. Also, this study is not a probability sample, but the result of actual TQ tests taken through 11/15/2005.)

Chapter 11

1. M. C. King and T. J. Kerr, "Academic Advising," in *Challenging and Supporting the First-Year Student,* ed. Upcraft, Gardner, Barefoot, and Associates, 320.
2. M. M. Watts, "The Place of the Library versus the Library as Place," in *Challenging and Supporting the First-Year Student,* ed. Upcraft, Gardner, Barefoot, and Associates, 339–55.
3. R. Vigoda, "On Today's Campuses, Stress Is a Major Subject," *Philadelphia Inquirer.* December 13, 1998, A1.

Chapter 12

1. W. McKeachie and M. Svinicki, *McKeachie's Teaching Tips* (Boston: Houghton Mifflin, 2006), 357.
2. J. Dewey, *How We Think* (New York: D. C. Heath, 1933), 118; retrieved September 18, 2006, from http://www.infed.org/biblio/b-reflect.htm.
3. T. K. Gamble and M. W. Gamble, *Contacts: Interpersonal Communication in Theory, Practice, and Context,* 398–400.
4. S. Brookfield, *Becoming a Critically Reflective Teacher* (San Francisco: Jossey-Bass, 1995), 13.

Glossary

Abstract conceptualization   Term used by David Kolb to describe how a person thinks and analyzes a situation to develop concepts, ideas, and theories about his or her experiences.

Academic resources   Services on a campus that directly relate to helping students achieve their academic goals. The key academic resources we discuss are academic advising, faculty, the library, and technology.

Active experimentation   Term used by David Kolb to describe what a person does when he or she is learning a new skill.

Active learning   Learning that engages all aspects of the learning process, including doing, watching, feeling, and thinking.

Active listening   Intentional listening that requires full attention and understanding on the part of the listener.

Agency   The power to decide how to use one's abilities to achieve desired results; also, an intentional action for a given purpose.

Andragogy   Philosophy of teaching and learning that focuses on specific needs of adult learners.

Application   Term used in the A-I mentoring model to describe learning activities that help students process new information.

Assumed similarity   The assumption that most people's beliefs and actions are similar to those of the dominant culture or that most people want their beliefs and actions to be like those of the dominant culture.

Authentic   Being truthful about who you are and not pretending to be something else.

Availability bias   The tendency to draw conclusions based on information that is readily available, rather than to seek accurate or complete information; also known as the fallacy of generalization.

Barriers   Obstacles that get in the way of effective communication.

Bias   An inclination toward a particular perspective or opinion.

Boundary   Condition that guides behavior and limits the extent of interaction in a mentoring relationship.

Campus resources   Programs and departments designed to relieve college students' stress and provide opportunities for learning.

Communication   Verbal and nonverbal interactions with other people.

Concrete experience   Term used by David Kolb to describe a person's initial response to actual experiences, including the person's feelings or reactions in a learning situation.

Confidentiality   Recognizing when something is shared in confidence and protecting the person by not sharing that information with unauthorized people.

Connecting link   The mentor's role that assists students to connect with extracurricular activities to enhance their education experience.

Credibility   The quality of being believable because the mentor is also a student and understands the challenges that other students face.

Critical reflection   According to John Dewey, "active, persistent, and careful consideration of any belief or supposed form of knowledge."

Cultural norms   Acceptable standards of thinking, feeling, and doing for a particular group.

227

Culture   A set of values, behaviors, tastes, knowledge, attitudes, and habits shared by a group of people.

Decision-making styles   The five common ways people tend to make decisions: rational, intuitive, dependent, avoidant, and spontaneous.

Dendrites   Branch-like extensions of the neuron that allow neurons to interconnect and form networks that represent knowledge in a person's brain.

Digital divide   The cultural and socioeconomic factors that influence a student's comfort with and access to technology.

Distress   Bad or negative stress caused by events such as a debilitating injury, the death of a loved one, or loss of employment.

Diversity   People in a community who represent a variety of different ethnic groups, races, languages, religions, genders, sexual orientations, socioeconomic backgrounds, levels of education, political views, ages, and physical and mental abilities.

Emotional awareness   Understanding how negative feelings such as fear, anger, and depression affect one's performance; how to cope with those feelings.

Empathy   The ability to understand and vicariously experience another person's thoughts and feelings.

Empowerment   Realization that one has the ability to improve his or her circumstances.

Ethnicity   Association with a particular group based on race, nationality, tribe, religion, or language.

Ethnocentrism   The belief that one's culture is superior to any other.

Eustress   Good or positive stress caused by events like getting engaged, buying a home, or earning a promotion at work.

Evaluation   The ability to assess the level of one's performance by seeking feedback from others and understanding the program's expectations.

Experiential learning   Education through hands-on experience; the opportunity to learn from one's own observations, interactions, decisions, and insights; in mentoring, which is a type of experiential learning, students learn teaching techniques and interpersonal skills through real experiences.

Facilitate   To make something happen or to make something easier; mentors facilitate learning when they teach students learning strategies and engage them in a variety of learning activities.

Facilitator   Someone who provides guidance to students that allows the students to meet their own needs.

Feedback   Information about one's performance as an individual or as part of a program.

First-year experience (FYE)   Campus-wide programs developed to increase retention and improve student success during the first year of college.

Formal mentoring   Appointment to be a mentor by an organization or an agreement.

Four Ms   Goal-setting method to define goals and track progress with motivation, making commitments, modifying environment, and monitoring actions.

Habits of mind   Term used by John Dewey to explain how people think without their conscious awareness; a consistent tendency or inclination to think in a certain way.

"I" messages   Communication strategy that takes away any threat to the person being spoken to and places responsibility on the speaker.

Informal mentoring   Fulfilling a mentoring role without an official appointment or agreement.

Information literacy   A student's ability to locate appropriate research materials and improve the quality of academic research for term papers.

Intellectual awareness   Knowledge of one's own thinking processes and effective learning strategies.

Intelligence   The ability to learn or understand.

Interdependence   State of being interconnected with a group of people and mutually dependent on one another for growth and development.

Interpretation   Term used in the A-I mentoring model to describe learning activities that allow students to clarify their own perceptions of what they are learning and consider alternative points of view.

Johari window   Diagram that illustrates one's self in four quadrants, including the open area, hidden area, blind area, and unknown area; it illustrates the importance of seeking feedback to recognize one's blind spots.

Learning coach   Mentor's role that focuses on having students understand their learning preferences and how they affect learning.

Learning community   Coregistration or block scheduling that enables students to take two or more courses, form study teams, and establish supportive relationships.

Mentor   Someone who is experienced and trusted as an adviser or guide.

Mentoring relationship   Relationship between mentor and student that typically follows six basic stages identified by asking Who are you? Why are we here? Where are we going? How are you doing? What is working? What is not working? and Are we there yet?

Metacognition   Awareness of one's own thinking and learning processes and the ability to consciously regulate those processes.

Multiculturalism   Theory that people should preserve their cultures, allow different cultures to coexist peacefully, and encourage opportunities to learn about different cultures.

Multiple intelligences   Identified by Howard Gardner as verbal-linguistic, musical-rhythmic, naturalist-adventurer, logical-mathematical, visual-spatial, bodily kinesthetic, interpersonal-social, and intrapersonal; people have different aptitudes for each of the eight intelligences.

Neural networks   Dendrite structures that grow out of neurons in the brain as a person learns.

Nonverbal communication   Messages sent to another person that are not spoken, such as body language, eye contact, and nodding the head.

Other-focused   Approach that centers on how the program will benefit the students.

Pedagogy   Philosophy of teaching and learning that focuses on specific needs of children.

Peer   Someone of equal standing, such as a friend, a colleague, or a fellow student.

Peer leader   The mentor's role that gives students good examples to follow so they can implement them in their own lives.

Peer mentor   Fellow student who demonstrates how to successfully navigate the college experience.

Personal space   A person's comfort zone regarding proximity to others while communicating.

Physical awareness   Consciousness of the positive and negative effects of certain behaviors on one's body.

Prejudice   An adverse opinion formed without sufficient knowledge about a person or group of people.

Problem-solving components   Defining the problem, generating possible solutions, gathering information, analyzing options, identifying obstacles, establishing a plan, taking action, and evaluating and revising.

Q-SPACE   Acronym for a strategy of using questions when presenting to a large group.

Reflective observation   Term used by David Kolb to describe what a person watches and sees in a learning situation.

Resource awareness   Recognition of time and money as resources that must be used responsibly.

Retention   Keeping students enrolled in an institution of higher education from the first year through graduation by providing adequate support and resources to ensure their success.

Role model   Someone who is an example and who others will want to copy or follow.

Schema   Background knowledge that exists as a type of structured framework in one's mind; a person can comprehend new concepts only if they fit in an existing framework of knowledge.

Schlossberg's transition theory   Theory that identifies four main factors that affect how well a person deals with change: situation, self, support, and strategies.

Self-awareness   Understanding one's thoughts, feelings, and actions.

Self-concept   One's perception of oneself in comparison to other people; strongly influenced by language, family, culture, religion, education, and media.

Self-efficacy   Confidence in one's ability to accomplish certain things.

Self-esteem   Value a person sees in herself or himself based on how the person's "real" self compares to a mentally constructed "ideal" self.

Self-focused   An approach that centers on how the program will benefit the peer mentor.

Self-system   An explanation of human identity developed by cognitive psychologists; three major dimensions are self-concept, self-esteem, and self-efficacy.

SMART goals   Goals that are specific, measurable, attainable, relevant, and time-limited.

Social awareness   Recognition of social influences and the effects they have on interpersonal relationships.

Spiritual awareness   Consciousness of one's attitudes and perspectives about life and reality.

Stereotype   Commonly accepted generalization that does not accurately represent individuals within the group; often based on oversimplifications or gross exaggerations.

Student advocate   The mentor's role that involves watching for students' needs and providing students with support and resources to meet the needs.

Student involvement   The amount of physical and psychological energy that students invest in their college experience.

Student support services   Services on a campus that help meet the personal interests and needs of students.

Think/pair/share   A large group presentation model that has students think about a topic, pair with other students, and share what they know.

Tolerance   Acceptance of people who have cultural beliefs and attitudes that are different from one's own

Transferable skills   Skills that will be useful in a future career or workplace

Transition   Event that results in changed relationships, routines, assumptions, and roles

Transition theory   Theory that a person's ability to successfully move through a transition is affected by situation, self, support, and strategies

Triune theory   Theory developed by Paul MacLean that explains how the brain is made up of three connected layers of increasingly sophisticated tissues: the reptilian complex (doing), the limbic structure (feeling), and the neocortex (thinking)

Trusted friend   The mentor's role that helps establish and maintain an open relationship with the student

Tutor   Person who assists students with the teaching or clarification of content specific to a particular course

Value   An ideal that a person cherishes or esteems

Verbal communication   Spoken messages sent to another person

Credits

Experts' Opinions

Chapter 2

Astin, Alexander W. *What Matters in College: Four Critical Years Revisited.*
San Francisco: Jossey-Bass, 1993. (p. 398)

Chapter 3

Covey, Stephen R. *The 7 Habits of Highly Effective People* training manual.
Published by Franklin Covey, 1998. (p. 7)

Chapter 5

Freire, Paulo, Fraser, James W., Macedo, Donaldo, McKinnon, Tanya, and Stokes,
William T., eds. "Mentoring the Mentor: A Critical Dialogue with Paulo Freire."
Counterpoints: Studies in the Postmodern Theory of Education, Vol. 60. Peter
Lang Pub., Inc. (June 1997). (p. 324)

Goleman, Daniel. *Emotional Intelligence.* Retrieved February 2, 2007 from Share
Guide: The Holistic Health Magazine and Resource Directory, Interview with
Daniel Goleman by Dennis Hughes, Share Guide Publisher. *http://www.
shareguide.com/Goleman.html.*

Chapter 6

Covey, Stephen R. *Principle-Centered Leadership.* New York: Simon & Schuster,
1990.

Lombardi, Vince. *What It Takes to Be #1.* New York: McGraw-Hill, 2001. (p. 54)

Chapter 7

Maya Angelou. Unsourced quote retrieved February 2, 2007 from http://en.wikiquote.
org/wiki/Maya_Angelou

Lake Jones, Mona. *The Color of Culture.* IMPACT Communications, Publications, Div.
(February 1993).

Helen Turnbull, president of Human Facets. "Interview with Helen Turnbull." Boone,
Louise E., and Kurtz, David L. *Contemporary Business Communication.*
Englewood Cliffs, NJ: Prentice Hall, 1994. (p. 643)

Chapter 9

Tinto, Vincent. "Enhancing Student Persistence: Connecting the Dots." Prepared
for presentation at Optimizing the Nation's Investment: Persistence and Success in Postsecondary Education, a conference sponsored by the Wisconsin
Center for the Advancement of Postsecondary Education, The University of
Wisconsin, Madison, Wisconsin, October 23-25, 2002. Retrieved February 5,
2007 from http://www.wiscape.wisc.edu/publications/attachments/419
Tinto.pdf.

Chickering, Arthur W., and Gamson, Zelda F. "Seven Principles of Good Practice,"
American Association for Higher Education bulletin, 39 (March 1987). (pp. 3-7)

Chapter 10
Teddy Roosevelt. Retrieved January 29, 2007 from
    http://rooseveltinstitution.org/about/theodore_roosevelt.

Chapter 11
McKeachie, Wilbert J. *McKeachie's Teaching Tips, Strategies, Research, and Theory
    for College and University Teachers.* Boston: Houghton Mifflin Company.
    (p. 165)

Chapter 12
Wheatley, Margaret. "It's An Interconnected World." *Shambhala Sun*, April 2002.
    Retrieved August 11, 2006 from http://www.margaretwheatley.com/articles/
    interconnected.html.

Photo Credits

Chapter 1
p. 3: © Marty Heitner/The Image Works; p. 5: © James Marshall/The Image Works.

Chapter 2
p. 18: © James Nesterwitz/Alamy; p. 28: © Jeff Greenberg/The Image Works.

Chapter 3
p. 34: © Franco Vogt/Corbis; p. 39: © David Young-Wolff/Photo Edit.

Chapter 4
p. 53: © Zave Smith/Corbis; p. 63: Bruce Laurance/The Image Bank/Getty Images.

Chapter 5
p. 73: Royalty-Free/Masterfile; p. 84: © Royalty-Free/Corbis.

Chapter 6
p. 91: © Bill Aron/Photo Edit; p. 97: © Charles Gupton/Corbis.

Chapter 7
p. 105: © Jeff Maloney/Stock Connection; p. 115: © Jeff Greenberg/Photo Edit.

Chapter 8
p. 125: © David Young-Wolff/Photo Edit; p. 135: © Colin Young-Wolff/Photo Edit.

Chapter 9
p. 146: © Bill Aron/Photo Edit; p. 159: Stockbyte Platinum/Royalty-Free/Getty Images.

Chapter 10
p. 171: Royalty-Free/Masterfile; p. 183: Les Todd/Duke University Photo.

Chapter 11
p. 191: © Joyce Choo/Corbis; p. 198: © Lee Snider/Photo Images/Corbis.

Chapter 12
p. 207: Les Todd/Duke University Photo; p. 219: Royalty-Free/Masterfile.

Acknowledgments continued from copyright page

term *The First-Year Experience* in association with educational programmatic approaches to enhance the first college year. This license is not transferable and does not apply to the use in any other programs or in any other literature without the written approval of the University of South Carolina. Pp. 95–98: Sections on purpose, adaptability, creativity, focus, perspective, open-mindedness, responsibility/choice, independence, service, dependability, positive thinking, humor, and balance; pp. 131–132: Verbal and Nonverbal Messages; pp. 160–162: Table on multiple intelligences; p. 165: Kolb's Learning Model: From *Becoming a Master Student*, 11th Edition. Reprinted with permission of Houghton Mifflin Company. P. 107: Student quote from M. Lee Upcraft, John N. Gardner, Betsy O. Barefoot and Associates (eds.), *Challenging and Supporting the First-Year Student*, Jossey-Bass, 2005, pp. 8–9. Reprinted with permission of John Wiley & Sons, Inc. Pp. 108–109: Ask Model Description from Joe Wittmer, "Valuing Diversity in the Schools: The Counselor's Role," *ERIC Digest*, (ED347475), 1992-12-00. Reproduced with permission of *ERIC Digest*. P. 110: Diversity Wheel adapted from "Cultural Sensitivity and Diversity Awareness: Bridging the Gap Between Families and Providers," *The Source*, Vol. 6, No. 3, p. 3. Reprinted with permission of Amy Price, Editor. P. 111: Prose poem "Expert's Opinion" from *The Color of Culture*, by Mona Lake Jones, Impact Communications, 1993. Reprinted with permission of the author. P. 129: Inffective/Effective Listening from T. K. Gamble and M. W. Gamble (2005), *Contacts: Interpersonal Communication in Theory, Practice, and Context*, pp. 109–110, 117–121. Reprinted with permission of Houghton Mifflin Company. P. 194: Academic advising quote; p. 197: Library quote and information literacy checklist: from M. Lee Upcraft, John N. Gardner, Betsy O. Barefoot & Associates (eds.), *Challenging and Supporting the First-Year Student*, Jossey-Bass, 2005, pp. 8–9. Reprinted with permission of John Wiley & Sons, Inc. P. 218: Johari window (graphic and description) from *Of Human Interaction*, by Joseph Luft, © 1969 Mayfield Publishing. Reproduced with permission of Joseph Luft. Pp. 156–157: Five Rules of How the Brain Learns from R. Smilkstein, *We're Born to Learn*, 2003, pp. 71–73, 103. Copyright © 2003 by Corwin Press, Inc. Reprinted by permission of Corwin Press, Inc. Pp.183–185: General Decision-Making Style Assessment from S. G. Scott and R. A. Bruce, 1995, "Decision-Making Style: The Development of a New Measure," *Educational and Psychological Measurements*, 55, pp. 818–831. Copyright © 1995. Reprinted by permission of Sage Publications, Inc.

Index

Cardenas, Sam, 21
career planning, 28, 194, 200
Carr, Rey, 54
change, self-awareness and, 82-84, 86
charisma, 37
Chickering, Arthur W., 162
Chin, Brian, 177
choices
    abundance of, 23-24
    in learning process, 150
    power of, 96
civic responsibility, 28
classes
    adjusting to college-level, 23-24
    catalogues and schedules for, 194, 195
    online, 198
college
    compared with high school, 23-25
    reasons for leaving, 29-30
commitment
    encouraging student, 26
    in goal setting, 177
    in mentoring relationship, 43, 55, 61
communication, mentoring, 125-143
    active listening skills, 128-131
    compared with other communication,
        126-127
    confidentiality in, 142
    contact lists, 143
    doing no harm in, 142
    general strategies for, 127
    giving and receiving feedback, 139-142
    one-on-one communication, 128-134
    personal space and physical contact
        in, 128
    presenting to large groups, 135-139
    recognizing barriers, 132-134
    for small groups, 134-135
    using electronic communication,
        142-143
    using "I messages," 132
    verbal and nonverbal messages, 131-134
competence, of peer mentor, 43
comprehensive listening, 129
computer technology, 198-199
concrete experience, 163
confidentiality, in mentoring relationship, 61,
    142, 205
connecting link role
    important attributes in, 55-56
    for mentors, 36, 38-40
    student involvement in, 48
contact lists, 143
Contacts (Gamble, Gamble), 129
conversation, in learning sessions, 167
cooperation vs. competition, 119

Counseling Adults in Transition (Schlossberg,
    Waters, Goodman), 21
courses. *See* classes
courtesy, 37
Covey, Stephen R., 38, 92
creative learning style, 42
creativity, power of, 95
credibility, 58
critical listening, 129
critical reflection, 215-216
cultural diversity and sensitivity, 28, 105-121
    ASK model for, 108-109
    avoidance of stereotyping, 116, 118
    awareness of cultural influences, 109-111
    benefits of experiencing, 107
    and cultural attitudes and biases, 111-115
    interaction strategies for, 115-118
    learning important cultural characteristics,
        118-121
    significance of, 107-108
cultural norms, 112
cultural perspectives
    biases and attitudes, 111-115
    recognizing, 109-111
culture, 109

decision-making styles, 182-186
delegation, in peer leadership, 44-45
dendrites, 155-156
dependability, power of, 97
dependent decision making, 182
depression, 85-86
Dewey, John, 82, 215
Diaz, Johann, 75
digital divide, 198
distress, 202
diversity, 98, 107-108. *See also* cultural
    diversity and sensitivity
Diversity Wheel, 109-110
Dollar, Jessica, 135
dropping out, 29
Duffy, Ben, 151
Dyer, Wayne, 95

Einstein, Albert, 82, 95
electronic communication, 142-143
Ellis, Dave, 131
e-mail, 142-143, 199
emotional awareness, 85-86, 88
Emotional Intelligence (Goleman), 86,
    97-98, 131
emotions
    in learning process, 154, 157-159, 163
    limbic brain and, 155
    self-awareness of, 80-81, 85-86
empathic listening, 131